THE ENCYCLOPAEDIA OF ATHLETIES

THE ENCYCLOPAEDIA OF ATHLETIES

By

Yog Raj Thani

The Encyclopaedia of Athleties

ISBN : 978-81-212-0390-6

First Published 1991, reprint 2013 in India by
Gyan Publishing House
23, Main Ansari Road, Daryaganj,
New Delhi - 110002
Phones : 23282060, 23261060
Fax : (011) 23285914
E-mail: books@gyanbooks.com
website: gyanbooks.com

Printed at : Sagar Color Scan, New Delhi.

Non-runners may find the slavish desire of others to get out and run somewhat mysterious. Strong association is now identified between exercise and a rise in the level of endorphins, which are brain chemicals produced by the pituitary gland. These have qualities similar to morphine in their pain-reducing effects. Certainly they are felt to be partly responsible for the euphoric feeling experienced by some runners during training. Runners therefore have to remain aware that their view of a training run as being indispensable may not necessarily be shared, or even understood, by non-runners.

ADRENALINE

Adrenaline and noradrenaline are hormones which are released by the adrenal glands when the body is faced with a stressful situation. In athletic terms, they are associated with the nervous anticipation of a competition, or a strenuous challenge like a marathon, and the heart rate and blood pressure are involuntarily increased in readiness for hard physical effort. If the anticipation of this sporting equivalent of fight or flight is insufficient to set off this chain reaction, the athlete may complain of feeling flat, and subsequently perform below his normal level. But there is little doubt that to a reasonable degree such nervousness will actually heighten the ability of the body to perform well through the release of these hormones into the bloodstream.

Other physical signs of nervousness are yawning before a race and an increased need to visit the toilets. In normal pre-race circumstances, neither is a cause for concern.

AEROBIC RUNNING

Running at a pace at which the athletes can inhale sufficient oxygen to replenish that being burned up by the muscles. Conversely, an aerobic running involves a rate of activity that burns up oxygen faster than the athlete can replenish it, as in sprint races.

AFRICAN GAMES

The first African Games, were contested in Brazzaville, Congo from 18 to

25 July, 1965. Subsequent Games were staged at Lagos, Nigeria in 1973 and Algiers, Algeria in 1978. Games scheduled for Kenya in 1982 were cancelled. African Championships, for athletics only, were first held at Dakar, Senegal in 1979, and have subsequently been held at Cairo, Egypt in 1982, Rabat, Morocco in 1984 and Cairo, Egypt in 1985.

African Players Record

Men

100m	10.00	Chidi Imoh (Nig)	1986
200m	20.31	Tsahakile Nzimande (Rsa)	1987
400m	44.17	Innocent Egbunike (Nig)	1987
800m	1:42.28	Sammy Koskei (Ken)	1984
1500m	3:29.46	Said Aouita (Mor)	1985
1 Mile	3:46.76	Said Aouita (Mor)	1987
3000m	7:32.23	Said Aouita (Mor)	1986
5000m	12:58.39	Said Aouita (Mor)	1987
10000m	27:22.47	Henry Rono (Ken)	1978
110mh	13.69	Fatwel Kimaiyo (Ken)	1974
	13.69	Godwin Obasogie (Nig)	1976
400mh	47.82	John Akii-Bua (Uga)	1972
High jump	2.28	Othmane Belfaa (Alg)	1983
Pole vault	5.34	Lakhdar Rahal (Alg)	1979
Long jump	8.25	Paul Emordi (Nig)	1987
Triple jump	17.26	Ajayi Agbebaku (Nig)	1983
Shot put	20.71	Nagui Asaad (Egy)	1972
Discus	68.48	John Van Reenen (Rsa)	1984
Hammer	73.86	Adam Barnard (Rsa)	1976
Javelin	82.06	Chris De Beer (Rsa)	1987
Decathlon	7934m	Ahmed Mahour B. (Alg)	1985
Marathon	2:08.08	Djama Robleh (Dji)	1985
20km walk	1:26.17	Abdelwahab Ferguene (Alg)	1987
50km walk	4:14.30	Eddie Michaels (Rsa)	1967

Women

100m	11.22	Evette Armstrong (RSA)	1986
200m	22.42	Evette Armstrong (RSA)	1986

400m	50.12	Myrtle Bothma (RSA)	1986
800m	1:59.39	Ilze Venter (RSA)	1983
1500m	4:01.81	Zola Budd (RSA)	1984
1 Mile	4:28.40	Sarina Cronje (RSA)	1980
3000m	8:37.50	Zola Budd (RSA)	1984
5000m	15:01.83	Zola Budd (RSA)	1984
10000m	32:50.25	Esther Kiplagat (Ken)	1984
110mh	13.09	Ina Van Rensburg (RSA)	1986
400mh	53.74	Myrtle Bothma (RSA)	1986
High jump	2.01	Desiree Du Plessis (RSA)	1986
Long jump	6.80	Maryna Van Niekerk (RSA)	1986
Shot put	17.32	Mariette Van Heerden (RSA)	1980
Discus	58.80	Nanette Van Der Walt (RSA)	1986
Javelin	62.34	Susan Lion Cachet (RSA)	1987
Marathon	2:35.43	Sonja Laxton (RSA)	1986

AGE GROUPS

Four - seniors, juniors, youths and boys. Seniors are at least 19, juniors 17, youths 15 and 16 and boys 13 and 14 on Sept., 1st in the year of competition. Those who are at least 40 on the day of competition take part in veteran events.

For Women - intermediate between 15 and 17 and junior between 11 and 15 at mid-night on Sept., 1st/2nd in the year of competition.

A.I.M.S.

An Association with the sole purpose of encouraging and fostering marathon running throughout the world, known as the Association of International Marathons, was founded in London in May 1982. In this sphere it work's with the International Amateur Athletic Federation.

Most of the world's leading marathons are members of the Association and the Association keeps strict watch on rules, standardization , efficacy on all aspects of the game.

AKABUSI KRISS

U.K. (born 28th Nov.,1958) - Has been an invaluable member of 4x400m relay teams, and consistently sub 46 seconds. Turned to 400m hurdling in 1987, and improved in his first three meetings. Made a great breakthrough with 48.64 and 48.74 at the World Championships.

AKII-BUA,JOHN

Uganda (born 1949) - Olympic 400m hurdles champion in 1972, Akii-Bua started his athletics career as an unsuccessful high hurdler, failing to qualify for the 1968 Olympic Games in Mexico. He topped the world rankings in 1973 with 48.5, but did not compete in the 1974 Commonwealth Games.

ALDER, J.N.C.

U.K. (born 10th June, 1940) - Won 1960 Olympic marathon gold in Rome in 2 hr. 22 min. 07.8 sec. Captured the world record of 30,000m during two hour track race at Walton.

ALL-WEATHER TRACKS

The traditionally constructed running tracks of cinder and grass have undergone momentous changes time to time. In 1950, the very first all-weather surface of rubberized track was laid. In 1963, American Bob Hayes (the 1964 Olympic champion) won the AAU National title of St. Louis in 1963 on a track made of a mixture of rubber, asphalt and crushed stones, laid on top of cinders and rolled to a thickness of 1/2 inches. Again the same year, Bill Baillie of New Zealand set world records on a bitumen track. In 1964, Tokyo Olympic games were destined to be the last staged on a cinder track. Today, many all-weather tracks consist of complex polymer compounds, usually applied in liquid form but allowed to solidify.

The tartan track consisting of rubberized surfacing became very popular. It was laid at the pan-American Games in Winnipeg in 1967, the Mexico City Olympics and Crystal Palace in Europe in 1968 , and the European Championships in Athens in 1969.

The initial cost of laying all-weather tracks is very high, but this is mitigated by the low maintenance requirements and the reliability of the surface.

ALTITUDE TRAINING

Training conducted by at especially sited high altitude training venues. This is of particular value to middle and long distance runners, for the thin air at high altitude causes an increase in the oxygen carrying capacity of the blood, ;thereby improving respiration and consequently enhancing athletic performance in the richer atmosphere at sea level.

AMATEUR (DEFINITION)

The Olympic definition is "one who participates and always has participated in sport solely for pleasure and the physical, mental or social benefits he derives therefrom and to whom participation in sport is nothing more than recreation without material gain of any kind, direct or indirect".

AMBROZENE, ANNA

U.S.S.R. (born 14th Aug.,1955) - Ambrozene's world record did not help her in Helsinki when she was beaten in Helsinki by her team mate. She earned silver in 400m 1983 World Championships. She also won a silver in European Cup 1981 and 1983, in 400m hurdles.

ANCHOR LEG

The final leg, or stage, of a relay race on the track, road or country often reserved for the fastest member of each team.

AOUITA, SAID

Morocco (born 2nd Nov.,1960) - The middle distance sensation of 1983, he took third place in World Championships in Helsinki.He won the Gold Medal in 1500m in 1981. In African Championship he won silver in 1982.

APPLEGARTH, W.R.

U.K. (1890-1958)- He did marvellously well in furlong. In this event he owned or shared the world record for all of 17 years.

APPROACH RUN

Field athlete's run preceding a jump or throw in any of the four jumping events and the javelin.

ARCH PROBLEMS

If you have trouble with the arch of your foot, such that it is too painful to run on, you should try to get a shoe with ample arch support or see a poediatrist about orthotics. In addition, you can strengthen your arches by rolling a towel in your toes or standing and rising on your toes while turning them inward.

ARKHIPENKO, VASILIY

U.S.S.R. (born 28th Jan.,1957) - One of Europe's most consistent performers in 400m. hurdles. He holds the Soviet record with 48.34 sec. In 1980 Olympic games he won silver in 400m hurdle. He was lucky to win silver in Moscow with the Americans' boycott of the games.

ASHFORD, EVELYN

U.S.A. (born 15th April,1957) - In the World Cups 1979 and 1981 she won gold in 100m and 200m sprints. She has an unorthodox heelflicking style, which she has refused to modify.

ASIAN GAMES (ASIAD)

Asian Games, as we know them today, were born largely as a result of the efforts of an inspired Indian, Prof. Guru Dutt Sondhi. To Sondhi, sports were a passion.

The first Asian Games were held at New Delhi, India from 8 to 11 March 1951, when ten nations took part. These multi-sport Games have since 1954 been held at four-yearly intervals, and a record number of (over 30) nations competed in 1990.

Venues:-

1951 New Delhi
1954 Manila

1958 Tokyo
1962 Djakarta
1966 Bangkok
1970 Bangkok
1974 Teheran
1978 Bangkok
1982 New Delhi
1986 Seoul
1990 Beijing

Asian Games best performances

Men	**hr:min:Sec**	
100m	10.26	LI Tao China in 1986
200m	20.41	Chang Jee Keun (Kor) in 1982
400m	45.00	Susumu Takano (Jap) in 1986
800m	1:46.81	Charles Boromeo (Ind) in 1982
1500m	3:43.49	Faleh Naji Jarallah (Iraq) in 1982
5000m	13:24.29	Toshihiko Seko (Jap) in 1986
10000m	29:37.56	Zhang Guo wei (Chn) in 1982
Marathon	2:15:29.70	Minetaku Sakamoto (Jap) in 1978
110mh	14.09	Yoshifumi Fujimori (Jap) in 1978
400mh	50.60	Takashi Nagao (Jap) in 1982
	metres	
High jump	2.33	Zhu Jian hua (Chn) in 1982
Pole vault	5.30	Tomomi Takahashi (Jap) in 1982
Long jump	8.07	T.C.Yohanan (Ind) in 1974
Triple jump	16.80	Zou Zhenxian (Chn) in 1982
Shot put	18.53	Bahadur Singh (Ind) in 1982
Discus	58.50	Li Weinan (Chn) in 1982
Hammer	71.14	Shigenobu Morofushi (Jap) in 1982
Javelin	79.24	Shen Mao Mao (Chn) in 1978
Women		
100m	11.76	Lydia de Vega (Phi) in 1982
200m	23.79	P.T. Usha (Ind) in 1986

400m	54.11	P.T. Usha (Ind) in 1986
800m	2:05.69	Chang Jong (N.Ko) in 1982
1500m	4:18.40	Chang Jong (N.Ko) in 1982
3000m	9:24.70	Kim Ok (N.Ko) in 1978
100mh	13.31	Esther Rot (Isr) in 1974
400mh	57.23	P.T.Usha (Ind) in 1986
	metres	
High jump	1.89	Zheng Da zhen (Chn) in 1982
Long jump	6.41	Liao When feng (Chn) in 1986
Shot put	17.17	Li Mei su (Chn) in 1982
Discus	57.24	Li Xiao hui (Chn) in 1982
Javelin	60.52	Emi Matsui (Jap) in 1982

Asian players best performances

Men

100m	10.26	Li Tao (Chn) in 1986
200m	20.41	Chang Jee Keun (Sko) in 1985
400m	45.00	Susumu Takano (Jap) in 1986
800m	1:45.77	Sri Ram Singh (Ind) in 1976
1500m	3:38.24	Takashi Ishil (Jap) in 1977
1 Mile	3:59.70	Takashi Ishil (Jap) in 1977
3000m	7:54.00	Takao Nakamura (Jap) in 1979
5000m	13:24.29	Toshihiko Seko (Jap) in 1986
10000m	27:35.33	Takeyuki Nakayama (Jap) in 1987
110mh	13.72	Yu Zhicheng (Chn) in 1987
400mh	49.20	Ryoichi Yoshida (Jap) in 1987
	metre	
High jump	2.39	Zhu Jianhua (Chn) in 1984
Pole Vault	5.57	Liang Xueren (Chn) in 1987
Long jump	8.23	Chen Zunrong (Chn) in 1986
Triple jump	17.34	Zou Zhenxian (Chn) in 1981
Shot put	19.09	Ma Youngfeng (Chn) in 1980
Discus	61.06	Djalal-Ali Keshmiri (Irn) in 1974
Hammer	75.94	Shigenobu Murofushi (Jap) in 1984
Marathon	2:07.35	Taishuke Kodama (Jap) in 1986
20km walk	1:21.39	Liu Jianli (Chn) in 1985
50km walk	3:52.51	Li Baojin (Chn) in 1987

Women

100m	11.22	Chi Cheng (Tai) in 1970
200m	22.62	Chi Cheng (Tai) in 1970
400m	51.61	P.T.Usha (Ind) in 1985
800m	1:58.00	Shin Keum Dan (NKo) in 1964
1500m	4:12.80	Zheng Lijuan (Chn) in 1987
3000m	8:50.68	Wang Xiuting (Chn) in 1987
5000m	15.27.44	Wang Xiuting (Chn) in 1987
10000m	31:27.00	Wang Xiuting (Chn) in 1987
110mh	12.89	Liu Huajin (Chn) in 1987
400mh	55.42	P.T.Usha (Ind) in 1984
	metre	
High jump	1.96	Yung Wenqin (Chn) in 1985
Long jump	6.70	Huang Zhihui (Chn) in 1987
Shot put	20.95	Li Meisu (Chn) in 1987
Discus	66.76	Yu Houruen (Chn) in 1987
Javelin	65.50	Li Baolian (Chn) in 1987
Marathon	2:30.30	Akemi Masuda (Jap) in 1983
5000m walk	21.20.20	Yan Hong (Chn) in 1987

ASIAN TRACK & FIELD MEETINGS

The first Asian Track & Field Meetings were held at Marakina, near Manila, Philippines in 1973.

Venues:-

1973	Marakina
1975	Seoul
1977	Not held
1979	Tokyo
1981	Tokyo
1983	Kuwait
1985	Djakarta
1987	Seoul
1989	N.Delhi

ATKINS, KEVIN

U.S.A. (born 27th January,1960) - At the age of 22 he won American Championship in shot put and won a gold in 1982.He could not get it in Helsinki and was a sensational non-qualifier.

AUDAIN, ANNE

New Zealand (born 1st Nov.,1955) - Has had considerable success in recent years on the US road running circuit. Ran the then fastest debut marathon for fourth at Chicago in 1983.

AUTOMATIC TIMING

Fully automatic electronic timing.

AYRTON, ZENIA

India (born 16th March, 1972) - A University student from Bombay, has represented the country in 100 m and won a Bronze medal in the Asian Junior Championships in 1990 in Beijing.

B

B.A.A.B.
British Amateur Athletic Board.

BAHADUR PRASAD
India (born 1st Sep., 1965) - He has represented the country in the Asian Track & Field meet in 1989 at New Delhi. Best performance 3:41.00 sec in 1500m.

BAHADUR SINGH
India (born 8th Feb., 1946) - He has represented the country in the Olympic Games, Asian Games, Commonwealth Games. An 'Arjuna Award' winner. Best performance in shot put 18.53m.

BALAS, I.
Romania (born 12th Dec., 1936) - 6ft. 0 1/4 in. tall. She has completely dominated the women high jumping ever since 1958. Won Olympic golds in 1960 and 1964, the European titles in 1958 and 1962 and have cleared 6 ft. or higher in more than 50 competitions since 1958.

BALCHA, KEBEDE
Ethiopia (born 9th Sept.,1951) - He won the Montreal marathon three times, and was fourth in the London Marathon in 1983 and also won silver in World Championships marathon.

BANKS, WILLIE

U.S.A. (born 11th March,1956) - Willie Banks has turned one of the track and field's more esoteric disciplines into a fun event with his bubbling personality. In World Championships 1983 he won silver in triple jump and bronze in 1981 World Cup.

BANNISTER, ROGER

U.K. (born 23rd March, 1929) - Although he only won one CG medal, it was in one of the Games' classic confrontations. In the 1954 mile he was matched against Australian John Landy the only two men in the world to have bettered four minutes and it was the Englishman who came out the winner as he ran his second and last sub-4 minute mile. In his only Olympics he finished 4th in the 1500 metres in 1952. He won 1954 European 1500 metres and as everyone knows,ran the first 4 minute mile at Oxford in 1954. He was knighted in 1975.

BARBOSA, JOSE LUIS

Brazil (born 27th May, 1961) - A very consistent 800m runner. He won silver in Pan American Games 1987, and gold in 1987 World Indoor Championships.

BAREFOOT RUNNING

Mostly the primary requirement of any runner is a pair of good shoes. This is to meet the contingency of the surface being too rough, stony or slippery. In spiked shoes, the grip is greater and likelihood of any injury due to any extraneous material or bad weather is eliminated. It also reduces the amount of impact on the feet of the runner. The runners have, however, to apply surgical spirits etc. to the soles of their shoes.

Some athletes prefer running barefoot because of lightness and freedom. Most barefoot running on most synthetic tracks is possible. Running barefooted on a well-kept grass surface on a summer evening is enjoyable.

In the barefoot category, the runners have also won great laurels. The Olympic marathon was won by an Ethiopian, Abobe Bikila in 1960. In 1962, Britain's Bruce Tulloh won the European Championships 500m title in barefoot. In 1985, Zola Budd, a British citizen, won the IAAF World cross-country title, the European Cup final 3000m and set a world record for 5000m in barefoot.

BARRIOS, ARTURO

Mexico (born 12th Dec.,1963) - Had an outstanding season on the 1986 US road running circuit, when he set a world 10km road best for a loop course of 27:41 at Phoenix and also had important 15km wins at Jacksonville and Portland. First major win was in 1980 Pan American Junior 5000m

BARRY, STEVE

U.K. (born 25th Oct., 1950) - The first British walker to approach true world class in almost a decade, he captured the Commonwealth Games 30 km title, ahead of a strong international field, in a fast time of 2h. 10min. 16sec. in 1982. He also set UK track records at 20 km and 10 km in 1981 and 1982, respectively. A super fast 20 km road walk of 1:22:51 early in 1983 suggested great things at the World Championships but injury eventually ruled him out of the reckoning.

BATON

The hollow aluminium or plastic cylinder which is passed from one runner to another during a track relay race.

BAUTISTA, DANIEL

Mexico (born 1952) - He won the I.A.A.F.Race Walking World Cup (the Lugano Trophy) twice, in 1977 and 1979, setting his world best 20 km mark at the latter event in Eschborn, West Germany. He retired soon after the 1980 Olympic Games.

BAYI, FILBERT

Tanzania (born 23 June,1953) - Bayi's 1500 metres Commonwealth Games metres win in 1974 was one of the all time great races, Bayi leading from start to finish in a new world record time of 3:32.2 to beat John Walker. He set second world record the following year when he lowered the mile record to 3:51.0. He lost his Commonwealth Games 1500 metres title to Dave Moorcroft in 1978 after coming back from a serious injury, though he led for almost whole the race. In 1980 he again lost in the last few strides in the Olympic steeplechase final to Poland's Bronislaw Manilowski.

BEAMON, BOB

U. S. A. (born 29th Aug.,1946) -His claim to fame was an incredible leap of 8.90 metres during the 1968 Olympics in Mexico- 29ft 2(1/2)in when the rest of the world were struggling to clear 27ft. It is a record that has only come under threat with the appearance of Carl Lewis. It was a leap that astonished everyone,including Britain's Lynn Davies who had won the gold medal four years earlier in Tokyo. It made nonsense of the previous 30 years, in which the gap had been increased by the nearest of decimals. It also became a one off, for never again did Beamon get near his achievement. According to the record books, he never got past 8.20 metres after Mexico. In fairness, he did suffer serious hamstring injuries to his right leg, and finally turned professional in 1973.

BEARDSLEY, DICK

U.S.A. (born 21st Mar.,1956) - He was the joint winner of the London Marathon in 1981, but a leg injury put stop to his world championship hopes.

BECKER, U.W.E.

West Germany (born 10th Dec.,1955) - He like everybody else in the 800 and 1500 metres,has suffered because of the excellence of Coe and Ovett. He was 11th in 1983 World Championships and 6th in European Championships.

BELL LAP

The final lap of a middle or long distance track race, the start of which is signalled by the ringing of a bell or, as in the USA, the firing of a gun.

BENNETT, TODD

U.K. (born 6th July,1962) - A precocious talent as a teenager, he won the European Junior Championships 400 metres title in 1981. He picked up gold and silver medals in the 4x400 metres relays in Brisbane and at the European Championships the same year.

BENOIT, JOAN

U.S.A. (born 16th March, 1957) - Already the third fastest woman marathoner at the end of 1982. She produced an astonishing run in the 1983 Boston race smashing the previous Women's world best by 2 min. 47 sec. with 2:22:43, which would have won the gold medal in the men's marathon at the 1956 Olympic Games.

BEYER, OLAF

East Germany (born 4th Aug.,1957) - His victory in the 1978 European Championships was one of the biggest shock of the decade.After that he won bronze in 800m European Cup 1981

BEYER, UDO

East Germany (born 9th Aug.,1955) - In Olympic Games 1976 and 1980, in shot he won gold and bronze respectively. He captured gold in European Championships. In the World Cup 1977,1979, and 1981 he won gold in shot. Still a sports student at the age of 28, has ruled world shot putting since he won a surprise gold in Montreal.

BIKILA, ABEBE

Ethiopia (1932-1973) -As a virtual unknown and running barefoot, Abebe Bikila won the 1960 Olympic marathon in 2hr 15min 16.2sec, a world's best time. In 1964 he became the first man to win the Olympic marathon twice, recording another world's best with 2hr 12min 11.2sec. In 1968 a serious leg injury forced his retirement from the Olympics. A year later he received severe injuries in a car crash, which left him paralysed and led to his death in 1973.

BISLETT

It is more than a shade ironic that the Bislett Stadium in Oslo has been the scene for many of the highlights of recent British athletics history. The world famous stadium with its tight bends,compact six lane track and enthusiastic crowds has become the perfect stage for setting world records- as many as 37 were set there between 1924 and 1982 and the most memorable of all was Dev Moorcroft's 5,000m record in 1982. His time of 13 minutes 00.42 seconds was 20 seconds faster than his previous best for the 12(1/2) lap distance and almost 6 seconds inside the previous world reord, which was held by Kenya's Henry Rono, who finished half a lap behind Coventry's Moorcroft. The stadium has also witnessed the main bouts in the curious arms length battle between Sebastian Coe and Steve Ovett for world middle distance supremacy. Coe has set world reords at 800m, 1,000m(twice) and the mile on the Scandinavian track. Ovett set 1500m and mile records there before the Moscow Olympics in 1980.

BLACK, ROGER

U.K. (born 31st Mar., 1966) - Made a brilliant start to his international career with six gold medals both 400m and 4x400m relay, in three international championships in 1985-6.

BLANKERS-KOEN, F.E.

The Netherlands (born 26th April, 1918) - She won four gold medals at the 1948 Olympic Games in London in 100m, 200m and 80m hurdles and enabled the Dutch 4x100m relay team to victory. Between 1938 and 1951, she set official world records in no fewer than seven individual events.

BLAZER, K.

East Germany (born 5th June, 1938) - Twice hurdles champion in the European Championships.

BLIND 100 METERS

The fastest time recorded for 100m by a blind man is 11.4 sec by Graham

Henry Salmon (born 5th Sep., 1952) of Loughton, Essex, England, at Grangemouth, Scotland, on Sept 2,1978.

BLISTERS

These skin injuries, caused by the heat of friction, can be prevented by wearing correctly fitting shoes and two pairs of socks, and keeping your feet dry by sprinkling powder in your shoes. If you get a blister, you should puncture it with a sterile needle, drain the fluid, and try to put some sort of protection around the blistered area.

BOARD, LILLIAN

South Africa (1948-1970) - She was born in South Africa, her family came to Britain in 1950, and, on moving to London, Lillian was soon running well for her club, London Olympiades. She first started placing at high level in 1966, coming fourth in the W.A.A.A. Championships 440 yards (in a very respectable 54.6), and fifth in the Commonwealth Games final at the same distance.

BOIT, MOKE

Kenya (born 1st Jan.,1949) - In 1981, he twice chased Sebastian Coe home in his two world mile record races, and in 1982 was still able to lift a medal in the Commonwealth 1500 metres. He won silver in 1979 World Cup 800 metres championship.

BOLOTNIKOV, P.

U.S.S.R. (born 8th March, 1930) - In 1957, won the Soviet 10,000m. championship. In 1960, he won the Olympic title and lowered the world record to 28 min. 18.8 sec. In 1962, he won the European title and improved his record to 28 min. 18.2 sec..

BOSTON, R.H.

U.S.A. (born 9th May, 1939) - Won the Olympic championship in long jump in 1960 breaking Jesse Owens' world record after 25 years, no doubt a most outstanding achievement, and became the first to leap over 27 ft. In 1964, he improved his mark to 27ft. 5in. He was an all-rounder of high order.

BOXER , CHRISTINA

U.K. (born 25th March, 1953) - In 1979, she set a UK mile record of 4:30.2 and became the first British woman to break 2 minutes for 800 metres. She had to wait until 1982 to win her first major international title, winning the 1500 metres at the Commonwealth Games. She also reached the 1980 Olympic 800 metres semi- finals and the 1500 metres final at the 1983 World Championships.

BRASHER, C.W.

U.K. (born 21st Aug., 1928). Won the 1960 Olympic race at Melbourne in record time of 8 min. 41.2 sec.He cut his mile time to 4 min. 09.0 sec. He was later known as Roger Bannister' pacemaker and training companion.

BREAK

The point at which the runners in the outside lanes cut into the inside lane of the track after a staggered start, during a race such as an 800 metres or 4x400 metres relay.

BRIGHTWELL, R.I.

U.K. (born 27th Oct., 1939) - He won the AAA junior title in 220 yd. in 1957. At the 1960 Olympics he just failed to reach the 400 m. final after twice breaking the UK record in the preliminary rounds.

BRILL, DEBBIE

Canada (born 10th March,1953) - A twelve year gap separated Brill's two Commonwealth Games triumphs and proved that even at twenty nine, and a mother, she can take on the best in the world.She won gold in High Jump in Commonwealth Games 1970, 1982 and silver in 1978. She won another gold in World Cup 1979.

BRITISH AMATEUR ATHLETIC BOARD (BAAB)
Founded in 1932, it is affiliated to the International Amateur Athletic Federation as the governing athletic association for the United Kingdom of Great Britain and Northern Ireland. The Board is responsible for the control of international athletics in Britain.

BRITISH ATHLETICS CUPS
Knock-out inter-club competitions for both men and women. The Men's Cup was first contested in 1973, from 1974 to 1976 it was the Pye Gold Cup and from 1977 to date the GRE Gold Cup. The Women's Cup was first contested in 1974 and from 1977 has been the GRE Jubilee Cup.

BRITISH ATHLETICS LEAGUE
First held in 1969. Contested by British men's teams.

BROWN, A.G.K.
U.K. (born 21st Feb., 1915) - In 1936 Olympic 400 m. final in Britain, he lowered the European record to 46.7 sec. only to lose by a mere two-hundredths of a second to the world record holder Archie Williams. He anchored the British team to an easy victory in the 4x400 m. relay . In his finest run just after the games, he was timed at 45.9 sec. for a 440 yd. relay leg. and snatched a win for his Commonwealth team. In 1938 he won the European 400 m. title.

BRUMEL, V.
U.S.S.R. (born 14th April, 1942) - In 1960, at the age of 18, he set a European record of 7 ft. 2 (1/2) in. in high jump and won the silver medal in the Olympic games . He shared the Olympic record of 7 ft. 1 in. He shared the 1964 Olympic title with John Thomas at 7ft. 1 (1/2) in. He is the highest jumper of all time both in terms of elevation [7 ft. 5 (1/)2 in] and the number of inches he has leapt above his own head.

BRYGGARE, ARTO

Finland (born 26th May,1958) - He became the first Finnish to win a medal in the 1983 110m hurdles World Championships.He competed like a man inspired. He also won bronze in 1978,1982 European Championships.

BUBKA, SURGEY

U.S.S.R. (born 4th Dec.,1963) - World champion in 1983 has gone on to dominate the world of Pole Vaulting, and has not been beaten in a championship since then. Has the speed and strength to manage a very high hold on the pole.

BUDD, ZOLA

South Africa (born 26th May, 1966) - Zola Budd was a marvellous bare foot runner. She made a series of unofficial world junior records at the age of 17, plus a 5000m time of 15;01.83 which was nearly seven seconds inside Mary Decker's world senior best. Because of being a South African and due to apartheid policy, she was banned from the Olympics and from international competitions. She, however, acquired British citizenship as her grandfather was a Londoner after great botheration. Physically protected and facing heavy opposition, she made her mark in many events. Her first Olympics in Los Angeles were to end in highly charged controversy.Watched by hundreds of millions on television, the do-or-die joust between Zola and American number one runner Mary Decker in the 3000 metres final climaxed in Decker's crashing fall, tears, and tension in the most debated debacle in modern Olympics. After humiliation, decided permanently to settle in South Africa but changed her mind and came again to England. Again she ran in the face of great opposition and heavy odds. In the European Cup final in Moscow, she led all the way in the 3000 m to record Britain's first European Cup final women's track win for eighteen years. Her time of 8;35.32 was a Commonwealth record and she reduced it to 8;28.83 in Rome, as well as becoming the first female UK runner to break four minutes for 1500m(with 3.59 in Brussels), had set a Commonwealth mile record of 4;17.57 in Zurich, and broken the world 5000m record.

BUGAR, IMRICH

Czechoslovakia (born 14th April,1955) -The ability of this country to produce world class discus throwers continued with Bugar, who took over from the great Ludvik Danek, holder of silver in discus at 1980 Olympics. He too had gold in 1983 World Championships. Again in European Championships 1978 and 1982 he captured gold and bronze.

BURGHLEY, LORD

U.K. (born 5th Feb.,1905) - Olympic 400 m hurdles winner in 1928 and fourth (in his fastest time) in 1932, silver medallist in the 1932 Olympic 4 x 400 m. relay, triple gold medallist at the 1930 Commonwealth Games - 120 yd. hurdles, 440 yd. hurdles and 4 x 440 yd. relay. He has been president of the AAA since 1936 and of the International Amateur Athletic Federation since 1946.

BURKI CORNELIA

Switzerland (born 3rd Oct., 1953) - Her two daughters were born in 1972, before she began her running career. Very consistent in major events, she achieved her best ever placings in Rome 1987.

BUTLER, G.M.

U.K. (born 25th Aug., 1899). For 40 years Guy Butler remained Britain's most bemedalled Olympian with one gold, one silver and two bronze awards to his name. In 1920 Olympics, he won silver in 400 m and brought the British team to victory in the 4 x 400 m relay. In 1924, he was third in the Olympic 400 m. Another bronze, he gained in the relay. He also worked as coach, writer and cine photographer.

BYKOVA, TAMARA

U.S.S.R. (born 21st Dec.,1958) - A fascinating racial mixture, half Greek/ half Russian, the statuesque blonde won the gold in high jump 1983 World Championships. Earned a silver in 1982 European Championships and another silver in European Cup 1983. In World Students Games she earned gold in 1983.

C

CAETANO DA SILVA, ROBSON

Brazil (born 4th Sept., 1964) - In 1987 World Championships he placed fourth in 200m and won gold in 1985 World Cup.

CAGE

A tall metal frame supporting a heavy hemp net that partially surrounds the throwing circles for the hammer and discus events, designed to prevent implements from flying in the direction of spectators if released accidentally.

CALHOUN, L.Q.

U.S.A. (born 23rd Feb., 1933) - He won the Olympics 110m hurdles twice in 1956 and 1960. He is co-holder of the world records for 110 m and 120 yd hurdles at 13.2 sec. in 1960 and is considered one of the finest hurdling exponent of all -time.

CALLISTHENICS

Stretching and suppling exercises used by sprinters, hurdlers, jumpers and throwers as part of the warm up routine to improve mobility for competition.

CALLUSES

Calluses are rough, thick areas of dead skin on the foot and are usually irritating to run on. An experienced person can shave them down with a razor blade, but caution is essential to avoid cutting live skin. You can also smoothen a callus with a pumice stone, but the best ounce of prevention is a good pair of running shoes.

CAMERON, BERT

Jamaica (born 16th Nov.,1959) - In 1982 he won his third NCAAA 400 metres title in 44.62, which was the fastest in the world that year. He won gold in 400m in World Championships and Commonwealth Games.

CAMPBELL, TONIE

U.S.A. (born 14th June, 1960) - He is reckoned by statisticians to be the best athlete who did not go to the World Championships.In 1981 World's Students Games he claimed 4th position in 110 metres hurdles.

CANTO, ERNESTO

Mexico (born 18th Oct.,1959) - Continuing Mexico's fine tradition in race walking, he captured the 20 km title at the 1983 World Championships at the age of 23 and quickly followed that with a second win, over the same distance, at the Pan American Games. One of the first walkers to clock sub 1h 20min. for 20 km he won his first major event,the Lugano Trophy.

CARBOHYDRATE LOADING

So much has been written about the dietary manipulation known as carbohydrate loading and its apparent benefits to marathon performance, that it has been wrongly regarded in some circles as an alternative to hard training. As long ago as 1939, it had been demonstrated in a classic study that while reducing the normal carbohydrate levels in an endurance competitor's diet lowered his endurance capacity, carbohydrate significantly prolonged it. In 1966, further laboratory tests were performed in Sweden using long distance cyclists riding bicycle. During the post-exercise period, in which the expected replenishment of glycogen is not forthcoming.

A successful formula for dietary manipulation seemed to be:

1. Hard exercise to deplete the glycogen stores.
2. Ignore the temptation to replace them immediately.
3. Allow the body to produce extra glycogen storing enzymes.
4. Re-introduce carbohydrates.

News of the Swedish experiment was sent by a friend to British marathon runner Ron Hill, whose analytical mind was always searching for ways of trying to improve performance. He developed his own version of the diet in 1969 AAA Marathon championship in Manchester and beat the holder of the world best Derek Clayton. Dietary preparation brought Hill his international honour when he won the European marathon title in Athens. Hill revealed details of the diet in a newspaper interview, and later progressed through a series of other racing successes, including victory in the Fukuoka classic marathon in Japan in December 1969.

His new found level of ability and consistency really gave the carbohydrate loading diet the public stamp of approval and recognition and everywhere marathon runners were trying it out,often with mixed fortunes.The diet at that time consisted of three phases .Firstly the 'bleed-out' of existing glycogen stores secondly after the run and for the following three days,the diet should consist of a high protein and fat content. The disadvantages soon began to become apparent . Not everyone noticed the same beneficial effects and for each one who did,there seemed to be someone else who had suffered from major digestive problems before and during the race. To feel sluggish,full and heavy is not always the best preparation for a long road race. So the emphasis should really be on a higher percentage of carbohydrate in the diet rather than an enormously increased volume.Also, during that second phase, when an iron will is needed to resist the temptation to eat sweet foods, the body may be weak and vulnerable to any germ or virus which may be around its natural defences are lessened, and there is a higher risk of contacting a cold or flu. Ron Hill, with the hindsight now of many marathons and experiments using high and low carbohydrate diets behind him, has modified his own views on the diet. During these first three days he still eats food like bacon, cheese,eggs, ham meat, butter, fish etc., together with green salads and vegetables. From midway through the fourth day, his emphasis switches to a much higher concentration of carbohydrates, but with care not to overdo the total quantity of consumed food, which should be normal.

As the man who bridged the gap between the research scientists laboratory and the road racing world, Hill is still, nearly twenty years later, having to explain and illustrate his dietary experiences.

Above all, though, nothing can replace training, there is little point in going to considerable extremes of dietary manipulation intended to help you over the last miles of the marathon if you are not basically fit enough to get that far in the first place.

CARISTAN, STEPHANE

France (born 31st May, 1964) - In 1986, European Championships he won gold in 110m hurdle. Two European 110m hurdle records in 1986. Operation on right knee in March held back his 1987 season.

CARR, H.

U.S.A. (born 27th Nov.,1942) - He established himself as the greatest furlong athlete the world had yet seen. He won over 400 m in 45.4 sec in the 1963 West Germany vs. USA match and over 440 yd. in 46.0 sec. in Australia shortly after the 1964 Olympics. He won two gold medals in 1964 Olympic -in 200 m in 20.3 sec and anchoring USA in the 4x400 m relay.

CARTILAGE TROUBLE

Cartilage trouble will have to be analysed by our doctors, but the consolation is that many ex-rugby and ex-football players whose cartilages ended their careers,are now running marathon.

CASTELLA, ROBERT DE

Australia (born 1957) - He became one of the world's most consistent marathon runners after he made his debut at the distance in 1979. He has since completed 16 marathons, six under 2:10 and all under 2:15, and has won eight of them. The only one he failed to finish was in Rome in 1987 at the I.A.A.F.World Championships, where he was strongly fancied to win.

CASTRO DOMINGOS

Portugal (born 22nd Nov.,1963) - Broke into top class in 1986, and continued the progress in 1987 when he was a surprise silver medallist at 5000m in Rome.

CAWLEY, W.J.

U.S.A. (born 6th July, 1940) - When 18, he made history by becoming the only athlete ever to place in the first six of all three hurdles finals at the American AAU Championships. He set a new world's 400 m hurdles record of 49.1 sec in the final US Olympic Trials and powered to victory in the Olympics (49.6 sec) in 1964.

CHAFING

The repetitive action in long distance running with thousands of identical strides in every race or training run leads to painful chafing.The cause of chafing may be clothing that is too tight or becomes an irritant when sweat soaked or has an inner seam which,when wet,may take on saw like properties. Prevention of paramount importance since races for which the runner has conscientiously prepared may otherwise be spoiled by a painful oversight. If you do suffer in a race, an unofficial stop by a first aid post may provide some petroleum jelly, and in some long races the organizers even provide Vaseline alongside the drinks and sponges at the later refreshment stations.

CHANGE DOWN

The transition, during a 400 metres hurdles race,from one astride pattern to another involving a greater number of strides between each of the hurdles.

"CHARIOTS OF FIRE"

In 1981, this film has been the most successful attempt so far by the cinema to portray the tensions of athletic performance. It followed the build up of two contrasting British sprinters, Harold Abrahams and Eric Liddell, to their eventual gold medal successes in the 1924 Paris Olympics.

There Abrahams, spurred on by his experiences of anti-semitism at Cambridge University, won the 100m while his great rival Scottish Liddell, whose Christian beliefs would not allow him to run the 100m which was held on Sunday won the 400m Director Huge Hudson and producer David Puttnam created a film which was spellbinding even to non - sporting audiences and while the fair number of dramatic liberties in terms of fact did not spoil the most pedantic athletics historian.

For example in the film, when Liddell discovers that the 100m heats will be held on a Sunday,he is just about to board the boat for Paris. In fact ,he knew a year before and his intention to run the 400m instead were well known. The romance between Abrahams and his wife Sybil did not actually happen until some time after the Paris Olympics.

Burghley, who became President of the AAA from 1936 to 1976, and of the IAAF from 1946 to 1976, was actually robbed of one of his achievements in the production. In an early sequence, Harold Abrahams is depicted as successfully running round the 370 yards of uneven flagstones of the great court at Trinity College, Cambridge including three right angled turns before the clock finishes striking noon. The feat was achieved by Lord Burghley during 1927 at Cambridge. Lord Burghley died shortly after the film release in 1981.

The sequences of 1924 Paris Olympics were staged at Bebington Oval,near Liverpool, which was cosmetically transformed into Colombes Stadium.

The film brought plaudits to action Ian Holm for his portrayal of Sam Musabini. The film ends with homecoming of the Olympic champions, before cutting to a recreation of 1978 memorial service for Abrahams. He died in 1925 following leg injury while long jumping. He went on to become a ubiquitous figure as an athletics administrator and elected to the AAA General Committee in 1926 and later he was the president. He was broadcaster on BBC radio.

Liddell who had been born of Scottish parents in China in 1902 did not compete seriously after 1925. He devoted rest of his life to missionary work in China and married to a Canadian missionary's daughter in 1934. They had three daughters. He died of brain haemorrhage when 43. His last words were: 'It is complete surrender'.

CHATAWAY, C.J.

U.K. (born 31st Jan., 1931) - Few athletes have enjoyed such widespread popularity as Chri Chataway. It was Chataway who pulled Roger Bannister to the first four minute mile and pushed John Landy to the second, and thereafter himself broke the barrier in 1955.

CHECK-UPS

The doctor's surgery is not the most exciting starting line for a sporting career, but for some it is an advisable port of call. If you have any doubts at all about your health you should go for a check up first, and if your own doctor is not prepared to do it, there are lots of other fitness testing centres that will. Even if you feel sure you are ready to run but if you fall into any of the following categories then a check up is a must:

(a) are seriously overweight,
(b) are over forty years of age,
(c) smoke or drink heavily,
(d) have not exercised for ten years,
(e) already have a medical condition,
(f) huff and puff after climbing the stairs,
(g) have high blood pressure,
(h) have a high pulse rate.

It is, after all, only a minor inconvenience and a small price to pay for an 'all clear' that can launch a new lifestyle.

CHICAGO MARATHON

From a modest beginning, the America's Marathon/Chicago grew rapidly to give its proper name in Status to threaten the New York City Marathon for prestige if not quantity. First held in 1977 as the Mayor Daley Marathon it became the world's biggest marathon. But New York bettered that 4000 figure a month later and then Chicago event drifted as just another U,S. marathon. Internal wrangling, and public controversy over the race threatened its very future.

The appointment of an exmarine, Bob Bright, as race director in 1982 made a significant difference and so did the result of 1983 race in which Kenyan Joseph Nzau and Britain's Huge Jones sprinted together for the finish line. Nzau was judged the winner though both shared the same time. New Zealand's Anne Audain fell and twisting her ankle and the three other runners passed her in women's race and she stood fourth. Her own $20000 first prize shrunk to a $4000.

Another drama followed in 1984 when Welshman Steve Jones shocked everyone by winning the world's best time of 2hr 8min 5sec which gave the event a new aura. And although Jones subsequently lost the record to Carlos Lopes the following year in Chicago, Jones again produced an astonishing performance with 2hr 7min 13 sec. In the same race the Olympic women's champion, Joan Benoit Samuelson gained revenge over Ingrid Kristiansen, Norwegian who had taken her world record in London six months earlier. Race between Benoit Samuelson and Kristiansen's had been confirmed by AIMS as accurately measured.

Despite 1985 frustrations for Bob Bright and his fellow organizers, this series of dramatic incidents helped to establish the America's Marathon/Chicago as a truly elite race.

CIERPINSKI, WALDEMAR

East Germany (borh 3rd Aug.,1950) - He managed fastest of 2:12.20 when finished 4th in the Prague Europeans marathon, but he emulated Bikila's feat of retaining the Olympic title with 2:11.03, the second fastest time of his life. He won marathon gold in 1976 and 1980 Olympic Games.

CLARK, DARREN

Australia (born 6th Sept., 1965) - Set world age 17 best to win 400m AAA title in 1983. Ran a 43.86 relay leg in 1984 Olympics. Three Australian 400m records in 1985-1986 and two Commonwealth 300m bests in 1985-86.

CLARKE, DAVE

U.K. (born 1st Jan., 1958) - One of the best and outstanding British cross-country runners in recent years. Finished second in 1981 and 1983. He is also an accomplished track runner.

CLARKE, R.W.

Australia (born 21st Feb., 1937) - He was setter of world records for seven events simultaneously - 3 mi, 500 m, 6 mi, 10,000 m, 10 mi, 20,000 m. and one hour. In 1964, he won the Olympic 10,000 m and in 1966 he won two silver medals in addition to the one he obtained in the 3 mi four years earlier. Altogether he won three silver medals at the Commonwealth Games from 1962 to 1966 and finally bowed out with yet another silver at the Commonwealth Games in the 10,000 metres in 1970.

CLAYTON, DEREK

Australia (born 1942) - One of only three men to have set two world bests in the marathon (the other two are Jim Peters of Great Britain and Abebe Bikila of Ethiopia). At the Olympics in 1968 he could only finish seventh,having been plagued by cartilage trouble earlier in the year.

CLOTHING & FOOTWEAR

In all events competitors must wear at least a vest and shorts clean and so designed and worn as not to be objectionable.The clothing must be made of a material which is non-transparent even if wet. Competitors may compete in bare feet or with shoes on one or both feet. The purpose of shoes is to give protection and stability to the feet and a firm grip of the ground. The shoes should not be so designed and constructed so as to give the competitor any additional assistance.

CLUBS

Athletic clubs form the backbone of the sports in Britain and most other countries. More than 1,800 clubs and associations in England and Wales alone are affiliated to the Amateur Athletic Association. Probably the first athletic club was the Necton Guild in Norfolk, founded in 1817, but no trace can be found of it after 1826.

COACHING

National Coaching Foundation, which is concerned with all sports, defines a coach as someone capable of filling the roles of instructor,manager, administrator,social worker,friend and student.

A runner progressing pre-teen novice to Olympic champion would probably learn the basic training at a local club from a more specialized coach. An experienced coach not necessarily attached to their club but would help them refine the ideal training programme for their talent for the entry into the territory of international competition.

Most athletics coaches, qualified and unqualified, are amateurs, working in their spare time at considerable personal expense. This is not understood by the athletes. Coaching is always helpful for the distance runners to have a chance to chat to a coach on occasions,or at least to a more experienced runner who may be able to offer advice without entering into a long term coaching relationship. There is a network of national,regional and county coaches in all events to provide general guidance to individual athletes to help them, if they wish, to find a coach in their area. A separate range of courses,booklets and video cassettes has been established by the National Coaching Foundation with a view to encouraging more people to become coaches.

COE, SEBASTIAN

U.K. (born 29 Sep., 1956) - When Sebastian Coe became the first man ever to retain the Olympic 1500m title in 1984 at Los Angeles it helped to reduce the painful memories in the intervening four years since he had first won the title at Moscow.

After Coe's decade in the top strata of international middle distance running,with a host of world records and big victories, it is still surprising to realize that upto the end of 1986 his tally of gold medals in major championships was just three. His rivalry with Steve Ovett, constantly if unconvincingly denied, helped to promote public awareness of the sports in the U.K. London born Coe joined the Sheffield Club Hallamshire Harriers at the age of 12. His father studied books and magazines and attended coaching courses, to learn all he could to devise a training schedule suitable for his son. At the age of 14 he was Yorkshire schools junior cross-country champion. Far from becoming a 1500/3000m specialist, Sebastian decided with his father that his competitive career should be moving down in distance rather than up. His further training,which now included a great deal of sprinting and mobility work was clearly paying off,and by 1978 it was certain that Coe would be a force at that year's European Championship in Prague especially when he improved his own UK record. Coe and Ovett met in the final at Prague. Coe stormed through the first lap in under 50 seconds with Ovett right on his shoulder. It was disappointing for both of them as the East Germany's Olaf Beyer passed them to snatch the gold. They finally met for only the second time on the track at the 1980 Moscow Olympics where both ran the 800m and 1500m, despite not having raced each other during the selection process. Yet on the eve of the games, in Oslo, both had set world records within an hour.But six days later in the 1500m final, the tables were turned . Coe, desperate to make amends for his disappointment in the 800m,turned in a last lap. Ovett, unable to mount a real challenge , was third.

As early as 10 June 1981, Coe produced a phenomenal world 800m record in Florence, and was so dominant on the stop-watch that the average of his five fastest 800m races at that moment (1:43.27) was faster than any other runner had achieved even once. Ovett, contented with his Olympic gold medal at the 800m,left the shorter distance records to Coe. The 1982 season offered chances of gold medals to both the champions, but for Coe it was to prove a dismal year. Following a stress fracture in his foot. He pulled out of the Commonwealth Games due to glandular fever. By the time of the European Championships Coe had recovered, and in a glorious moment for British Athletics, he, Cram, and the young Scot Tom Mckean battled out the 800m medals down the home straight. This time at last,Coe was the winner in 1:44.50, but a few days later, attempting the double, he had to give best to the determined Cram in the 1500m, losing in a furious last 800m run in 1:46.0. Coe was ready to explore a new chapter of his career, while combining his running with a part-time post as Vice Chairman of the Sports Council.

COGHLAN, EAMONN

Ireland (born 21st Nov.,1952) - Eamonn's delight at winning gold in Helsinki was understandable; he finished Ist in the major championships. He finished 4th in 5000m and 1500m in Olympic Games 1976 and 1980 respectively. He claimed gold medal in 1983 World Championships and World Cup.

COMMONWEALTH GAMES

The first British Commonwealth Games were played at Hamilton, Canada in 1930. In the second Commonwealth Games in London in 1934, women's events were introduced. The games are held in various Commonwealth countries every four year.

The centrepiece of the Games,where the Olympic greats and world-record holders mingle with emerging world-class competitors. Africa, West Indies, Canada, Australia and New Zealand usually play apromient part, and with Steve Cram, Seb Coe, Steve Ovett and Daley Thompson to call on, England will be favourites to win a crop of gold medals. But this is where unknown Africans descend from altitude to upset the dedicated long-distance runners from lowland countries. Commonwealth Games athletics provide a platform for a host of world-class athletes to display their talents at the very highest level, whilst giving stage to those who, if only for a fleeting moment, capture the attention of millions.

Commonwealth Players Records

Men

100m	9.83	Ben Johnson (Can) in	1987
200m	19.86	Donald Quarrie (Jam) in	1971
400m	44.17	Innocent Egbunike (Nig) in	1987
800m	1:41.73	Sebastian Coe (UK) in	1981
1500m	3:29.67	Steve Cram (UK) in	1985
1 Mile	3:46.32	Steve Cram (UK) in	1985
3000m	7:32.10	Henry Rono (Ken) in	1978
5000m	13.00.41	Dave Moorcroft (UK) in	1982
10000m	27.22.47	Henry Rono (Ken) in	1978
110mh	13.23	Mark Mckoy (Can) in	1987
400mh	47.82	John Akii-Bua in	1972
	metre		
High jump	2.33	Milt Ottey (Can) in	1986
Pole vault	5.65	Keith Stock (UK) in	1981
Long jump	8.27	Gary Honey (Aus) in	1984
Triple jump	17.57	Keith Connor (UK) in	1982
Shot put	21.68	Geoff Capes (UK) in	1980
Discus	67.32	Rob Gray (Can) in	1984
Hammer	77.54	Martin Girvan (NI) in	1984
Javelin	85.24	Mick Hill (UK) in	1987
Marathon	2:07.13	Steve Jones (Wal) in	1985
20km walk	1:19.22	Dave Smith (Aus) in	1987
50km walk	3:46.34	Willi Sawall (Aus) in	1980

Women

100m	10.87	Merlene Ottey (Jam) in	1987
200m	21.93	Merlene Ottey (Jam) in	1985

400m	49.43	Kathy Cook (UK) in	1984
800m	1:57.42	Kirsty McDermott (Wal)in	1985
1500m	3:59.96	Zola Budd (UK) in	1985
1Mile	4:17.57	Zola Budd (UK) in	1985
3000m	8:28.83	Zola Budd (UK) in	1985
5000m	14.48.07	Zola Budd (UK) in	1985
10000m	31:19.82	Liz Lynch (Sco) in	1987
110mh	12.87	Shirley Strong (UK) in	1983
400mh	53.76	Debbie Flintoff (Aus) in	1986
	metre		
High jump	1.99	Debbie Brill (Can) in	1982
Long jump	6.90	Beverley Kinch (UK) in	1983
Shot put	19.74	Gael Martin (Aus) in	1984
Discus	67.48	Meg Ritchie (Sco) in	1981
Javelin	77.44	Fatima Whitbread (Eng) in	1986
Marathon	2:26.06	Lisa Martin (NZ) in	1986
5000m walk	21:16.00	Kerry Saxby (Aus) in	1987

COMMON COLD

Common cold is more of a problem for runners because they experience frequent changes in temperature and weather and are often in between being wet and dry. They also run down their reserves, so more care should be taken in showering and changing quickly, with an intake of vitamin C as an added insurance. Once you have got a cold, the best policy is to rest and certainly not to run. It could turn to something much worse. Running should never be considered if you have temperature. On the other hand, asthma and hay fever should not stop you getting out, but ensure you always have your inhaler with you.

CONNOR, KEITH

West Indies (born 16th Sept.,1957) - Connor went into the World Championships as favourite but he came out as a non-qualifier. He was fourth in Olympic Games 1980 triple jump. In European Games he won a gold in 1982.

CONSOLINI, A.

Italy (born 5th Jan., 1917) - He had a consistent long career in the top flight as discus thrower. He broke the world record three times - in 1941 (175ft. 0in.), 1946 (177ft. 11in.) and 1948 (181ft. 6(1/2)in.). However, his throw (186ft. 11(1/2)in) in 1955 was his best. He was Olympic champion in 1948 and silver medallist in 1952. In 1946, 1950 and 1954 he was European champion.

COOPER, BRAD

Bahamas (born 30th June,1957) - An immense man, Cooper shows the difference in throwing event standards between the Commonwealth, the USA and Eastern bloc. He won gold in Commonwealth Games 1982 and silver in 1978 for discus throw.

COOPER, J.H.

U.K. (born 18th Dec., 1940). He was the sole holder of the U.K. 400 m hurdle record in 1963 when he won against the Russian Federation Republic in Volgograd in 50.5 sec. In 1964 Olympics he won 400 m hurdle in 50.5 sec. and semi-final in 50.4 sec. and in the final he got Olympic silver medal with yet another U.K. record - 50.1 sec. Later in the Games with his official personal best 440 yd. time of 47.9 sec., he stormed through his 400m in 45.6 sec., making Britain take second place.

COVA, ALBERTO

Italy (born 1st Dec.,1958) - He will be a favourite for the 5000m and 10,000m. He won the gold in 1983 World Championships and 1982 European Championships in 10,000m. He also won silver in 1983 European Cup.

CRAMP

Cramp is one of the most common, usually in the calf muscles, which occurs when you are overtired or have lost a lot of minerals in your sweat. You can treat it by grabbing hold of your leg and gradually stretching it in the opposite direction of the contraction. Cramp can be prevented by taking in adequate amounts of electrolytes before and during your run.

CRAM, STEVE

U.K. (born 14 Oct.,1960)- It seemed unlikely, at a time around 1980, when British athletics was still marvelling at its good fortune in simultaneously having two such brilliant 1500m runners as Steve Ovett and Sebastian Coe, that a third runner of similar stature could emerge.

He followed both his countrymen as a holder of the world record but to reach that position, he passed through a number of obstacles which could have sidetracked him. His attention became focused more on running and encouraged by Jimmy Hedley, coach. Some encouraging performances in 1975, notably in the English Schools junior championships,where he was third in the cross-country and fourth in the 1500m, helped reassure Cram that he had made the right choice of sport, and guided by Hedley he soon made his mark as one of Britain's leading young middle distance prospects. In May 1977 Cram surprised the athletics world by running a UK age 16 best of 3:47.7 for 1500m at Gateshead. During the Durham School Championships in June ,passing 400m in 58 seconds during a self-made run in a race which he won by over 15 seconds. His time was 2.2 seconds faster than the UK best set by Steve Ovett. A month later with the Commonwealth Games approaching, the Scottish selectors did not send Williamson and Cram was picked for England and although he did not get through his heat, it was the start of an international apprenticeship which was to continue for some years, but then pay valuable dividends. At the UK Championships in June ,the main trial, disaster struck Cram, who tripped and fell just after the bell, and jogged home a dejected last, while Williamson finished second to Dave Moorcroft. But with Moorcroft opting for the 5000m in Moscow instead, and Cram a few days later in Norway running the fastest time by a British athlete in 1980 with a 3:37.3 to ease his frustration the selectors asked Williamson and Cram to race again during a Dream Mile in Oslo in July Cram finished second. In 1981, he continued to be rather overshadowed by the Big Two, but he was getting closer. But if,in 1982, he was able to step out of the shadow a little, he still did not feel he was fully accepted although he won both the titles that year as Coe was ill. A year later,at the inaugural World Championships in Helsinki, he added another gold medal to his collection as Coe was again absent and Ovett had run an uncharacteristically poor tactical race.

Most memorable race for British fans that season came in the IAC Coca Cola Floodlit event at Crystal Palace on 9th Sept. Ovett announced that he,too, would run the mile. He wanted another crack at Cram before the end of the year. Ovett had lost the World title, but he wanted to even the score,especially as his world 1500m record had shown him he was in terrific form. Cram made the first move from 350m out, and Ovett chased him all the way to the finish, just a stride behind. In the home straight, he could not get on terms and Cram remained just in front,to win. Meanwhile,Cram was being treated for an injury to his right calf, which had seriously interrupted his Los Angeles preparation. He finished second to Coe in Los Angeles. He set his first world record for 1500m narrowly beating Olympic 5000m champion Said Aouita of Morocco in July 1985 and take revenge on Seb Coe by beating him in Oslo and taking his world mile record away on 27th July. He even narrowly missed setting a world 1000m record in poor weather conditions at his native Gateshead on 9 August,and while he was still getting faster in training, beat Olympic 800m champion Joaquim Cruz in Zurich in his fastest ever 800m time of 1:42.88. But a hamstring injury, frustratingly, ended his phenomenal season.Cram turned the tables again on Coe, outsprinting him on the final lap of the 1500m final, to end the championship season on a high note, with at least three of his four gold medals.

In some ways, not winning the 1984 Olympic title may have been a godsend to Cram. Trying to win the one 1500m title to have eluded him keeps him motivated. "I have got to try to win it in Seoul, otherwise when I am 50 people will still come up to me and say you weren't as good as Coe because you never won the Olympics."

CRAWFORD, HASELY

Trinidad (born 1950) - He was the winner of the 100m title in Montreal in 1976. Facing an impressive field, including defending champion Valeriy Borzov of the Soviet Union, Don Quarrie of Jamaica, and Havey Glance of the USA, his winning time of 10.06 seconds placed him sixth on the all time list.

CROSS-COUNTRY CLUBS

For those contemplating a season in the mud, many running clubs organise come-and-try-it cross country events at the end of the autumn. If you have trouble in finding such an event, a letter to any of the following addresses should help.

England Men: Barry Wallman, 7 Wolsey Way, Cherry Hinton,Cambridge.
Women: Vera Duerdin, 10,Anderton Close, Bury, Lancs.

Scotland Men: Ian Clifton, 38 Silverknowes Drive,Edinburgh 4.
Women: Mrs. J.Ward, 144 Canberra Avenue, Dalmuir West, Clyde bank.

Wales Men: G. Collins, Harriers Haunt, 40, Twyniteg, Killey, Swansea.
Women: Margaret Elgie, 19 Coedbach, Highlight Park, Barry, South Glamorgan.

N.Ireland Men: Northern Ireland Sports Council (Athletics), 2 Upper Malone Road, Belfast 9.
Women: Pam Reece, 28, Ravelston Avenue, Glengormley, N.Ireland.

CROSS-COUNTRY RUNNING

What exactly constitutes 'cross-country' has been interpreted differently over the years. Even the IAAF conceded in its rules that owing to the extremely varying circumstances in cross-country running in regard to different seasons, climatic conditions and distances, it is not possible to lay down any rigid legislation for internal standardization of this sport. For championship and international events, it is ,however, laid down that the race shall be run over a course confined, as far as possible, to open country, fields, heathland, commons and grasslands. A limited amount of ploughed land may be included. If the course passes through woodland without any clearly defined path or track, it must be clearly marked for the runners. The traversing of roads of any description should be limited to the minimum.

It is much more difficult to measure distances as accurately as on road. Further, the exact distances even on the same course may vary year to year , according to the lances where the flags are placed. Time is slower because of mud, uneven ground, and long grass. Spiked or studded shoes are necessary to retain some grip. It is actually a game of stamina and strength. The first English Cross-Country Championship as such was staged in Epping Forest in 1876, but all thirty-two competitors went off course and the race was declared void. The 1988 race, held over eleven and a quarter miles at

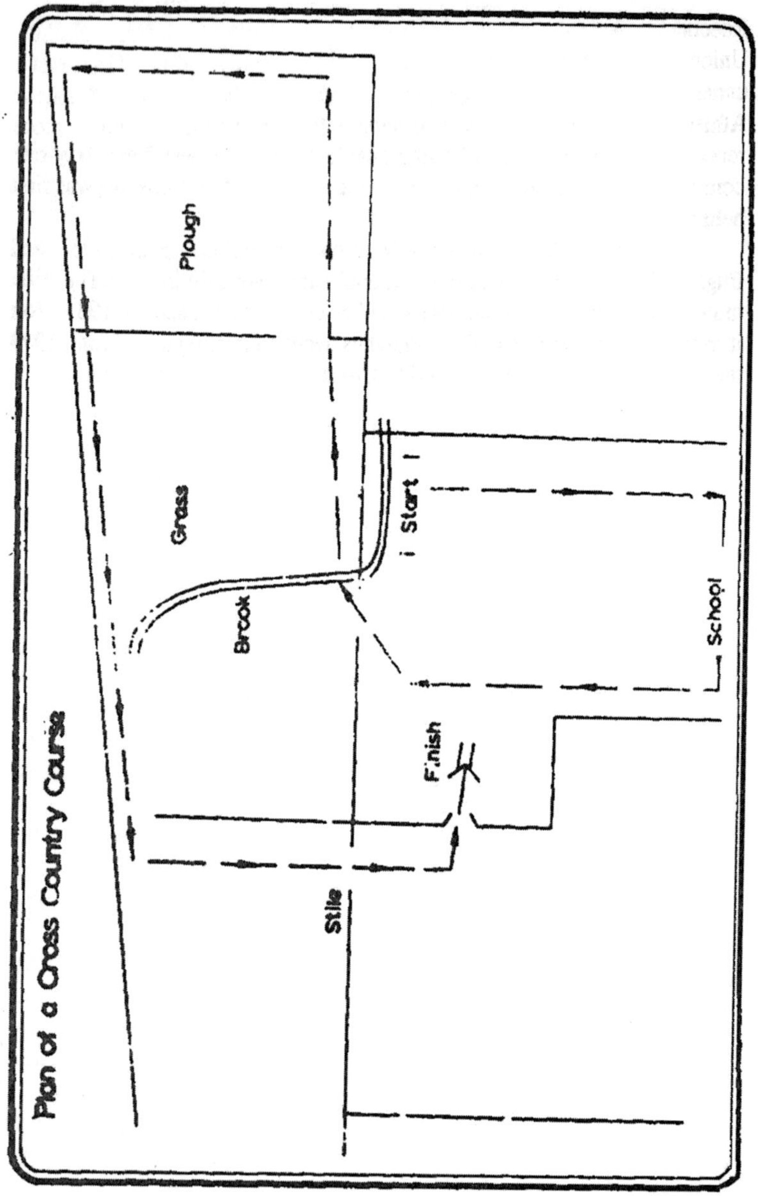

Plan of a Cross Country Course

Roechampton was won by Percy Stenning. The English Cross-country Union (ECCU) was founded in 1883, it grew steadily and in 1973 it came under the wing of the world governing body., the International Amateur Athletic Federation, which has subsequently helped expand it into a more representative annual World Championship. In 1986 runners from sixty-one countries took part. The Junior Men's race in these championships was first held in 1961.

France held a Women's National Championship in 1923 and England held its first Women 's National Championship in 1927. The first international women's match was held at Douai, in France, in 1931. But it was not until 1967, that their matches were held regularly. From 1973 they became a part of IAAF World Cross-country Championship.

WORLD CROSS-COUNTRY CHAMPIONSHIPS

Year	Winner	Nationality (Venue)
1903	Alf Shrubb	England(Glasgow)
1904	Alf Shrubb	England(St Helens)
1905	Albert Aldridge	England(Dublin)
1906	Charles Straw	England(Caerleon)
1907	Alfred Underwood	England(Glasgow)
1908	Arthur Robertson	England(Paris)
1909	Edward Wood	England(Derby)
1910	Edward Wood	England(Belfast)
1911	Jean Bouin	England(Caerleon)
1912	Jean Bouin	England(Edinburgh)
1913	Jean Bouin	England(Paris)
1914	Arthur Nichols	England(Chesham)
1915-19	(not held)	
1920	James Wilson	England(Belfast)
1921	Walter Freeman	England(Newport)
1922	Joseph Guillemot	France (Glasgow)
1923	Charles Blewitt	France (Paris)
1924	William Cotterell	England (Gosfoth)
1925	Jack Webster	England (Dublin)
1926	Ernest Harper	France (Brussels)

1927	Lewis Payne	France (Caerleon)
1928	Harold Eckersley	France (Ayr)
1929	William Cotterell	France (Paris)
1930	Tom Everson	England (Leamington)
1931	Tim Smythe	England (Dublin)
1932	Tom Everson	England (Brussels)
1933	Jack Holden	England (Caerleon)
1934	Jack Holden	England (Ayr)
1935	Jack Holden	England (Paris)
1936	William Eaton	England (Blackpool)
1937	James Flockhard	England (Brussels)
1938	Jack Emery	England (Belfast)
1939	Jack Holden	England (Cardiff)
1940-45	Not held	
1946	Raphael Pujazon	France (Ayr)
1947	Raphael Pujazon	France (Paris)
1948	John Doms	Belgium (Reading)
1949	Alain Mimoun	France (Dublin)
1950	Lucien Theys	France (Brussels)
1951	Geoff Saunders	England (Caerleon)
1952	Alain Mihalic	France (Hamilton)
1953	Franjo Mihalic	England (Paris)
1954	Alain Mimoun	France (Birmingham)
1955	Frank Sando	England(Sansabastian)
1956	Alain Mimoun	France (Belfast)
1957	Frank Sando	Belgium(Waregem)
1958	Stan Eldon	England (Cardiff)
1959	Fred Norris	England (Lisbon)
1960	Abdesselem Rhadi	England (Glasgow)
1961	Basil Heatley	Belgium (Nantes)
1962	Gaston Roelants	England (Sheffield)
1963	Roy Fowler	Belgium(Sansabastian)
1964	Francisco Arizmendi	England (Dulin)
1965	Jean Fayolle	England (Ostend)
1966	Assou El Ghazi	England (Rabat)
1967	Gaston Roelants	England (Barry)
1968	Md. Gammoudi	England (Tunis)

1969	Gaston Roelants	England (Clydebank)
1970	Mike Tagg	England (Vichy)
1971	Dave Bedford	England (Sansabastian)
1972	Gaston Roelants	England (Cambridge)
1973	Pekka Paivarinta	Belgium (Waregem)
1974	Erik de Beck	Belgium (Monza)
1975	Ian Stewart	New Zealand (Rabat)
1976	Carlos Lopes	England (Chepstow)
1977	Leon Schots	Belgium (Dusseldorf)
1978	John Treacy	France (Glasgow)
1979	John Treacy	England (Limerick)
1980	Graig Virgin(USA)	England (Paris)
1981	Graig Virgin(USA)	Ethiopia (Madrid)
1982	Mohd. Kedir(Eth)	Ethiopia (Rome)
1983	Bekele Debele(Eth)	Ethiopia (Gateshead)
1984	Carlos Lopes(Por)	Ethiopia (New York)
1985	Carlos Lopes(Por)	Ethiopia (Lisbon)
1986	John Ngugi(Ken)	Kenya (Neuchatel)
1987	John Ngugi(Ken)	Kenya (Warsaw)

Women

1967	Doris Brown(USA)	England (Barry)
1968	Doris Brown(USA)	U.S.A. (Blackburn)
1969	Doris Brown(USA)	U.S.A. (Clydebank)
1970	Paola Pigni(Itl)	Holland (Vichy)
	Doris Brown(USA)	England(Frederick,Md)
1971	Doris Brown (USA)	England (San Sebastian)
1972	Joyce Smith (Eng)	England (Cambridge)
1973	Paola Cacchi (Ita)	England (Waregem)
1974	Paola Cacchi (Ita)	England (Monza)
1975	Julie Brown (USA)	U.S.A. (Rabat)
1976	Carmen Valero (Spa)	U.S.S.R. (Chepstow)
1977	Carmen Valero (Spa)	U.S.S.R. (Dusseldorf)
1978	Grete Waitz (Nor)	Rumania (Glasgow)
1979	Grete Waitz (Nor)	U.S.A. (Limerick)
1980	Grete Waitz (Nor)	U.S.S.R. (Paris)
1981	Grete Waitz (Nor)	U.S.S.R. (Madrid)

1982	Maricica Puica (Rom)	U.S.S.R. (Rome)
1983	Grete Waitz (Nor)	U.S.A. (Gateshead)
1984	Maricica Puica (Rom)	U.S.A. (New York)
1985	Zola Budd (Eng)	U.S.A. (Lisbon)
1986	Zola Budd (Eng)	England(Neuchatel)
1987	Annette Sergent (Fra)	U.S.A. (Warsaw)

CROUCH START

The starting position used by sprinters and hurdlers in which the athlete adopts a bent leg position, with the foot of one leg and both the knee and foot of the another leg in contact with the track.

CRUZ, JOAQUIM

Brazil (born 12th March,1963) - He was World Junior record holder in 1981. He won bronze in the World Championships of 800m. in 1983. Missed 1986 season due to Achilles tendinitis and had surgery, although he came back in 1987, also had to miss World Championships.

CUSMIR, ANISOARA

Romania (born 28th June,1962) - She won silver in 1983 World Championships of long jump event. In 1982, she got silver in European Championships, and a gold in 1983 in World Students Games.

CUTHBERT, B.

Australia (born 20th April, 1938) - In the 1956 Olympic games in Melbourne, she won three gold medals - 100 m., 200 m. and 4x100 m. relay. In the 1962 Commonwealth Games, she got victory for the Australian relay team. At the 1964 Olympics, she won the 400 m. in 52.0 sec.

D

DAMILANO, MAURIZIO
Italy (born 6th April,1957) -He won 20km walk gold in 1980 Olympic games and was seventh in 20 kilometre walk World Championships.His twin brother Giorgio; coached like Maurizio by brother Sandro, was eleventh in Moscow.

DANEK, L.
Czechoslovakia (born 29th Sept., 1927) - A brilliant discus thrower. He was world record holder with 211ft. 9 1/2in. He finished second , 19in. behind in 1964 Olympics. In 1965, he raised his world record to 213 ft. 11 1/2in. He exceeded 60 m. in more than 80 different meetings, no other thrower reached even 30.

DASH
An American team referring to the shorter sprints of 100 metres or less.

DA SILVA, A.F.
Brazil (born 29th Sept., 1927) - He won every major triple jump he participated. He was Olympic champion in 1952 and 1956, Pan-American champion in 1951, 1955 and 1959. He held the world record from 1950 to 1953 and from 1955 to 1958. His best was 54ft. 4in. in 1950.

DAUTE, HEIKE
East Germany (born 16th Dec.,1964) - Two gold medals, at the age of only eighteen, including a shock first place in World Championship 1983 in long jump.

DAVIES, L.

U.K. (born 20th May, 1942) - In 1964 Olympics in Tokyo he won championship in long jump - 26ft. 10in. In 1966, he won gold medals in both the Commonwealth (26ft. 2 3/4in.) and European (26ft. 2 1/4in.) competitions.

DAVIS, G.A.

U.S.A. (born 12th July, 1932) - He set many world records in hurdles - 440yd. flat (45.7 sec.), 400m. hurdles (49.2 sec.), 440 yd. hurdles (49.9 ,sec.), equalled the world record of 22.5 sec. for 200 m. hurdles(turn) and anchored the USA team to win the 4x400 m. relay in the world record of 3 min. 02.2 sec. Both in 1956 and 1960 Olympics he won gold medals in 400m. hurdles.

DAVIS, O.C.

U.S.A. (born 12th July, 1932) - In the 1960 Olympics, he shared the world record time on 44.9 sec. in 400 m with Germany's Carl Kaufmann. He anchored the USA to victory in 4x400m relay in a world record of 3 min. 02.2 sec.

DEAD HEAT

A race finish in which two or more athletes reach the finish line at exactly the same instant a rare occurrence but most likely in sprint events.

DE CASTELLA, ROBERT

Australia (born 27th May,1957) - De Castella has proved himself to be the hardest and toughest event competitor on Los Angeles marathon with the second fastest time in history of 2h 08:18. He won marathon gold in 1983 World Championships and Commonwealth Games 1982.

DECATHLON

Ten events played on two consecutive days constitute a decathlon. First day: 100m., long jump, shot, high jump and 400m. Second day: 110m. hurdles, discus, pole vault, javelin and 1500 m. The athlete has to take part in all

the events and placing is determined in accordance with the scores obtained as per the International Amateur Athletic Federation scoring tables.

World record performances at ten-yearly intervals

1915	Jim Thorpe (USA)
1925	Jim Thorpe (USA)
1935	Hans-Heinrich Sievert (Ger)
1945	Glenn Morris (USA)
1955	Rafer Johnson (USA)
1965	Yang Chuang-kwang(Tai)
	Phil Mulkey (USA)
1975	Bruce Jenner (USA)
1985	Daley Thompson (UK)
	Jurgen Hingsen (GFR)

DECKER, MARY

U.S.A. (born 4th Aug.,1958) - At the age of 14 she pigtailed with a race on her teeth, delighted the whole of the USA by beating Soviet Olympic silver medallist Niele Sabaite . In World Championships of 1500m and 3000m 1983 she won gold.

DE LA HUNTY, SHIRLEY

Australia (born 18th July,1925) - Collected seven gold medals. It was in the London Olympics of 1948 that she appeared to have finished third in the 200m. only to be given fourth place. She was third in the 180m. hurdles in the 1948 Olympics Games but became champion in 1952 and retained the title in Melbourne. She was also bronze medallist in the 100m. in 1948 and 1952 and collected a silver for the sprint relay. She earned a gold in the same squad. In addition, she won two gold and two silver medals at the Commonwealth Games.

DELEZE, PIERRE

Switzerland (born 25th Sept.,1958) - Moved upto 5000 metres and ran fast times, although only seventh in Stuttgart. Progressed to fourth in Rome in 1987. Fast finisher.

DELIS, LUIS

Cuba (born 6th Dec.,1957) - In discus he won bronze in 1980 Olympic Games, silver in discus World Championships 1983 and bronze in 1979 World Cup and again a gold in World Students Games 1983.

DESRUELLES, RONALD

Belgium (born 14th Feb., 1955) - After winning 1980 European Indoors title was disqualified on a positive drugs test. Now concentrates on sprints rather than long jump. His brother Patrick is Belgian pole vault record holder.

DIAZ CRUZ MARIA

Spain (born 24th Oct.,1969) - Was the youngest ever Spanish international at the age of 13 in 1983 World Race Walking Cup and the youngest ever individual European champion in 1986.

DICKERSON, MARIANE

U.S.A. (born 14th Nov.,1960) - She ran only marathon in June 1982. Her career best was World Championships 1983 when she picked up a silver. She is a Master's degree holder from University of Michigan.

DIDRIKSON, MILDRED

U.S.A. (1914-1956) - One of the most remarkable female athletes of all time. Won the American Women's team championships in 1932 single handed. Restricted to three events at the 1932 Olympics, she won golds in the hurdles and javelin and was relegated to second place in the high jump by a dubious judging decision. She took up golf, and as Mrs. "Babe" Zaharias she became the best woman golfer in the world, winning tournament after tournament in the 1940s and early 1950s. She died of cancer in 1956.

DIET

The good news is that most runners have a healthy appetite and stay trim. The bad news is that a poor diet can adversely affect performance. In this context poor meals lacking in nutrients rather than quantity, even if ample quantities are consumed, will be of only limited help unless they are properly balanced. It would be possible to fill several volumes on the subject of diet, but as most people in the West already enjoy a diet which is adequate to sustain a moderate amount of training, guidelines only are offered here.

Some athletes see diet as a possible short cut to improve performance,and many exaggerated claims have been made for particular foods. Even in the so-called lands of plenty, there is considerable confusion and ignorance about this basic, fundamental facet of our existence, and with the increasingly hectic pace of life and advent of convenient foods, many people are not getting the best out of the food stuffs available. On the other hand there are others who perhaps put too great a store by their plates and not enough in their training.

DILLARD, HARRISON

U.S.A. (born 8 July, 1923) - Inspired to become an athlete with the sight of Jesse Owens being paraded through the streets of his home town after the 1936 Olympics, Dillard achieved his first world record in the 220 yards in 1946. Between May 1947 and June 1948, he won 82 successive sprint and hurdles races,yet he fell in the US Olympic trials that year and failed to make the hurdles squad. But his third place qualified him for Wembley at 100 metres and he equalled Owens' Olympic record of 10.3sec and four years later won the hurdles title in Helsinki.

DINA RAM

India (born 6th Aug., 1964) - He is working in Defence Services. Winner of Gold medal in the Asian Track & Field meet in 1989 in New Delhi, with a timing of 8:48.46 sec in 3000 m Steeplechase.

DINSUMO, BELAYNETH

Ethiopia (born 1965) - He won Ist major Ethiopian marathon race in 1986. Second in Tokyo and Rotterdam marathons, and won at the Goodwill Games, Rotterdam and African Games 1987.

DIP FINISH

A lunging dive executed just before the finish line, particularly by sprinters and hurdlers, to gain vital inches over opponents.

DISCUS THROW

Discus throwing was one of the original Olympic contests. The discus is made of wood or plastic, with a rounded metal rim. Modern discuses weigh 2kg(4.5lb) for men and 1kg (2.25lb) for women.

The discus throw has attracted the most colossal of athletes through the ages, yet all have been dwarfed by one man and his supreme competitive instincts. Al Oerter, four times Olympics champion and four times world record holder, is the personification of the will to win. As fellow American Jay Silvester once said with considerable feeling, "when you throw against Oerter, you don't expect to win,you just hope."Even at the age of 43 and after a seven year retirement Oerter was back, throwing further than ever and aiming for a place in the 1980 Olympic team. His dream was wrecked only by President Jimmy Carter's Moscow boycott. Oerter claimed his first Olympic title in 1956 at the age of 20 and his second in 1960. But it was not until 1962 that he broke his first world record, becoming the

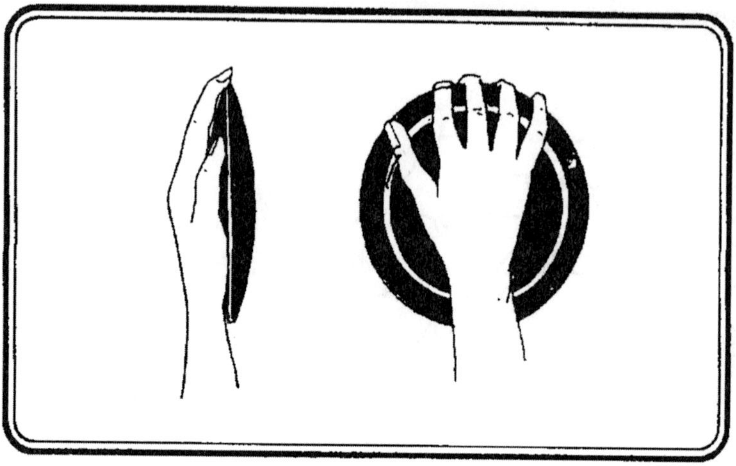

first man through the 200ft barrier with 61.10. Oerter's third Olympic victory, in Tokyo 1964, was also his bravest. For a year he had been suffering from the effects of a slipped disc and throwing in a surgical collar. Then, eight days before the final, he slipped in training and tore cartilages in his rib cage as well, the worst possible injury for an event demanding rotational power.

The doctors told him it would be eight weeks, never mind eight days, before he could throw again. But in the morning of the qualifying

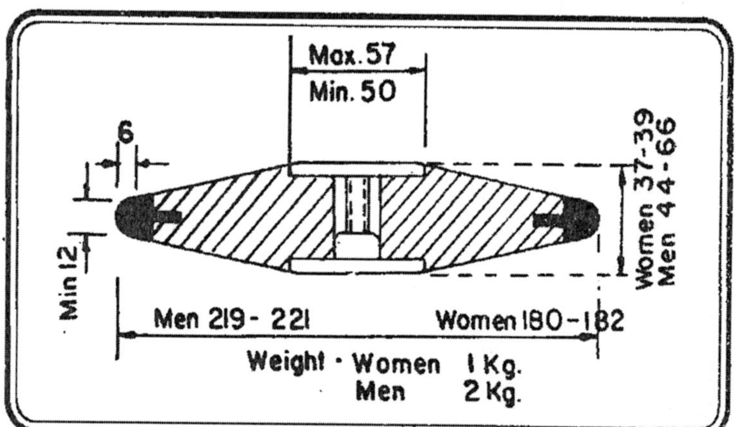

Discus Throw

round he was there, wrapped in strapping and packed in ice, to throw an Olympic record. In the final, crippled by the pain, he was facing world record holder Ludvik Daek of Czechoslovakia. By the fifth round Daek had established a commanding lead and Oerter was back in fourth. He forced himself to slow down, to endure a longer stretch of agony and took the gold medal with a 61.00m throw. Pushed back to fourth that day was Jay Silvester, who four years later would arrive in Mexico City as the world record holder and favourite for the 1968 Olympics title. It made no difference ... Oerter produced the finest throw of his life so far, 64.78m to take his fourth title.

Rules of Discus Throw:

1. The competitor may adopt any position of throw as per his convenience.
2. For a valid throw the discus must fall so that the point from which the measurement is to be made is within the inner edges of lines making a sector of approximately 65 degrees set out on the ground so that the radii lines touch, with their edges,the extremities of the stop board and cross at the centre of the circle.

DISCUS WORLD RECORD AT TEN YEARLY INTERVALS

1905	49.66m	Martin Sheridan (USA) New York 10 Sept, 1905 7feet circle.
1915	48.27m	Unofficial- Armas Taipale (Fin)Copenhagen 14 Aug 1913(and 48.90m exhibition in 1914) 47.58 Oficial- James Duncan (U.S.A.)New York 27 May, 1912
1925	47.89m	Official Glenn Hartranft (U.S.A.)Cambridge, Mass,31 May, 1924.
1935	53.79m	Unofficial Gordon Dunn(USA) Eureka 24May 1935
	53.10m	Official Wilhelm Schroder (GFR)Magdburg 28 April, 1935.
1945	53.34m	Official Adolfo Cosolini(Ita)Milan 26 Oct,1941.
1955	59.28m	Fortune Gordien (U.S.A.) Pasadena,Cal. 22 Aug, 1953

1965	65.22m	Ludvik Danek(Cs) Sokolov 12 Oct, 1965
1975	69.08m	John Powell (U.S.A.) Long Beach 4 May, 1975
1985	71.86m	Yuriy Dumchev (U.S.S.R.)Moscow 29 May, 1983.

DISTANCE AND TIME MARKERS

For distances of 20,000m or less, and in World Championships, Olympic Games, Area Games and World Cup competitions, large distance markers should be displayed every kilometre. In longer road races markers may be displayed every two kilometres or each mile.

The elapsed time shall be called out or displayed every 5 km, or more frequently if possible.

DIXON, ROD

New Zealand (born 7th July,1950) - After running a 2:11 marathon in 1982 in Christchurch, he realized he can yet chase Olympic glory. He followed it with a 2h 09mi victory in New York. He was first in New York Marathon.

DOMBROWSKI, LUTZ

East Germany (born 25th June,1959) - He is a long jumper.He won a gold in 1980 Olympic Games in long jump. He again captured a gold in European Championships 1982 long jump event. He broke his leg in a car accident and missed World Championships 1983.

DONKOVA, YORDANKA

Bulgaria (born 28th Sept., 1961) - Displayed the finest ever sprint hurdling by a woman in 1986, with very sharp speed and technique, running ten sub 12.50 times. She ran a further four such times in 1987. She had lost three fingers on her right hand in an accident on her fifth birthday.

DOPING

The use of drugs to enhance athletic performance artificially.

DORIO, GABRIELLA

Italy (born 27th June,1957) - The fastest 1500m runner in free Europe, she won silver in 1500m in 1981 World Cup. She is also among the prettiest 1500m. runners.

DRUPPERS, ROB

The Netherlands (born 29th April,1962) - He was fifth in Athens European Championships of 800m. In 1983 World Championships of 800m he claimed silver.

DRUT, GUY

France (born 1950) - He became the first Frenchman in 56 years to win an Olympic gold medal on the track when he won the 110mh in Montreal in 1976. He readily accepted that he was the favourite to win the gold medal in Montreal.

DUMAS, C.E.

U.S.A. (born 12th Feb., 1937) - In 1956, at the age of 19, he made world record by jumping 7ft. He also won Olympic championship in that year. For five successive years (1955-59) he won US championship. He also won Pan-American championship in 1959. He was also a useful high hurdler with a best time of 14.1 sec. for 120 yd.

DUMBADZE, N.

U.S.S.R. (born 23rd Jan., 1919) - In discus throw, she was European champion in 1946 and 1950. She made a world record at 174ft. 8 1/2in. and later raised it to 187ft 1 1/4in. Surprisingly, it exceeded the previous world record by 11ft. 3in. Her new record remained unchallenged for eight years.

E

EASTMAN, B.B.

U.S.A. (born 9th July, 1911) - The world record of 440 yd. in 47.4 sec. set up by Ted Meredith (USA) in 1916 remained unbeaten for 15 years though it was equalled by three athletes but in March 1932, Eastman broke the record by running 440 yd. in 46.4 sec. A few months later he created world record of 880yd. in 1 min. 58sec.

EIGHT HUNDRED METRES

Eight Hundred Metres World Record at ten-yearly intervals

1905	1:53.4y	Charles Kilpatrick (USA) New York 21 Sept 1895
1915	1:51.9	Ted Meredith (USA)Stockholm 8 Jul 1912
1925	1:52.2y	Ted Meredith (USA) Philadelphia 13 May 1916
1935	1:49.8y	Ben Eastman (USA)Princeton 16 Jun 1934
	1:49.70	Tom Hampson (UK)Los Angeles 2 Aug 1932
1945	1:46.6	Rudolf Harbig(Ger)Milan 15 Jul 1939
1955	1:45.7	Roger Moens (Bel)Oslo 3 Aug.1955
1965	1:44.3	Peter Snell (NZ) Christchurch 3 Feb 1962 (in 1:45.1 880y)
1975	1:44.1y	Rick Wohlhuter (USA)Eugene 8 Jun 1974
	1:43.7	Marcelo Fiasconao(Ita)Milan 27 Jun 1973
1985	1:41.73	Sebastian Coe (UK) Florence 10 Jun 1981

EKIDEN ROAD RELAY

Ekiden was the name given to the old Japanese transportation system for government documents and officials by relay of horses or men. The women run legs of 5km, 10km, 7.195km, 5km.

ELECTRONIC TIMING

The electronic timing apparatus is started automatically when the starter fires his pistol. The finish times, and the finishing places, are read from a photo-finish picture taken from a moving film. There is now also a videotape system. Such systems can be linked with scoreboards and television. This enables you to see the official time flashing on the screen as the race is run.

ELLIOT, H.J.

Australia (born 25th Feb., 1938) - Continuously for nine years (1954 to 1962) Herb Elliott never lost a mile or 1500 m race. In the three major championships he contested, he won 880 yd and mile at the 1958 Commonwealth Games and 1500m. in the 1960 Olympics.

ELLIOTT, PETER

U.K. (born 9th Oct.,1962) - In 1982 he won the AAA 800m title.He deservedly won a place in the Helsinki team and finished a gutsy fourth. In 800m 1983 World Championships he stood fourth and claimed bronze in European Cup in 800m in the same year.

EL HASSAN, KHASHIEF

Sudan (born 26th March,1956) - He stood 7th in the 400m. World Cup of 1979, and claimed gold medal.

EMMELMANN, FRANK

East Germany (born 15th Sept.,1961) - His best event was 200 sprints, when he claimed fifth place in World Championships 1983.

EUROPEAN CHAMPIONSHIPS

First held in 1934 (men) and 1938 (women). The European championships are now contested over a full range of events every four years.

Venues

1934	Turin
1938	Paris
1946	Oslo
1950	Brussels
1954	Berne
1958	Stockholm
1962	Belgrade
1966	Budapest
1969	Athens
1971	Helsinki
1974	Rome
1978	Prague
1982	Athens
1986	Stuttgart

European players best performances

Men			
100m	10.00	Marian Woronin (Pol) in	1984
200m	19.72	Pietro Mennea (Ita) in	1979
400m	44.33	Thomas Schonlebe (E.Ger.) in	1987
800m	1:41.73	Sebastian Coe (UK) in	1981
1500m	3:29.67	Steve Cram (UK) in	1985
1Mile	3:46.32	Steve Cram (UK) in	1985
3000m	7:32.79	Dave Moorcroft (UK) in	1982
5000m	13:00.41	Dave Moorcroft (UK) in	1982
10000m	27:13.81	Pernando Mamede (Por) in	1984
110mh	13.20	Stephane Caristan (Fra) in	1986
400mh	47.48	Harald Schmid (FRG) in	1982
	metre		
High jump	2.42	Patrik Sjoberg (Swe) in	1987
Pole vault	6.03	Sergiy Bubka (SU) in	1987
Long jump	8.86	Robert Emmiyan (SU) in	1987
Triple jump	17.92	Khristo Markov (Bul) in	1987
Shot put	22.91	Alessandro Andrei (Ita) in	1987
Discus	74.08	Jiirgen Schult (GDR) in	1986

Hammer	86.74	Yuriy Sedykh (SU) in	1986
Marathon	2:07.12	Carlos Lopes (Por) in	1985
20km walk	1:19.12	Axel Noack (GDR) in	1987
50km walk	3:38.17	Ronald Weigel (GDR) in	1986
Women			
100m	10.81	Marlies Gohr (GDR) in	1983
200m	21.71	Marita Koch (GDR) in	1979
		Heike Drechsler (GDR) in	1986
400m	47.60	Marita Koch (GDR) in	1985
800m	1:53.28	Jarmila Kratochvilova in	1983
1500m	3:52.47	Tatyana Kazankina (SU) in	1980
1 Mile	4:15.80	Natalya Artyomova (SU) in	1984
3000m	8:22.62	Tatyana Kazankina (SU) in	1984
5000m	14:37.33	Ingrid Kristiansen (Nor) in	1986
10000m	30:13.74	Ingrid Kristiansen (Nor) in	1986
110mh	12.25	Ginka Zagorcheva (Bul) in	1987
400mh	52.94	Marina Stepanova (SU) in	1986
	metre		
High jump	2.09	Stefka Kostadinova (Bul) in	1987
Long jump	7.45	Heike Drechsler (GDR) in	1986
Shot put	22.63	Natalya Lisovskaya (SU) in	1987
Discus	74.56	Zdenka Silhava (CS) in	1984
Javelin	78.90	Petra Felke (GDR) in	1987
Marathon	2:21.06	Ingrid Kristiansen (Nor) in	1985
5000m walk	21.30.92	Oksana Shchastnaya (SU) in	1987

EUROPA CUP

A European Cup, featuring qualifying semi-finals and one athlete per nation per event, was conceived by Bruo Zauli, a former president of the IAAF's European Committee. During that period they failed to win only one of the fourteen trophies contested. They narrowly lost the women's competition to the Soviet Union in 1973.

Venues

1965 Stuttgart (men)

	Kassel (women)
1967	Kiev
1970	Stockholm (men)
	Budapest (women)
1973	Edinburgh
1975	Nice
1977	Helsinki
1979	Turin
1981	Zagreb
1983	London
1985	Moscow

EUROPEAN INDOOR CHAMPIONSHIPS

The major winter event for non-distance athletes in Europe. These championships have been held annually - usually in February or March since 1966. They acted as a springboard to international stardom for Valery Borzov, the powerful Russian sprinter who has been the championships' most successful competitor. Borzov, who became the first European to land the coveted Olympic spring double when he won the 100m and 200m at the 1972 Games. He took the European indoor 50m or 60m title seven times between 1970 and 1977.

EUROPEAN JUNIOR CHAMPIONSHIPS

European Junior Championships recognized as official by the European AA A were staged in 1966 and 1968 as European Junior Games and since 1970 competitions have been the European Championships for Juniors. Junior men must not reach 20 and junior women 19 during the year of competition.

Venues

1966	Odessa
1968	Leipzig
1970	Paris
1973	Duisberg
1975	Athens

1977	Donyetsk
1979	Bydgoszcz
1981	Utrecht
1983	Schwechat
1985	Cottbus

F

FALLEN ARCHES
Also require plenty of support to build up what are commonly known as flat feet.

FALSE START
A false start is committed when an athlete moves or begins to run before the starter's gun is fired to signal the commencement of a race.

FARTLEK
A form of training, of Swedish origin, for middle and long distance runners in which the athlete alternates periods of fast and slow running during a training run, preferably in open country.

FASTEST LOSERS
Track athletes who have qualified for later rounds or finals of their events by achieving one of the fastest times in the heats, outside of an actual qualifying placing in a particular heat.

FELL, GRAEME
U.K. (born 19th March,1959) - In 1982 and 1983 he claimed silver in the Steeplechase of European Championships and Commonwealth Games.

FESEKO, EKATERINA
U.S.S.R. (born 10th March,1956) - She won 400m hurdles gold in 1983

World Championships, and won a gold of World Students Games also.She says, "I didn't think I would win, but my performance was technically perfect."

FIBINGEROVA, HELENA

Czechoslovakia (born 13th July,1949) - Fibingerova's exuberant delight in winning the first world title in World Championships 1983 was not surprising. She won silver in 1981 World Cup and in 1983 she earned gold in European Cup.

FINISHING KICK

A runner's sprint finish over the last lap, or part of the last lap, of a middle or long distance race.

FINLAY, D.O.

U.K. (born 27th May, 1909) - In 1932 Olympics, he was third in the 110m hurdles. In 1936 Olympics, he came second. In the European Championships in 1938 he was at the top with his best time of 14.3 sec. He also won the Commonwealth title.

FIVE THOUSAND METRES

Five Thousand Metres World Record

1905	15:20.0	Charles Benett (UK)Paris 22 Jul 1900
1915	14:36.6	Hannes Kolehmainen (Fin)Stockholm 10 Jul 1912
1925	14:28.2	Paavo Nurmi (Fin)Helsinki 19 Jun 1924
1935	14:16.9	Lauri Lehtinen (Fin)Helsinki 19 Jun 1932
1945	13:58.1	Gunder Hagg (Swe)Goteborg 20 Sep 1942
1955	13:40.6	Sandor Iharos (Hun)Budapest 23rd Oct.1955
1965	13:24.2	Kipchoge Keino (Ken)Auckland 30 Nov 1965
1975	13:13.0	Emiel Putemans(Bel)Brussels 20 Sep 1972
1985	13:00.40	Said Aoquita (Mor)Oslo 27 Jul 1985

FIXX, JAMES

U.S.A. (1932-1984)- James was the son of a New York magazine editor and adopted the same career. In 1964, at the age of 32, he started playing tennis to remove his stress. He suffered a tennis injury in 1967 and became interested in running and entering races. He ran 60-80 miles a week. He completed eight Boston Marathons, with a best time of 3 hours 12 minutes. It was an irony of fate that he collapsed and died while on a ten mile run in Northern Vermon at the age of 52.

His contribution to the game as a writer is notable. He created hundreds of runners by his writings. He wrote about his enthusiasm in running in his classic *'The Complete Book of Running'*. It sold around 1 million copies and had sixteen foreign editions. Other books followed and these further added to his laurels.

FLANAGAN, J.J.

Ireland/U.S.A. (1873-1938) - A marvellous hammer thrower. He held seven American titles. In 1900,1904 and 1908 Olympics, he won gold medals. He raised the world record 14 times ending up with 184ft.

FLYER

An exceptionally fast start in a sprint race resulting either from the athlete marginally anticipating the start without detection or due to his unusually sharp reactions.

FOOT

The foot consists of twenty six bones varying greatly in size and shape,supported by ligaments and muscles, which allow both a considerable range of rotation and a strong leverage, as well as absorbing shock. Overall, the bones of the foot also form two longitudinal arches to assist in transmitting forces during movement. If the arch has a degree of abnormality, an orthopaedic support may be needed to correct its mechanical function in running,for what might pass unnoticed in many people could lead to possible injuries to the leg or lower back in the serious runner. Along the length of the underside of the foot, just below the skin surface, lies the *plantar fascia,* which is a firm connective tissue linking the heel to the base of the toes. Pain in this band, often beginning near the underside of the heel, is a potential problem for the runner and may be caused by *plantar fasciitis.*

FOSBURY, DICK

U.K. (born 6th March, 1947) - With famous flop style of jumping that won him the 1968 Olympic title it has now become the accepted style for the event. He began the experiments that were to win him the gold, as a 16 year old and by the time he had left school he was clearing two metres and recorded 7ft as a 20 year old.

In 1968, he cleared 2.24 metres to win the title, a height that is still only one centimetre below the current British record, but he was lost to the sport five years later when he turned professional.

FOSTER, GREG

U.S.A. (born 14th Aug.,1958) - His first big win came in the 1981 World Cup but two years later he reached the pinnacle in his event taking the 110m hurdles gold medal in a time of 13.42 at the World Championships in 1979 he figured in a unique indoor world best dead heat with Nehemiah for 60 yards hurdles.

FOUR HUNDRED METRES

Four Hundred Metres World Record at ten yearly intervals

1905	47.8y	Maxie Long (USA) New York 29 Sept, 1900 Long ran 47.0y on a straight track at Guttenburg, NJ on 4 Oct, 1900
1915	47.8y	Maxie Long (USA)
1925	47.4y	Ted Meredith(USA) Cambridge, Mass 27 May, 1916
	47.4y	Binga Desmond (USA) Evanston 3 Jun, 1916.
1935	46.2	(46.28 auto timing) Bill Car (USA) Los Angeles 5 Aug, 1932

1945	46.0	Rudolf Harbig (Ger)Frankfurt/main 12 Aug, 1939
	46.0	Grover Klemmer (USA) Philadelphia 29 June, 1941
1955	45.4	Lou Jones (USA)Mexico City 18 Mar, 1955
1965	44.9y	Adolph Plummer (USA)Tempe 25 Mar, 1963
1975	43.86	Lee Evans(USA) Mexico City 18 Oct,1968
1985	43.86	Lee Evans (as above)

FOUR-MINUTE MILE

It is a common feature now to make a mile in less than four minutes, the world record now standing around the three and three-quarter minute mark but for a long time it was considered to be a herculean task. All great runners had this dream which always eluded them.

In 1937, Blackheath Harrier Sydney Wooderson 4:6.4 at Sydney, made the sub-four minute mile a distinct possibility. In 1945 two Swedes, Gunder Haegg and Anne Anderson reduced Wooderson record to 4:1.3 but this was not accepted as both the Swedes were declared professional.

At the end of 1952, an Australian John Landy, who was not selected for the final at Helsinki, made a mile in 4:2.1 in Melbourne. Hectic efforts were being made to cross the four minute mile barrier. Landy ran 4:2.8 in Melbourne and then 4:4.2 in Perth. Britain's Roger Bannister made a run of 4:3.6 at Oxford in May 1953. The same year, 21 year old Wes Santee made a run of 4:2.4 in California and 4:3.7 in Nebraska. Bannister's time of 4:2, the third fastest mile ever, was inside his own British record. In 1953, John Landy made his personal best of 4:2 in Melbourne.

Bannister was availing of every opportunity to be the first to make four minute mile. At last the day dawned. In the match between Oxford University and the AAA at Iffley Road track, Oxford. Bannister made the achievement in 3:59.4, leaving Chatawat, runner up a little behind.

G

GARDERUD, ANDERS

Sweden (born 1946) - He won the European Junior 1500m steeplechase title in 1964, it was assumed, in Sweden at least, that he would go on to one day win an Olympic gold medal.He finally made it with his last attempt at the age of 30, after one of the most thrilling Olympic steeplechase finals of all time. In the meantime he repeatedly had to overcome being branded a failure after poor performances at major championships.

GARDNER, M.A.

U.K. (born 12th Nov.1928) - In 1948 Olympics Gardner made the 80m hurdles in the Olympic record time 11.2 sec. Koen of Holland, who was declared first but she lost to Mrs.Fanny Blankers Koen of Holland by inches. She was again runner up to Fanny in the European hurdles final in 1951.

GASSER, SANDRA

Switzerland (born 27 July,1962) - Made superb breakthrough to top world class in 1987, but suspended for drugs abuse in Rome, and thus lost her bronze medal and in the Grand Prix, third overall and the mile first place. She is however vigorously protesting against this ban.

GATESHEAD

In 1973, Gateshead Stadium was little more than a dirt track, which found difficulty in attracting local athletics events. But Brendan Foster took over as the town's sports and recreation manager that year and marked the opening of a new synthetic track in August 1974 by setting a world 3,000m record at the inaugural Gateshead games. Since then the stadium has staged many top international fixtures, including the IAAF Golden 5,000m race in June 1981, which was fittingly won by a Gateshead harrier,Barry Smith. Gateshead also stages an annual international cross-country event on the Riverside Park Bowl course, adjacent to the stadium, and the IAAF World cross-country championships were held there in March 1983.

GAUDER, HARTWIG

East Germany (born 10th Nov., 1954) - He won gold in 50 km walk in 1980 Olympic Games and 1987 World Cup. The feat of winning European junior and senior, Olympic and World titles is matched only by Daley Thompson.

GEORGE, W.G.

U.K. (1858-1943) - He made world records in 1884 for the mile (4min.18.4sec), 2 miles (9min.17.4sec), 3 miles (14min.39.0 sec), 6mi(30 min.21.5sec.), 10mi (51min.20.0sec) and one hour (11mi.932yd.) In 1886, he made a mile in 4min 12 1/4 sec. a record unbeaten until 1915.

GERSCHLER, WOLDEMAR

Germany (born 1904) - A famous German coach and physiologist who innovated the unique interval training method, which is presently being used by most of the middle- and long-distance runners. Born in 1904, he graduated from Leipzig University and qualified as a school teacher. He was offered the job of chief coach to Dresdner, one of Germany's top sports clubs before War. He coached the German Rudolf Harbig to a world 800m record of 1:46.6 in 1939 which survived until 1955. He was at the zenith of his career when under his training Josy Barthel won the 1952 Olympics 1500m title. Gerschler made tough demands on the athletes. On the basis of physiological research he carried out while in charge of the Freiburg University Institute of Education, he proved that athletes could undergo a great deal more training if it was rightly monitored.

GIVENS, RANDY

U.S.A. (born 27th March, 1962) - She finished 4th in the 1983 American Championships. She also won gold in 200 sprints of World Students'Games 1983 and a silver.

GOATER, JULIAN

U.K. (born 12th Jan.,1953) - He finished 2nd in the European Cup 10,000m and at the end of the 1976 season became the second fastest British 5000m runner of all time with 13:15.59. He won the bronze in 1982 Commonwealth Games 10,000m.

GOHR, MARLIES

East Germany (born 21st March,1958) - She cracked 11 seconds for the 100m. at the East Germany Championships in 1977. In the World Cup 1977 she won a gold for 100m sprints. She was beaten in the 1980 Olympics final, but she fought back to win Helsinki title.

GOOD START

Getting off to a good start is more important in sprints than in longer races. The time it takes a runner to move off after hearing the starter's gun is called the reaction time. Some people have faster reactions, or reflexes, than others. That is, they are quicker to respond to a signal 'quicker on the draw'. But you can improve your reaction time by practice and by concentrating on what you are going to do, not on listening for the gun.The best sprinters take little more than a tenth of a second to react to the gun.

The start of a big race is always exciting. Some runners might try to 'beat the gun'. But a good starter will always bring the runners back if he considers that any of them anticipated the gun. If a runner makes a false start, he is warned. If he is responsible for another false start, he will be disqualified.

GORCHAKOVA, Y.

U.S.S.R. (born 17th May, 1933) - She came third in the 1952 Olympic javelin encounter. In 1963,she won the U.S.S.R. title at 182ft 5 1/2 in. In the qualifying round at the Tokyo Olympics, she reached the world record distance of 204ft.8 1/2 in. In the Olympics final due to an injury, she finished third with 187ft.2 1/2in.

GRATTON, MIKE

U.K. (born 28th Nov.,1954) - He won the marathon London Race in 1983. He had to drop out of the World Championships marathon because of the back trouble. In Commonwealth Games he took bronze in 1982.

GUAN PING

China (born 1st. Feb.,1966) - Worlds best 5000m and 10000m walk records in 1986. She won gold in 1986 Asian Games. Placed 2nd in 10km walk 1985 World Cup.

GUNTHOR, WERNER

Switzerland (born 1 June, 1961) - Had a brilliant season 1986, with European titles both indoors and outdoors. In the latter he added 56cm to his Swiss record. Carried this form over to 1987, when he was defeated only once outdoors.

H

HAGG, G.

Sweden (born 13th Dec.1918) -Hagg set 15 world records in different distances. In 1945 ,he made a mile in 4 min.01.3sec. breaking the previous record by 3.3 sec.

HALBERG, M.G.

New Zealand (born 7th July,1933) - In racing he gained title in the 1958 and 1962 Commonwealth Games and in the 1960 Olympics 5000m.

HAMMER THROW

The hammer weighs the same as the men's shot, but the addition of the wire and the different throwing techniques mean that it can be thrown four times as far. Because the hammer has been known to land on the track, the event is now usually held at a different time to the other events. Women do not compete in the hammer event.

Throwing the Hammer

The thrower swings the hammer around his head several times and then rotates his whole body before releasing the handle. 'The round the head style' of hammer throwing was devised by Highland Games expert Donald Dinnie in the 1860s and he remained virtually unbeaten for 30 years. Then came the dynasty of Irish born Americans who monopolised the world record from 1885 to 1949.The first of these so-called Irish Whales was John Flanagan, three times Olympic champion, who took the record from a meagre 44.46m in 1895 to 56.18m in 1909. He was succeeded by Matt McGrath with 57.10m(187ft 4in) in 1911 before Pat Ryan set the first official IAAF record with 57.77m in New York on 17 Aug.1913. It was to stand for 25 years and ten days. Officially Ryan's successor was

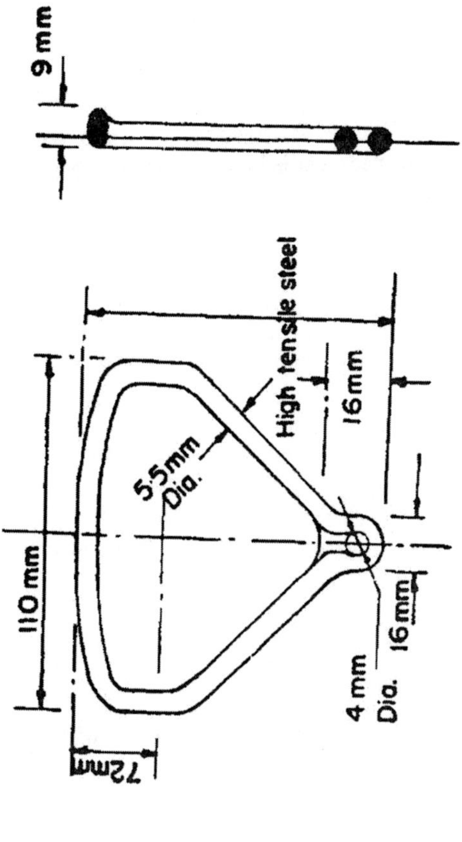
9 mm
High tensile steel
5.5mm Dia.
16mm
110 mm
4 mm Dia.
16mm
72mm

Germany's Erwin Blask with 59.0m, but a year earlier the last of the great Irishmen, Pat O'Callaghan had thrown 59.55m at the Cork County Championships. The performance was never put forward for ratification because the circle was fractionally too small and the hammer a few grammes over weight,factors which, of course,would have hindered rather than helped O'Callaghan. O'Callaghan never did hold the world record, but Olympic gold medals in 1928 and 1932 assured his immortality. It had taken 43 years for the record to progress from 55 to 60 metres, when Hungary's Jozsef Csermak threw 60.34m in 1952. Yet within eight more it had soared through the 70m barrier with America's Harold Connolly,the 1956 Olympics champion. Nine years on and the Soviet Union's Anatoliy Bondarchuk was over 75m and in 1978 another Soviet, Boris Zaichuk, unleashed the 80m era.

As the Irish -Americans had dominated,so did the Soviets now. From 1980 they remorselessly drove the record forwards eight times in four years through three athletes namely Yuriy Syedikh, Juri Tamm,and Sergey Litviow.

Syedikh, 191cm and 110kg. had been denied his opportunity of three successive Olympic gold medals by the East European boycott of the 1984 Los Angeles Games. He took a measure of revenge at the unlikely gathering of the Cork City Sports Day on 3rd July, 1984 when, with his opening throw, he mustered an incredible 86.34, an improvement of 2.20 on the previous best.

Rules of Hammer Throw

1. The competitor may choose any position for initial stance.
2. For a valid throw, the hammer must fall so that the point from which measurement is to be made is within the inner edges of lines marking a sector of approximately 65 degree set out on the ground so that the radii lines touch, with the edges, the exremities of the stop board and cross at centre of the circle.
3. Immediately after the throw all measurements should be made.

World record at ten-yearly intervals

1905	52.71m	John Flanagan (USA)
1915	57.77m	Pat Ryan (USA)
1925	57.77m	Pat Ryan (USA)

Hammer
1
2
3
4
5
6
7
8
9

1935	57.77m	Pat Ryan (USA)
1945	59.00m	Erwin Blask (Ger)
1955	62.52m	Mikhail Krivonosov (USSR)
1965	73.74m	Gyula Zsivotzky (Hun)
1975	79.30m	Walter Schmidt (GFR)
1985	86.34m	Yuriy Sedykh (USSR)

HAMSTRING INJURY

Common athletics injury, especially in sprinters and hurdlers, in which the tendon located behind the knee is wrenched or even torn, usually when the athlete is running full speed.

HANSEN, F.M.

U.S.A. (born 29th Dec.,1940) - He was the first Olympic pole vault champion to utilise fibre glass at the 1964 Games. He cleared 16ft.8 3/4 in. at his final attempt for victory. In 1963 he cleared 17ft.1in. and 17ft.2in. for a pair of world records in June and 17ft.4in. for another global mark in July's USA vs USSR match.

HARBIG, R.

Germany (born 8th Nov.,1913) - Rudolf Harbig made record for 800m in 1min.46.6sec. in1939. It was broken only after a long period of 16 years. He broke another world record in 1939 i.e. 400m in 46.0 sec. In 1941 he broke a 1500 metre record for 2min.21.5sec. He won a bronze medal in Berlin Olympics and in 1938 he captured the European 800m title as well assisted Germany to victory in the relay. He won 55 consecutive races at all distances from 50 to 1000m between Aug.1938 to Sept.1940.

HARDIN, G.F.

U.S.A. (born 1st July,1910) - His world record of 50.6 sec. for 400m hurdles remained unbroken for 10 years from 1934 to 1953. He was the second fastest in 46.8 sec. and tied the 220 yds. hurdles (straight) record of 227. In the 1936 Olympics final he equalled the world record of 52.0sec. He won the Olympic title at the second attempt in 1936.

HARE

An athlete who is entered in a middle or long distance track race, not with the intention of winning but specifically to set a fast pace in the early stages of the race, in order to lay the foundations for a record attempt or at least a fast over all time by the other runners in the field.

HARY, A.

West Germany (born 22nd Mar.1937) - In 1960 Olympics he won the title in 100m. He won another gold medal in the 4x100m relay to bring his total to 4 since he scored in the same event at the 1958 European Championships.

HAYER, R.L.

U.S.A. (born 20th Dec., 1942) - In 1959, he was only a tenth of a second outside the straight 220 yds. record of 20.0sec. Next year he matched the world record of 9.2 sec. of Frank Budd and in 1963 he made his own world record of 100yd. in 9.1 sec. Earlier in the season, he had tied the world records for 200m and 220 yds.(turn) of 20.5 sec. In 1964 Olympics he won 4x100m relay for the USA in world record time of 10.10sec.

HEAT

Track race serving as a preliminary elimination rounds before a final in a track-and field meet.

HEATLEY, B.B.B.

U.K. (25th Dec.1933)- He won the English Cross-Country title in 1960,1961 and 1963, the international championship in 1961. In 10,000m track breaking world record of 48m.120sec. by 25 sec. in 1964 Olympics, he won the marathon in a world's best time of 2hr.13min.55sec. He gained the silver medal in 2hr.16min.19sec.

HEINO, VILJO

Finland (born 1914) - He was the leading Finnish distance runner of the 1940s, folowing in the footsteps of the great Paavo Nurmi. Double world record holder at six miles and holder of eight world records at distances from six-miles to 20,000m. He is credited as being the first amateur to break 50 minutes for ten miles, recording 49:41.6 in Turku, Finland on 30 September 1945. He retired from racing in 1951.

HERRIOTT, M.

U.K. (born 8th Oct.,1939) - He won the AAA Junior titles in 1957 and 1958. He became the first under 19 in the world to break 9min for the 3000m steeplechase. In 1959 he began his sequence of AAA Championship victories. Even not keeping in good health, he was 4th in the 1966 Commonwealth Games and 8th in the European Championships.

HEWSON B.S.

U.K. (born 4th April,1933) - In 1958 Commonwealth Games, Hewson was selected to run for the 1500m instead of 800m. No doubt a disturbing shift, but Hewson won the title. In both the Commonwealth Games in 1954 and 1958, he was runner up. On 26 occasions he beat 1min.50sec. for 800m and for five years he held the European 880 yd. record.

HIGH JUMP

High jump is an important and popular field event. To be a successful high jumper one must have proper leg spring off the bounce. Moreover, he should have as light build and light weight. In other words, a well coordinated man of average height and weight can develop himself to be a good high jumper.

Style of High Jump: Although the most popular,natural and easy style of jump is the "scissors style" but it is not much encouraged.There are generally three established styles of high jump:

(a) The Straddle
(b) Western Roll
(c) Eastern Style

Rules of High Jump

1. The uprights or the posts shall not be moved during the

Straddle

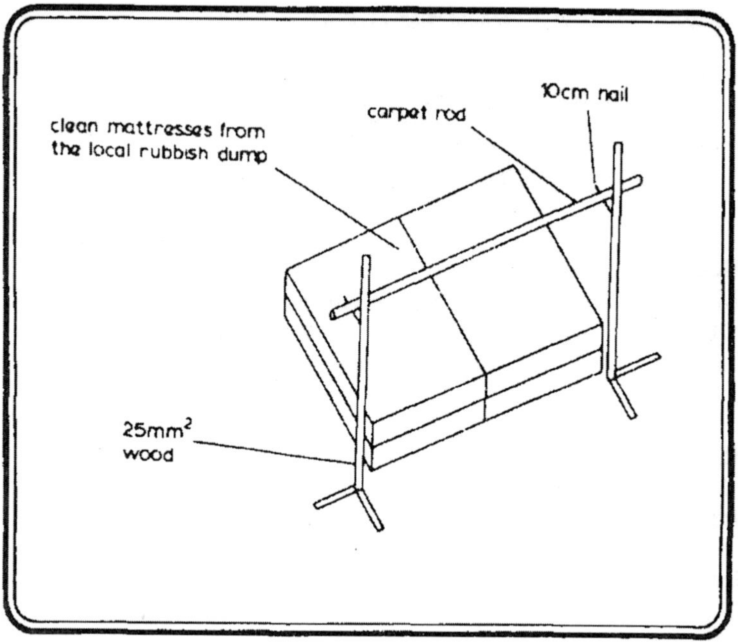

competition unless the judges consider the take off or landing ground has become unsuitable. Such a change shall be made only after the round is completed.

2 The judges shall decide the height at which the competition shall start, and the different heights to which the bar will be raised at the end of each round.

3. An athlete fails in the competition if
   (a) in the course of jump he dislodges the bar so that it falls peg, or
   (b) he touches ground or landing area beyond the plane of the uprights without clearing the bar, or
   (c) he takes off from both feet.

High Jump World Record:

1905	1.97m	Michael Sweeney(USA)	1895
1915	2.01m	Edward Beeson (USA)	1924

1935	2.07m	Walter Marty (USA)	1934
1945	2.11m	Lester Steers (USA)	1941
1955	2.12m	Walt Davis (USA)	1953
1965	2.28m	Valeriy Brumel (USSR)	1963
1975	2.30m	Dwight Stones (USA)	1973
1985	2.41m	Igor Paklin (USSR)	1985

HILL, A.G.

U.K. (born 24th March,1889) - He won both the 800m and 1500m at the 1920 Olympic Games.He ran a totai of four races winning 800m in 1min.53.4sec. and 1500m in 4 min.01.8sec.

HILL, R.

U.K. (born 25th Sept.,1938) - He is one of the most versatile of the world's distance runners. He broke world record of 15 mile and 25,000m and won a number of National titles. He has yet to do himself justice in a major championship. He was 19th in the 1964 Olympic marathon, 18th in the 10,000m and 5th in the 1966 Commonwealth Games .

HILL TRAINING

Training on hills is often characterized solely as runners punching their way up a steep gradient,sometimes in loose sand, and is considered to be a relatively short, explosive exercise. Firstly running, jogging or walking backdown after each effort as a form of recovery. This training is primarily for track runners for improving their sprinting ability.

The second method of hill running affects the road runner more significantly. It is to run a series of hills, which would ideally be spaced around a repeatable road circuit, in as relaxed a style as possible. By running a continuous circuit, and consciously relaxing on the hills, while working the arms a little harder where necessary. In trying to evaluate the more suitable style of hill training for himself, the runner has to consider whether he is training for a relatively short race which he wants to complete as fast as possible, or a longer race which he wants to complete as economically and efficiently as possible.

HINES, JIM

U.S.A. (born 10th Sept.,1946) - He ran 9.9sec at the AAU Championships in Sacramento in 1968, he staked his claim to a place in the history of the sport, for he was the first man to break the 10sec. barrier with a legal time after earlier running a wind assisted 9.8sec. He won the Olympics 100m title in Mexico the same year with 9.95sec.

HISTORY OF ATHLETICS

Athletics is the modified and disciplined form of many natural inherited skills of man like running, jumping, throwing, etc. Though evidence of Egyptians practising running as far back as B.C. 3500 is available, only the efforts of Greeks had much influence upon the shape of modern athletics.

The first Olympic champion we know by name was Coroebus. In the Olympia Games of B.C. 776 he won the straight or sprint race over a distance of about 180 metres, close enough to our 200 metres run round one curve of the modern 400 metres track.

We have some more evidence of these ancient athletics. The Pentathlon was decided on the number of first places gained in five events. Long jumpers often carried small weights in their hands to heave themselves forward and it has been suggested that they made not one leap but a multiple jump, rather like the present-day triple jump. The Greek javelin thrower was allowed to put his fingers through the loop of a leather thong at the end of his light wooden spear so that he could achieve greater pulling power.

As we see, the Games of ancient Greece greatly stimulated the modern revival of the Olympics, although they had fallen into decline and were eventually abolished by the decree of the Roman Emperor Theodosius. But, howsoever rich the inheritance from the distant past, it is true to say, in the words of the athletics historian Dr Roberto Quercetani, that 'Track and field athletics, as we know it today, was born in the British Isles'

HITOMI, KINUE

Japan (1908-1931) - He was perhaps the greatest female all-rounder. In the Women's World Games, organized by the Federation Sportive Feminine Internationale at four yearly intervals from 1922 to 1934, she won eight medals, more than any other woman. In 1926 she was first in the long jump and the standing long jump, second in the discus, and third in the 100 yards. In 1930 she won the long jump, came third in the 60m and the javelin.

HITTING THE WALL

During all prolonged running event, such as a marathon, the body's natural energy source of glycogen which is stored in the muscles and liver will usually be completely used after several hours of hard exercise.A form of dietary manipulation, called carbohydrate loading has helped some runners postpone this point in the race, but the system also has its drawbacks.

HOFFMAN, ZDZISLAW

Poland (born 27th Aug.,1959) - He was one of several surprise field events winners. In 1983 World Championships in triple jump he won gold and silver in European Cup 1983.

HOGGAN, J.J.

U.K. (born 28th May, 1933) - In his most distinguished Cross-Country career, he was the winner of many English titles in 1938 and 1939 and the International Championship in 1933, 1934,1935 and 1939. In Track running he won four AAA titles to his credit. In 1948, he won five marathon races including the AAA Championship in his best time of 2hr.31lmin.0.4sec.

HOLDOF, W.

West Germany (born 17th Feb.,1940) - A brilliant all-rounder. In Tokyo Olympics in 1964, he set personal record in three events and finished with a best score of 7,887 points. He was co-holder of unofficial European holder of 60yds. best of 60sec. He took part in racing, hurdles, high jump, long jump, pole vault, shot, discus. A talented all-rounder.

HOLTOM, MARK

U.K. (born 6th Feb.,1958) - He was a favourite for the Commonwealth Games in 1982 . He won gold in 1981 European Cup 110m hurdles.

HONEY, GARY

Australia (born 26th July,1959) - A great competitor, Honey's best may be only 8:13, but in major events he seems to be able to beat rivals. Won gold in long jump in 1982 Commonwealth Games. Before that he had earned silver in 1979 World Cup.

HOPKINS, T.E.

U.K. (born 16th March, 1936) - In 1952 Olympics, while only 16, she finished fourth. In 1952 she won the Commonwealth and European titles and in 1956 she tied for the silver medal at the Olympics. In high jump she broke the world record at 5ft.8 (1/2). In 1954 she was runner up in 1954 Commonwealth long jump, won WAAA titles at 100m. hurdles as well as in the jumps and is a best holder of the British Pentathlon record hurdles.

HURDLES

Hurdle race is not a jumping event. You do not jump hurdles, you clear them. In the words of Mr. G.H.G.Dyson, one of the world's greatest athletic Coaches, 'Hurdling is running with obstacles in the way'.

There are three forms of hurdle racing - high (3ft. 1in.) hurdling over (120yd. and 110m.), intermediate (3ft. 0in.) hurdling over 440 yd. and 400 m. and low (2ft. 6 in) hurdling over 220 yd. and 200 m. Ten flights of hurdles are negotiated in each of these races.

Following are six fundamental points about all hurdling:

1. Hurdling is running, and fast hurdling is sprinting.
2. Lift the hips and the body not higher than is absolutely necessary to clear the hurdle.
3. Drive as hard as possible across the top of the hurdle. In other words, spend as little time as you can off the ground.
4. Land in such a position that you can sprint 'all out' immediately.
5. All movements of the legs, arms and trunk must be made as near as possible parallel to the direction of run.
6. Treat every hurdle as a winning post, and try to get there first.

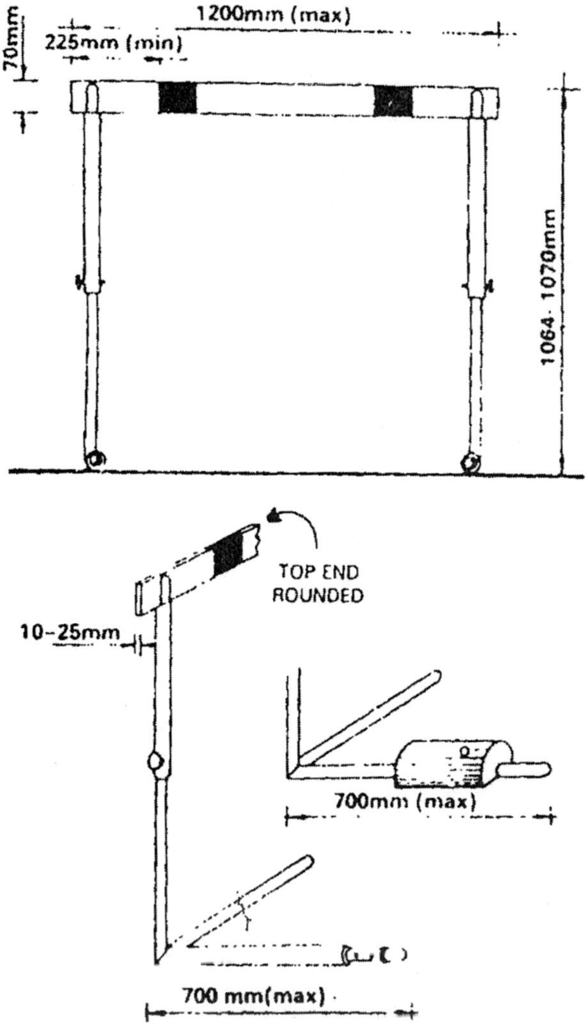
1200mm (max)
70mm
225mm (min)
1064-1070mm
TOP END
ROUNDED
10-25mm
700mm (max)
700 mm(max)

100m Hurdles (Men) and 100m Hurdles (Women)

The same principles apply to the start as in the 100m event. Some hurdles may offset their blocks slightly from the centre of their lane towards the side of their leading leg. This allows for the swing back action of the leading arm and minimises the possibility of clashing with the hurdler in the adjacent lane; others may adjust their blocks to a position closer to the starting line where they feel they can get up into their running quicker than with the setting they have for the flat distance. These are, of course, matters for individual interpretation. In both men's and women's events eight strides to the first hurdle and three strides between each subsequent hurdle is the usual number of strides taken. The leading leg at hurdle clearance will be to the rear in the starting blocks. This means that the hurdler who normally starts with his left leg forward in the blocks and who wishes to lead with the same leg has the option of changing his feet position to bring the right leg forward. This may appear awkward at first but, unless the athlete is particularly tall and can reach the first hurdle in seven strides, it is the only solution and should eventually prove effective with practice.

Any fault in hurdle clearance can be traced back to take-off and, in the case of the first hurdle, usually to the start itself. The hurdler should be able to run over the first hurdle 'in his sleep'and in fact, all subsequent hurdles as well. As the take-off foot hits the ground there is an explosive lift of the leading knee combined with a corresponding body dip and vigorous drive of the hips across the hurdle. At take-off the foot of the leading leg should be behind the knee and not in front.

Four Hundred Metres Hurdles World Records

1915	54.6y	William Meanix (USA)
1925	52.1	Ivan Riley (USA)
1935	50.6	Glenn Hardin (USA)
1945	50.6	Glenn Hardin (USA)
1955	50.4	Yuriy Lifuyev (USSR)
1965	49.1	Rex Cawley(USA)
	49.3y	Gert Potgieter (SAF)
1975	47.82	John AkilBua (Uga)
1985	47.02	Edwin Moses (USA)

HYPOTHERMIA

Hypothermia is normally associated with elderly people whose bodies have lost much of their ability to retain heat in cold weather. Even fit, experienced long distance runners have been known to fall victims to this chilling of the body.

In March 1972, hundreds of competitors in the English National Cross-Country Championships at Sutton Coldfield suffered mild hypothermia when a sudden bitter storm of snow and sleet descended during the senior nine mile event. As it gets colder, the body tries to retain some of its heat by forming goose pimples on the skin, and starting to shiver. But if these early symptoms of hypothermia are ignored, the body temperature will start to fall. A warm bath, with the legs and arms raised out of the water, is an effective way of restoring the body to normal temperature. Alcohol should be avoided because this will actually provoke further heat loss by sending more blood towards the skin, rather than to the brain, where it is urgently needed. Usually the medical officer will be in a much better position to make such a decision, as a runner suffering from hypothermia may be irrational.

I

I. A. A. F. (International Amateur Athletic Federation)

The world track and field athletics, road and cross-country running race and walking is the International Amateur Athletic Federation which was formed in Stockholm on 17th July, 1912. The I.A.A.F. promotes its own World Championships in track and field every four year. I.A.A.F. is also responsible for the track and field programme at the Olympic Games. The I.A.A.F. Headquarters is at 3 Hans Crescent, Knightsbridge, London.

The international Amateur Athletic Federation shall comprise duly elected national governing bodies for amateur athletics which agrees to abide by the rules and regulations of the I.A.A.F.

The rules and regulations of an elected national governing body must be in conformity with and not wider than I.A.A.F. eligibility rules. A Bureau shall be established in London to carry out the administration of the I.A.A.F. in accordance with the decision of Congress and Council. The location may be changed only with the approval of Congress.

The objects of the Federation shall be:

1. To establish friendly and loyal cooperation between all members for the benefit of amateur athletics, peace and understanding between nations throughout the world.
2. To strive to ensure that no racial, religious, political or other kind of discrimination be allowed in athletics, and to take all practicable measures to stop such discrimination.
3. To strive to secure that there shall be no hindrance to the participation of any country or individual in International athletic competitions on racial, religious or political grounds, and to ensure that there be no such hindrance in international meetings over which the I.A.A.F. has control.
4. To compile rules and regulations governing international competitions for men and women, of all ages in amateur athletics.

5. To ensure that all contests between Members, including Area and Group Championships or Games, shall be held under the laws and rules of the I.A.A.F.
6. To affiliate national governing body for athletics which may be recognised by the respective National Olympic Committee, where sucn a Committee exists.
7. To decide any dispute that may arise between members, if called upon to do so.
8. To cooperate with the Organising Committees of the Olympic Games in carrying through the organisation of the athletic competitions, and, as delegated by the I.O.C., to supervise and control all the technical arrangements.
9. To frame regulations for the establishment of World and Olympic records, and such other amateur athletic records as Congress agrees may be recognised.

Rules of I.A.A.F. competitions.

The Manager

The Manager shall be responsible for the correct conduct of the Meeting. He shall check that all officials have reported for duty, appoint substitutes when necessary and, in cooperation with the appointed Marshal, arrange that only authorised persons are allowed in the centre of the arena.

Umpires (Track Events)

1. Umpires are assistants to the Referee without authority to make final decision.
2. The Umpire shall be placed by the Referee in such a position that he may observe the competition closely and, in the case of a foul or violation of the rules by a competitor or other person, make an immediate written report of the incident to the Referee.
3. Any such breach of the rules should be indicated by the raising of a red flag.
4. A sufficient number of Umpires should also be appointed to supervise the take over zones in relay races.

The Recorder

The recorder shall collect the full results of each event, details of which shall be provided by the Referee, the Chief Time keeper or Chief Photo Finish Judge and the Wind gauge Operator. He shall immediately relay these details to the Announcer, note the time this is done,record the results and hand the result sheet to the Manager of the meeting.

The Announcer

The Announcer shall inform the public of the names and numbers of the competitors taking part in each event, and all relevant information such as the composition of the heats, lanes or stations drawn, and intermediate times. The result of each event should be announced at the earliest possible moment after receipt of the information from the Recorder.

The Indoor Stadium

1. The stadium shall be completely enclosed and covered. Lighting, heating and ventilation shall be provided to give satisfactory conditions for competition.
2. The arena should include an oval track, a straight track for sprints and hurdles, runways and landing areas for high jump, pole vault and long/triple jump. In addition, a circle and landing sector for shot put should be provided, either permanently or temporarily.
3. All the tracks, runways or take-off surface areas shall be covered with a synthetic material or have a wooden surface. The former should preferably be able to accept 6mm spikes in running shoes.

I.A.A.F. WOMEN'S WORLD ROAD RACE

This annual event was first held at 10km at San Diego, California on 4 Dec., 1983. The 1984 venue was Madrid and in 1985 Gateshead, when the distance was increased to 15km.

I.A.A.F. WORLD CUP MARATHON

This event was first staged at Hiroshima,Japan on 13-14 Apr., 1985. With three team members to score, 41 men's teams and 17 women's teams completed the course. The men's race was of exceptionally high standard, with the first three running times in the world's fastest six of all times.

I.A.A.F. WORLD JUNIOR CHAMPIONSHIPS

The inaugural championships were held at Athens on 16-20 July 1986.

I.A.A.F. WORLD RACE WALKING CUP

This competition is held biennially for the Lugano Trophy (Men) and the Eschborn Cup (Women). Lugano, Switzerland was the first venue for this competition, which was then for men's European teams, the first team from the rest of the world to take part was the USA in 1967. From 1977 the event has been officially recognized by the IAAF with the above name. The finalists are nations from each continent, with additional European nations qualifying for the final from three qualifying matches.

I.A.A.F. WORLD VETERANS CHAMPIONSHIPS

The first major veterans championships were the US Masters in 1968, although the Veterans Athletic Championships had been formed in London back in 1931. In recent years veterans athletics has flourished, the World Veterans Championships in Rome in 1985 attracting over 4000 athletes from 50 countries. This event was the sixth such championships- the first, then entitled World Masters, was held in Toronto in 1975. The other venues have been: 1977 Goteborg, 1979 Hanover, 1981 Christchurch, 1983 Puerto Rico. Veterans compete in five year age bands, from the minimum ages of 40 (men) and 35(women)

I.A.C.

International Athletes Club.

IBBOTSON, G.D.

U.K. (born 17th June,1932) - He won the bronze medal in 1956 Olympics in 5000m. However, in a mile he equalled Roger Bannister's British record of 3 min.

I.C.A.A.A.A.

Intercollegiate Association of Amateur Athletes of America.

IHAROS, S.
Hungary (born 10th March,1930) - He is one of the all time great on a stop watch basis. During 1955 and 1956 he broke world records at not less than seven distances, from 5,000 to 10,000m.

IKANGAA, JUMA
Tanzania (born 19th July, 1957) - First African to better 2hrs. 10min. for marathon, when second to de Castella in epic Commonwealth duel in 1982. Improved his African best when second at Fukuoka in 1983. Has won 7 of his 19 marathons including Melbourne 1983-84, Tokyo 1984 and 1986, Fukuoka 1986, Beijing 1987.

ILG, PATRIZ
West Germany (born 5 Dec., 1957) - The former World and European steeplechase champion missed most of the 1979 and 1984 seasons through injuries. A great finisher who did run all out for fast times. He is the only steeplechaser to win medals at three European Championships.

INDOOR ATHLETICS
The Amateur Athletic Union of the United States instituted natural indoor championships in 1906. English Championships were organised by the AAA at Wembley from 1935 to 1939 and were revised in 1962. An inaugural European Indoor Game was held in Dortmund in 1966. Two types of surfaces are used for major indoor competitions. Wood where the track is usually banked around the bends, and dirt, clay or cinders. The size of the track varies from eight to twelve laps to the mile.
In 1985, they were contested by representatives of 70 nations, each of whom had been allocated by the IAAF a number of places based on their athletics strength.

World Indoor Games Records

Men		
60m	Ben Johnson (Can)	6.62
200m	Aleksandr Yevgenyev (USSR)	20.95
400m	Thomas Schonlebe (GDR)	45.60

800m	Coloman Trabado (Spa)	1:47.42
1500m	Mike Hillardt (Aus)	3:40.27
3000m	Joao Campos (Por)	7:57.63
60mh	Stephane Caristan (Fra)	7.67
High Jump	Patrik Sjoberg (Swe)	2.32
Pole Vault	Sergey Bubka (USSR)	5.75
Long Jump	Jan Leitner (CS)	7.96
Triple Jump	Khristo Markov (Bul)	i7.22
Shot Put	Remigius Machura (CS)	21.22
50kmW	Gerard Lelievre (Fra)	19:06.22
Women		
60m	Silke Gladisch(GDR)	7.20
200m	Marita Koch(GDR)	23.09
400m	Diane Dixon (USA)	53.35
800m	Cristina Cojocaru(Rom)	2:04.22
1500m	Elly Van Hulst (Hol)	4:11.41
3000m	Debbie Scott (Can)	9:04.99
60mh	Xenia Siska (Hun)	8.03
High Jump	Stefka Kostadinova (Bul)	1.97
Long Jump	Helga Radtke (GDR)	6.86
Shot Put	Natalya Lisovskaya (USSR)	20.07
30kmW	Giuliana Salce (Ita)	12:53.42

INFIELD

The area of an athletics arena situated inside the main track which accommodates all of the throwing events facilities and sectors plus many, if not all, of the jumping event facilities.

INJURY

Vast majority of distance runners experienced injuries caused through constant repetition of an exercise(running). Other sport injuries are direct, involving physical contact, such as in a crushing soccer tackle. Indirect injury is caused by a violent force involving physical contact such as twisting an ankle by stepping in a hole.

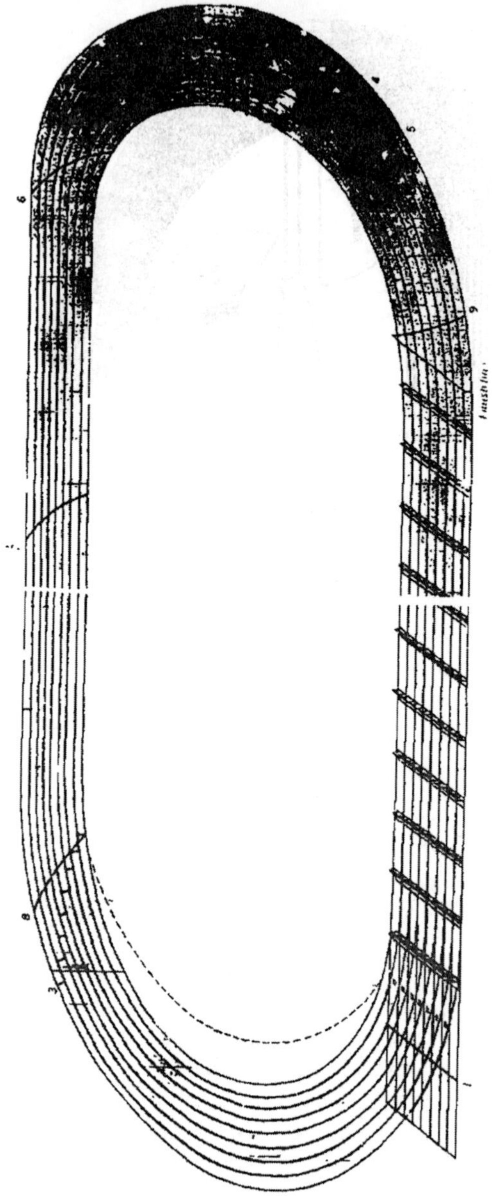

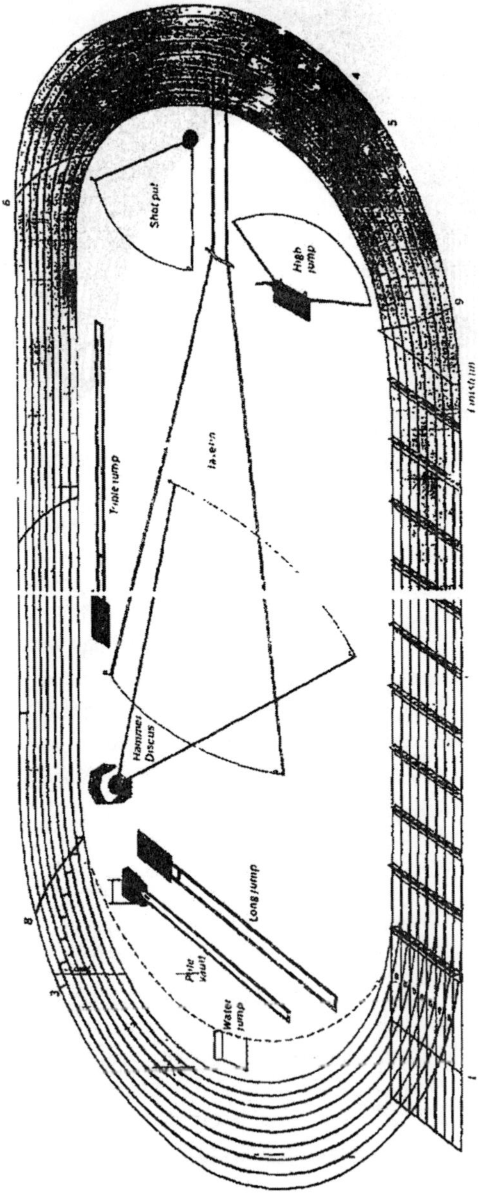
Shot put
High jump
Triple jump
Hammer
Discus
Long jump
Pole vault
Water jump

The human body is designed to work in symmetry, but if one small aspect of the machine goes wrong, the whole work is thrown out of synchronization.

INTERNATIONAL OLYMPIC COMMITTEE

The IOC, to which the Congress of Paris on June 23rd, 1894 entrusted the control and development of the modern Olympic Games, is responsible for the regular celebration of the Games and ensuring they live up to the ideals of Baron Pierre de Coubertin (the man behind their revival) by promoting friendship between the amateur sportsmen of all countries.

INTERVAL TRAINING

Interval training is a physically demanding and effective method of improving oxygen debt tolerance. It was introduced by German coach Woldemar Gerschler (1904-82) and his physiologist colleague,Dr. Hans Reindell. Their principles were based on the fact that physical exercise increases the heart rate, and rest slows it down. A normal untrained healthy adult may have a pulse rate of around 70-74 beats per minute, for instance but a highly trained international athlete's larger, more efficient heart may need only 32-34 beats per minute to pump the equivalent amount of blood at rest. Some runners believe, erroneously, that interval running sessions have to be performed on a track, the advantage of doing so is to measure the distance accurately, but the basic principle of interval training is that always run hard, recover, and then run hard again.

I.O.C.

International Olympic Committee.

ISO-HOLLO,VOLMARI

Finland (1907-1969) - A long-distance runner with an equal liking for the flat and the steeplechase. Between 1984 Los Angeles and the 1936 Berlin Games he ran the second fastest 3000m race ever, finishing in 9:03.8, an Olympic record that was not beaten until 1952. In the 10,000m he finished third in 30:2.2 in a race where the Finns took a clean sweep of the medals.

I.T.A.
International Track Association.

J

JACKSON, M.

Australia (born 13th Sept.,1931) - In Commonwealth Games in 1950 she won in 100m breaking world record . Again in 1952 Olympics she was champion in 100m and 200m race breaking world record.

JAHN, BETTINE

East Germany (born 3rd Aug.,1958) - She excelled at the 1983 World Championships winning the 100 metres hurdles gold medal in a wind assisted 12.35, faster than the world record. Amazingly, this was her first major success, although she had missed the bronze medal at the 1982 European Championships by only 0.01 sec. and finished 7th in the 1980 Olympic final.

JAHN, DETTINE

East Germany (born 3rd Aug.,1958) - In World Championships 1983 she won gold for 100m hurdles. In the same year she captured another gold for 100m hurdles in European Cup.

JARVINEN, M.H.

Finland (born 18th Feb.1909) - He raised the world record in Javelin ten times from 234ft 9 1/2 in to 253ft.4(1/2)in. during 1930 to 1936. He won the Olympic title in 1932 and the European titles in 1934 and 1938. He was also a brilliant all rounder.

JAVELIN

A Javelin weighs minimum of 800 grammes 1(3/4)lbs and consists of three parts, a pointed metal head, a shaft and a cord grip. The shaft may be

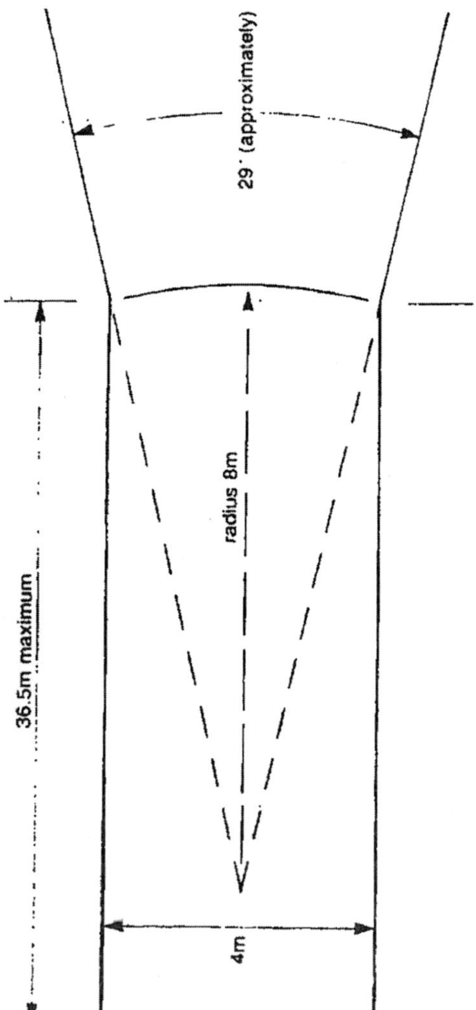
29° (approximately)
radius 8m
36.5m maximum
4m

constructed of either wood or metal. The complete javelin measures between 8ft 6(1/2)in. and 8ft.10 (1/4)in. in length. It is thrown following a running approach. It must be thrown over shoulder or upper part of the throwing arm and must not be slung or hurled. At no time after preparing to throw until the javelin has been discharged into the air may the competitor turn completely around so that his back is towards arc. A throw is not valid unless the point strikes the ground before any part of the shaft, but it need not necessarily stick in.

Rules of Jevelin Throw

1. The competitor may adopt any position to suit his convenience.
2. The javelin must not be held with one hand only, and at the grip, so that the little finger is nearest to the point. The javelin shall be thrown over the shoulder or upper part of the throwing arm, and must not be slung or hurled.
3. The throw shall not be measured if the point of the javelin does not strike the ground before any part of the shaft or if the competitor crosses the scratch line or its extension. The competitor must not place his foot or feet upon the scratch line or board.
4. For a valid throw, the javelin must fall so that the point from which the measurement is to be made is within the inner edges of lines marking a sector of approximately 65 degree set out on the ground and so that the radii line touch, with their edges, the extremities of the stopboard and cross at the centre of the circle.
5. All measurements should be made immediately after the throw.
6. The length of the runway shall not be more than 120 ft. (36.5 metres) but not less than 98 ft. 6 in. (30 metres)and shall be marked by parallel lines 2 in. (5 cm.) wide and 13 ft. 1(1/2)in.(4 metres) apart.
7. The throw shall be made from behind an arc of a circle drawn with a radius of 26 ft. 3in. (8 metres). Such arc shall consist of a strip made of wood or metal 2 (3/4)in. (7cm.) wide painted white and sunk flush with the ground.
8. Lines shall be drawn from the extremities of the arc at right angles to the parallel lines marking the runway. These lines shall be 5 ft. (1.5 metres) long and 2 (3/4) in. (7cm.) wide.
9. All throws to be valid must fall within the inner edge of lines

marking the sector set out on the ground by extending for a distance of 95 yards of the lines from the centre of the circle, of which the arc is a part,through the points at which the arc joins the lines marking the run way. The outer ends of sector lines should be marked .vith flags.

10. A competitor's throw must not be marked and measured if he steps on the arc or extended scratch lines or if he crosses the scratch line on the ground marked N at any time, before a fair throw has been indicated by the judge at the throwing end. He is allowed to run on or outside the run-up lines provided that at the moment of throwing he is behind the arc and between the run up lines.

World record at ten-yearly intervals

1905	53.79m	Eric Lemming (Swe)
1915	65.81m	Jonni Myyra (Fin)
1925	68.55m	Jonni Myyra (Fin)
1935	76.66m	Matti Jarvinen (Fin)
1945	78.70m	Yrjo Nikkanen (Fin)
1955	81.75m	Franklin Bud Held (USA)
1965	91.72m	Terje Pedersen (Nor)
1975	94.08m	Klaus Wolfermann (GRF)
1985	104.80m	Uwe Hohn (GDR)

JAZY, M.

France (born 13th June,1936) - He set nine world middle distance records (including two relays) during an International career of ten years. He was a runner up in the 1960 Olympic 1500m. In 1962, he won the European Championships. In 1964 Olympics 5000m he finished fourth. In 1966, he won the European Championships in 5000m.

JENNER, BRUCE

U.S.A. (28th Oct.,1949) - Jenner was considered the greatest all-rounder until Daley Thompson appeared on the scene. He won the decathlon title at the 1976 Olympics with a world record score adding more than 160 points to the total which had brought the title in Munich. He is said to be one of the athletes who have moved into the millionaire status.

JERMORE, H.W.

Canada (born 30th Sept.,1940) - At the Tokyo Olympics,he gained bronze medal in 100m and finished 4th in the 200m. In 1966, at the Commonwealth Games he won the title in 100yd.

JIAN-HUA, ZHU

China (born 29th May.,1963) - In 1983 high jumping, he became the first male athlete from the People's Republic of China to set official athletics world records. His major high jump victories prior to 1983 camé at the 1981 Asian Championships and 1982 Asian Games where he cleared the second highest jump in the world that year. He gained only country medal at the 1983 World Championships.

JOGGING CLUBS

Beginners, and those without any pretensions to competition at this stage, may prefer the friendly take-it-or-leave-it informality of the local jogging club. These, too, are numerous; some are well established and flourishing, others come and go at the whim of a small membership. Both *Running Magazine* and *Today's Runner* have published lists of established jogging clubs,and updated their lists time to time. *Running Magazine* published main list in their April 1984 issue. *Today's Runner* list published in their issue dated October 1985.

JOHNSON, D.I.N.

U.K. (born 5th Jan.,1933) - He won the half mile championship in the 1954 Commonwealth Games. In the 1956 Olympics, he won silver medal in the 800m final. In 1959, he displayed his potential as a miler by topping the British 1500m list with a 3m.42.9sec.

JOHNSON, R.L.

U.S.A. (born 18th Aug.,1934) - He was a marvellous all-rounder. In 1955, he set world record in decathlon at 7985 points. He was second at the 1956 Olympic decathlon and was first in the 1960 Olympic decathlon. His best score was 8683 points. Of the eleven decathlons he competed, he won nine.

JOHNSTON, T.F.K.

U.K. (born 11th March, 1941) - He won his first international vest in 1963. In 1965 he beat the world record for 30000m. by 1/4min. He covered 18mi 1128 yds.distance in 1hr. 32min.34.6sec. in a record time.

JONES COUNTER

A device which is attached to the front axle of a bicycle being used to accurately measure road race courses. Invented by a New York runner, Clain Jones it measures by counting the number of wheels revolutions of the bicycle when ridden over the shortest possible line the runner could take.

JONES, H.W.

U.S.A. (born 4th Aug.,1938) - At the 1960 Olympic hurdles he secured a bronze medal and in the 1964 a gold at hurdles. His best time of 13.4 sec. at hurdles has been shattered by only a few athletes so far. He was unbeaten in not less than 55 indoor meetings during four years between 1960 and 1964. His most brilliant record was 6.8 sec. for 60 yds. He was also a world class sprinter. He was member of the USA team that set a world record of 39.1sec. in the 4x100m. relay in 1961.

JONES, HUGH

U.K. (born 1st Nov.,1955) - He won the AAA title in Rugby in 1981, finishing fifth in the European Cup and then third in New York.He also won the London Marathon in 2:09.24, his fastest till date.

JONES, STEVE

U.K. (born 4th Aug., 1955) - World marathon best 1984 and a further Commonwealth record 1985. UK half marathon best 1986.

JORDAN, J.W.

U.K. (born 15th Nov.,1935) - Her performance in half mile has been brilliant. She won the WAAA 880 yds. for five years between 1958-62 and won 11 of her 14 international races for Britain securing 63 out of a possible 70 points. She broke the world record in 880 yds. in 1954 at 2min.09.0sec. Again She held the world record with 2min.06.1sec in 1960.

JUANTORENA, ALBERTO

Cuba (born 11th Nov.,1950) - In Olympic Games 1976,1980 he won the gold for 800m and 400m. He was the winner of gold medals in the same event (800m and 400m) of World Cup of 1977. A severe Achilles tendon injury stopped him defending both Olympic titles in Moscow, but he attempted the 400 metres and although not fully fit stood fourth in 1980 Moscow Olympics.

JUMP OFF

A contest in which tying athletes at the end of a high jump or pole vault competition attempt progressively higher or lower heights until the tie is resolved deciding the winner.

JUNIOR

General term applying to young male or female athletes still in their teens.

JUNIORS

Under AAA laws, juniors (17-19) throw the same javelin model as seniors, youths (15-17) use an implement weighing 700 grammes (1lb.5 1/4 oz). The women's Javelin is of the same specifications as the boys', 600 grammes in weight, 7ft. 2 5/8 in to7ft 6 1/2 in length.

JUNIOR MEETINGS

There are several important international competitions for juniors. Such meetings have been held in Europe since the 1960's. The age limits are 20 for men and 19 for women. The American Athletic Union (AAU) introduced Junior Championships in 1972. These are for men under 19 and women under 18. Junior matches between the US and the USSR have also been held since 1972. The Americans have had the better of the men's matches. The Russians have done better in the women's matches.

K

KALEK, LUCYNA

Poland (born 9th Jan.,1956) - She has one of the finest competitive records. Reaching world class in 1979 with a 100 metres hurdles victory at the World Students Games in a fast 12.62, she went on to take the sprint hurdles bronze medal at the 1980 Olympic Games. Two years later she crowned her career with a resounding 100 metres hurdles win at the European Championships in one of the fastest recorded time of 12.45.

KAZANKINA, TATYANA

U.S.S.R. (born 17th Dec.,1951) - The greatest middle distance runner that the Soviet Union has yet produced, she won the 800/1500 metres double at the 1976 Olympic Games and retained the latter title four years later in Moscow. Of her four world records at 800/1500 metres her last mark of 3:52.4 at the longer distance represents one of the finest performances in athletics history.

KEDIR, MOHAMMED

Ethiopia (born 6th Sept.,1953) - He dutifully set up Yifter's victories in the Moscow 5000 and 10,000 metres, but was a disappointment in the next World Cross-Country Championships at Gateshead.

KEINO, K.

Kenya (born Jan.,1940) - In the 1962 Commonwealth Games in Australia, he finished 11th in the 3mi. in 13min.50.0sec. and set a national record of 4min. 07.0sec. in the mile heats. In the 1964 Tokyo Olympics he returned 13min. 49.6sec. in his 5000m heat (a 23 sec. improvement) 3in.45.8sec.in his 1500m heat, 13min.50.4 sec for 5th in the 5000 m final and a sub-four mile (3min. 41.9 sec). In 1965 in 3000m. he set a phenomenal world record of 7min.39.6sec. He won the 1500m and 5000m at the first African Games. In New Zealand he beat 5000m world record with 13min 24.2 sec. In the 1966 Commonwealth Games he returned 12min.57.4sec. in 3 min. and secured fastest mile in history (3min.53.4 sec.).

KHALIFA, OMER

Sudan (born 18th Dec., 1956) - As the torch bearer in the Sport Aid Run 1986, he set out from a relief camp in the Sudan to reach the United Nations via 12 European cities in eight days.

KHARLOV, ALEXANDER

U.S.S.R. (born 18th March, 1958) - In 400m hurdles he won bronze of the World Championships held during 1983. He was sixth in 400m European Championships of 1982. He claimed gold medal of World Students Games in 1983 of 400m hurdles.

KILBY, B.L.

U.K. (born 26th Feb., 1938) - He was a distinguished marathon runner. In 1962 he captured both the European and Commonwealth titles. He finished fourth in the Tokyo Olympics.

KINCH, B.E.V.

U.K. (born 14th Jan., 1964) - Bev Kinch became the girl at last to beat Mary Rand's nineteen year old British long jump record. She won the only gold in World Students games of 100m. long jump.

KIPKOECH, PAUL

Kenya (born 1963) - He is becoming known more through his road and cross-country running than for his massive talent over 10,000m on the track. His talent encompasses many distances. He was fifth in the 1984 Olympic 5000m final behind Said Aouita, and has a best 1500m time of

3:41.41. Three times he has finished runner-up in the World Cross-Country Championships, once to Lopes of Portugal in 1985 and twice, in 1987 and 1988, to Ngugi.

KIRSZENSTEIN, I.

Poland (born 25th May,1933) - In the Tokyo Olympics she won silver medals in the long jump (with a Polish record of 21ft.7 1/2 in.) and 200m (in a European record of 23.1 sec). She put Poland to victory breaking world record in 4x100m. relay. At the 1966 European Championships, she won the 200m (23.1sec) and long jump (21ft.6in.) and helped Poland to victory in relay.

KISELEYO, VLADIMIR

U.S.S.R. (born Ist Jan.,1957) - He won gold in 1980 Olympic Games shot event and finished seventh in 1982 European Championships.

KLIM, R.

U.S.S.R. (born 25th May,1933) - He won gold medal in hammer throw in 1964 Olympics. In 1966, European Championships, he was European record holder.

KLOBUKOWSKA, E.

Poland (born 1st Oct.,1946) - In 1964 Olympics she equalled the European 100m. record of 11.3 sec. and gained bronze (100m) and gold (4x100 relay)medals. Next season she achieved a world record of 11.1 sec.for 100 m and cut her fastest 200m from 24.5sec. to 23.0sec. In the 1966 championship she won the 100m and came second in the 200m. She secured victory in relay for her country.

KNEE

The knee is one of the three great stabilizers for the runner, along with the ankle and hip. Knee pain can take frustrating form of injury, because of the inaccessibility of its complex working. The knee is the joint where the lower end of the thigh bone meets the upper end of the shin bone to form what is basically a hinge, but with some limited rotational movement.

Within the knee are two semilunar shaped cartilages, or menisci, which act as cushioning. It is this type of cartilage, rather than the normal connective tissue on joint surfaces, which may be surgically removed if damaged. The growing use of arthroscopy in knee surgery has meant that the joint is not quite the stubborn challenge to the medical world it used to be, but it is still the area in which specific expertise is most needed for diagnosis of injury.

KOCEMBOVA, TATYANA

Czechoslovakia (born 2nd May,1962) - In 1983 became the world's third fastest female 400metres runner with her 48.59 in second place in the World Championships final, before earning another silver medal with the Czech 4x400 metres relay team.

KOCH, MARITA

East Germany (born 22nd Feb.,1957) - Perhaps the most celebrated female athlete of the last decade, Marita Koch first emerged as a threat to Irena Szewinska's domination of women's 400m running in 1977 when, at the age of 20, she won the European indoor crown and triumphed in the European Cup final. She then fought a terrific duel with Szewinska in the 1977 World Cup final in Dusseldorf, losing to the "Polish princess" by less than a quarter of a second. However, she made amends in the 1978 European Championships final with a world record of 48.94sec.

But only another twelve months elapsed before she eclipsed Szewinska. After twice breaking the world 400m record and setting new figures for 200m, she set her fourth world record of the year in the European Championships to take the gold medal in 48.94 secs and thus became the first woman to break the 49sec.barrier. In 1979, she emulated the record-smashing feats of Sebastian Coe by twice breaking her world 200m record (22.02 secs. and 21.71 secs) and doing likewise in the one lap event before winning the Olympic title in Moscow in 1980.

KODAMA, TAISUKE
Japan (born 26th July, 1958) - Has run 11 marathons, winning Beppu and Beijing in 1986.

KONCHELLAH, BILLY
Kenya (born 20th Oct., 1961) - The masai man made a great impact as a Junior in 1979-80, then until his Olympic fourth place in 1984. In 1985, he contacted tuberculosis, but came back as the world's number one 800m runner in 1987.

KONDRATYEVA, LYUDMILA
U.S.S.R. (born 11th April,1958) - She was a shock winner of the Moscow Olympics 100m, when she beat the overwhelming favourite and then world record holder Marlies Gbhr of East Germany. She had been best known as a 200m runner winning the Prague European title. She earned silver in 100m of European Cup in 1979.

KOSTADINOVA, STEFKA
Bulgaria (born 25th March,1965) - Won 34 successive high jump competitions 1984-6, her one loss in 1986 followed by 19 further wins. Lost three times in 1987, but showed brilliant form to set world record in Rome. Has jumped 2 metres in 46 competitions.

KOZAKIEWICZ
Poland (born 12th Dec.,1953) - There can be few more satisfying moments for a Pole than to win Olympic gold medals in pole vault . He won gold in 1980 Moscow Olympics. In World Cup 1977 he won a silver.

KPALEMAIINEN, H.
Finland (born 23 Feb.,1891) - He won three Olympic gold medals in 1912, in 5000m, 10,000m and cross-country. In 5000m he created world record with finish in 14 min. 36.6 sec. which lasted for 10 years. In 1920 Olympics,

he won marathon and held world records at numerous events from 3000 to 30,000 m.

KRAENZLEIN, A.C.

U.S.A. (1928 - 1976) - In Olympics, he won gold medals in four events- 60m, 110m hurdles, 200 m. hurdles and long jump. His world records for 120 yds (152.2 sec.) and 220 yds.

KRATOCHVILOVA, JARMILA

Czechoslovakia (born 1953) -This powerfully built Czech girl became the sensation of the first World Championships in Helsinki in 1983, by winning the semi-final of the 400metres and then less than 30 minutes later, returning to the track to win the 800m gold medal. By a series of injuries her arrival on the world scene was delayed until she was 25 and it was not until 1978 that her name began to appear regularly. The major medals eluded her again in 1980 at the Moscow Olympics when she was well beaten in the 400 metres by Marita Koch. In 1981, at the age of 30 she gained her revenge over Koch, by beating her in both the European and World Cup finals.

KRISTIANESEN, INGRID

Norway (born 21st Mar.,1956) - Won Houston marathon just five months after giving birth to son. Has won 11/20 marathons and all five track 10km races. She is the only athlete to hold world records at 5,000m, 10,000m and marathon.

KRZESINSKA, ELZBIETA

Poland (born 1934) - The only woman to have won two medals in Olympic long jump competition, winning the gold in 1956 with world record 6.35m and coming second eight years later in 1964. She was ranked number one in the world in 1956, and set another world record of 6.35m several months before the Olympics prior to equalling that mark in the final. In the 1960 Olympics in Rome she lost by ten centimetres to Vera Krepkina (URS),6.27m to 6.37m.

KULA, DANIUS

U.S.S.R. (born 28th April,1959) - A javelin gold in 1980 Olympic Games, bronze in World Championships 1983, again a gold in World Cup 1981. He was fortunate to win in Moscow. His third round throw landed in the opinion of most experts,flat as a pancake. But the officials, who were ludicrously accused of opening the Lenin stadium doors to create a favourable draught, ruled his throw was valid.

KUTS, V.

U.S.S.R. (born 7th Feb.,1927) - In 1953, he ran 5000m in 13 min 31 .4 sec., a second faster than the world record. In 1954 in the European 5000m championship he won in the world record time of 13min. 56.6 sec. Again in London he won 5000m race in 13 min. 51.2 sec. Just before the 1956 Melbourne Olympics, he set world records of 28 min 30.4 sec for 10,000m and 13 min 35.0 sec for 5000m In the Olymics he won the 5000m and 10000 m Next year he made 5000m. in world record time of 13 min 350 sec. which remained unbeaten for seven years.

KUTTY, ROSA

India (born 3rd Jan.,1964) - She has represented the country in the Asian Track & Field meet in 1989. Best performance 2:05.7 sec in 800 m and 4:20.56 sec in 1500 m.

L

LADIES' SHOES

Some companies have introduced shoes built on special women's lasts which they report are narrower than men's. As far as the U.K. market is concerned the majority of women runners appears to find the small sized shoes built on standard lasts quite suitable. If they require cosmetic changes, that is, fashionable feminine colours, this need is also being catered for by most companies.

LANDY, J.M.

Australia (born 4th Apr., 1930) - Landy made hectic efforts to become the first four minute miler but failed. In 1952 he ran a mile in 4 m. 02.1 sec. In May 1954, when Roger Bannister made that achievement, he made a mile in 3 min. 57.9 sec. taking 1 1/2 sec. more than Bannister. He created a world record of 3 min. 41.8 sec. for 1500m. In the Commonwealth Games 1954 he was second and in the 1956 Olympics he won a bronze medal in 1500 m.

LANE DRAW

The sequence of competitors' starting positions in track races run in lanes, determined randomly by officials or perhaps by computer at major international meetings.

LARRABEE, M.D.

U.S.A. (born 2nd Dec., 1930) - He won the first national title 400 m in 45.4 sec. in Europe and equalled the world record of 44.9 sec. in the US Olympic Trials. He won two gold medals in the 1960 Olympics - 400m in 45.1 sec. and anchored USA relay team to world record victory.

LATTANY, MEL

U.S.A. (born 10th Aug.,1959) - In 1981, he won both 100m and 200m World Students Games and World Cup 200 metres titles. He hit the top form in 1983 to lose a shoe during the vital 200 metres trial race for American World Championships team. He underlined what he might have achieved in Helsinki by smashing the world figures for 300 metres.

LAUER, K.M.

Germany (born 2nd Jan., 1937) - In 1956 Olympics high hurdles finals he came fourth. In 1958, he won 110m hurdles in European Championships. In 1959, he set world record of 13.2 sec. for 110 m. high hurdles and 22.5 sec for 200m low hurdles (turn). He anchored Germany in 4x100m relay victory and won a gold medal. In 1959 in decathlon he got 7,955 points, fourth best score ever made at that time.

LEADING LEG

In the steeplechase and hurdles events, the athlete's leading leg is the one which precedes his torso in clearing the obstacles, whereas the trailing leg,as the name suggests, trails the rest of the body over the barriers.

LEATHER, D.S.

U.K. (born 7th Jan., 1933) - In 1954, she became the first female five minute mile runner (4 min 59.6 sec). Next year she reduced her timing to 4 min 45.0 sec. In 880 yd. she broke world record in 2 min 09.0 sec in 1954. In 1957, she secured W.A.A.A. titles in 880 yd and mile.

LEGS AND LUNGS

Distance running has little to do with style or skill. Look at any group of distance runners doing their laps. You will see many kinds of styles and different stride lengths. There are tall and short runners, well-built and skinny ones. But they all run in a relaxed manner. To do this at good speed, lap after lap requires a lot of training. Training, or conditioning, develops the legs and lungs, and helps the heart adjust to the strain.

LEITAO, ANTONIO

Portugal (born 22 July, 1960) - Had posted several fast times but little of major success until the Olympics, when he ensured that the pace was fast in the final, and reaped his reward with a bronze medal.

LERWILL, S.

U.K. (born 16th Aug., 1928) - In high jumping she won the European title in 1950 and broke the women's record in the event at 5 ft. 7 1/2 in. The record remained unbeaten from 1951 to 1954. In 1952 Olympics she got silver medal. She won the W.A.A.A. title four times.

LEWIS, CARL

U.S.A. (born Ist July,1961).At the age of 19 Carl Lewis clocked the fastest ever 100m time. In 1983,Lewis began his magnificent season by achieving three individual wins at the US championships.Lewis went on to complete another famous hat trick at the inaugural World Championships in Helsinki. He became the star of the strongest ever athletics championship by winning gold medals in 100m and long jump. He won gold in long jump of World Cup 1981. Lewis, set to become one of the millionaires of athletics, has brought the day closer when it may be possible that someone will break the long jump record that Bob Beamon set in Mexico in 1968. Lewis has cleared the 28 ft. mark on numerous occasions and his 28ft. 10 in. in 1983 in Indianapolis at the US Championships, is the best ever at sea level. Earlier in the same meet he had recorded 19.75 sec, again the fastest 200 metres at sea level. He went to Helsinki for the World Championships with all the flare of a super star, and he proved he was . He outran Calvin Smith, the world 100 metres record holder, in the final with Olympic champion Allan Wells in fourth. In the long jump he killed off all the opposition with his first effort of 8.55 metres and then produced another of 8.42 metres which would also have won him the gold, just for good measure. Then with Emmit King, Willie Gault and Calvin Smith, produced 37.86 sec against the world relay record of 38.03 sec. It is likely that he could have won the 200 metres as well. He took four gold medals in Los Angeles 1986 and equalled the 1936 record of his childhood hero Jesse Owens.

LIDDELL, E.H.

U.K. (1902-1945)- Liddell won a gold medal in the 400 m in 47.6 sec and a bronze medal in the 200 m in the 1924 Olympics. His 100 yd in 9.7 sec in 1923 remained unbeaten as the U.K. record for 35 years. In China in 1925 he made 400 m in 49.0 sec.

LIFTING

The illegal practice in race walking of breaking continuous contact with the ground by raising the rearmost foot clear of the ground fractionally before the foremost foot has regained contact.

LILLAK, TINA

Finland (born 15th Apr.,1961) - She won the only gold in javelin in 1983 World Championships. The javelin soared beyond the 70m mark and the title was her's. The crowd went wild and Tina danced around the track in a premature lap of honour. She was fourth in 1983 European Championships.

LISOVSKAYA, NATALYA

U.S.S.R. (born 16th July, 1962) - Undefeated in 1987, when she won the world titles indoors and outdoors and made up for her disappointing showing in Stuttgart the previous year.

LITVINOV, SERGEY

U.S.S.R. (born 23rd Jan.,1958) - In World Championships 1983 his first throw was 82.68 and no one could get anywhere near that he won the gold in that Hammer throw,beating the Russian. In 1980 he got silver. In European Cup 1979 he had to satisfy with silver.

LONG, D.C.

U.S.A. (born 13th June, 1940) - In 1960 he raised the world record twice in the shot. He won the bronze medal in Rome Olympic. In 1962 he raised the world record by half an inch with a put of 65ft 10 (1/2)in. In 1963 he was in the best performers list. In 1964 he made a put of 67ft. 10in. and in the Olympics that year won the gold medal.

LONG DISTANCE RUNNING

In the middle and long distance running, there is some controversy as the dividing line between the two sprints. But for our purpose we will say that 5000 metres is the transition and certainly everything from, and including, 10,000 metres is clearly long distance. Athletes seem to draw a line at 5000 metres, a distance they will run almost as regularly and often as an 800 metres runner will race his speciality, but they are more wary about fast 10,000 metres races, spacing these out with several weeks in between. Marathon runners restrict themselves to only a few races per season, with intervals of months in between. The ultra-long distance involved in the marathon brings with it several new factors - road conditions, gradients, feeding stations, large number of competitors etc.

LONG JUMP

The long jump takeoff is marked by a board sunk level with the runway and the surface of the landing area (sand pit), the edge of which nearer to the landing area is called the take-off line. A competitor can take off wherever he pleases before the line. Jumps are measured from the nearest break in the sand made by any part of the athlete's body or limbs to the take off line and at right angles to such line. The long jump competition for women in Olympics was introduced in 1948.

Rules of Long Jump and Triple Jump

(i) Each competitor may be allowed 3 to 6 trials as agreed upon by judges.

(ii) The best of all the 3 or 6 trials will be considered for credit.

(iii) The take-off shall be from a board, the edge nearest the landing area shall be called the 'scratch line'.

(iv) If a competitor takes off before reaching the scratch line, it shall not be counted as a failure but the competitor will be at a disadvantage for the distance.

(v) The distance of run through, recommended as 35-40 metres, is

unlimited.

(vi) If any competitor touches the ground beyond the scratch line or scratch line extended, with any part of his body, the jump is considered a failure.

(vii) The measurements of his jumps shall be made at right angles from the nearest break in the ground in the landing area made by any part of the competitor'body on the scratch line.

(viii) The use of any additional weights or grips is not permitted.

World record at ten-yearly intervals

1905	7.61m	Peter O'Connor (Ire)
1915	7.61m	Peter O'Connor (Ire)
1925	7.89m	William DeHart Hubbard (U.S.A.)
1935	8.13m	Jesse Owens (U.S.A.)
1945	8.13m	Jesse Owens (U.S.A.)
1955	8.13m	Jesse Owens (U.S.A.)
1965	8.35m	Ralph Boston (U.S.A.)
1975	8.90m	Bob Beamon (U.S.A.)
1985	8.90m	Bob Beamon (U.S.A.)

LOPES, CARLOS

Portugal (born 18th Feb.,1947) - In 1982, at the Athens Europeans he finished fourth. He took second place in the World Cross-Country Championships in Gateshead. He won silver in 1976 Olympic Games marathon.

LOS ANGELES

Staged the highly successful 1932 and 1984 Olympic Games. Built in 1923, Los Angeles, of course, also has some of the most polluted air in the world and that is bound to affect distance runners- in particular the marathon competitors . There is even a joke circulating that the smoke and permanent traffic congestion in Los Angeles will make it hard for competitors to get from their living accommodation to the Coliseum and other centres of competition. A new Rekortan synthetic track was laid at the stadium in 1983.

LOSCH, CLAUDIA

West Germany (born 10th Jan., 1960) - A superb competitor, who has made a habit of winning important competitions. Since his first major success when he won the 1979 European Cup Final high jump at the age of 17 in 1987 he was below par through injury, but cleared a season's best in Rome.

LOVELOCK, J.E.

New Zealand (born 28th Dec., 1909)- In 1932, he set a British mile record of 4m. 12.0 sec and was seventh in the Olympic 1500m final. In 1933, he made a world record of 4m in 07.6 sec and in 1934 won the Commonwealth mile. In 1936 Olympic 1500m , Lovelock won victory in record time of 3 min 47.8 sec.

LOWER-BACK PAIN

Sometimes lower-back pain stems from foot problems; the feet and legs adjust to the problems, but the runner's gait changes, altering the centre of gravity in the lower back and causing strain. Adequate stretching can prevent foot problems and, thus, lower-back problems.

Lower-back pain may also arise from having weak abdominal muscles, which is why a cornerstone exercise for all athletes is the bent-knee sit-up.A regular regimen of bent-knee sit-ups, along with other conditioning exercises, is an excellent means to keeping both abdominal and back muscles in proper shape.

LOWE, D.G.A.

U.K. (born 7th Aug., 1902) - In 1924 Olympics 800m he won gold medal and in 1928 Olympics he again won gold medal lowering the Olympic record to 1 min 51.8 sec. In Berlin after the Olympics he scored the fastest 800m in 1 min 51.2 sec.

LUNCH TIME RUNNING

Lunch time running is becoming increasingly popular for many sound reasons. You are (hopefully) fully awake, it breaks up the day in the dark days of winter, it offers the only chance of daylight running and it keeps you out of the pub. The disadvantages are fitting it into a tight lunch hour, and how to get clean and changed if there are no facilities at work.

M

MACHURA, REMIGIUS

Czechoslovakia (born 3rd July,1960) - Disqualified for 18 months on a positive drugs test when second at the 1985 European Cup final. She won gold in 1985 World Indoor Championships. His brother Martin is the decathlon record holder.

MALINOWSKI, BRONISLAW

Poland (1951-1981) - A tragic car accident brought an end to the career of possibly the greatest steeplechaser the world is ever likely to see. A popular figure in Britain, Malinowski who boasted of a Scottish mother and said at one time he would like to run for that country. He went on to win the European senior 3,000 metres title in 1974 and 1978 but had to wait for three Olympics before finally winning the gold as he did in Moscow, coming back from over 30 metres behind to win in 8 min 9.7sec. He had a best of 1min 49.8 sec for the 800 metres and 28min 25.2 sec for the 10,000 metres.

MAMINSKI, BOGUSLAW

Poland (born 18th Dec.,1955) - In 1980 Olympic Games he was placed seventh in 3000 metres steeplechase. He won silver in 1983 World Cup and again in European Championships he claimed silver.In 1981 World Cup of 3000 metres steeplechase he fetched gold. He has stoutly defended the memory of his father who died in a car crash in 1982.

MANOLIU, LIA

Bulgaria (born 1932) - She won the gold medal for throwing the discus in her fifth Olympics. In 1956 she came ninth, before winning two bronze medals in 1960 and 1964.

MARATHON

It is the longest of all races at all the international competitions, Olympic, European and Commonwealth. The race was first started at the 1908 Olympics and comprised 26 mi 385 yd and this is taken as a standard distance for a marathon race. This category of race is full of incidents and is watched very eagerly.

World best at ten-yearly intervals

1915	2:36:06.6	Alexis Ahlgren (Swe)
1925	2:29:10.8	Al Michelsen (U.S.A.)
1935	2:26:42.1	Sohn Kee Chung (Kor)
1945	2:26:42.1	Sohn Kee Chung (Kor)
1955	2:17:39.4	Jim Peters (U.K.)
1965	2:12:00.0	Morio Shigematsu (Jap)
1975	2:08:33.6	Derek Clayton (Aus)
1985	2:07:11.6	Carlos Lopes (Por)

MARATHON HISTORICAL HIGHLIGHTS

25 Nov.1892 Baron Pierre de Coubertin made a statement at the Sorbonne in Paris regarding the revival of the ancient Olympic Games. Michel Breal wrote to de Coubertin suggesting that the Olympic programme include a distance race in 1894.

Two runners left Athens at 8am to run to Marathon.G Grigoriou finished in 3:45:00,ten minutes after J.Vanoulis who had taken a lift in a cart for 5km during the run on Feb.1896.

The first official marathon to be held over the Marathon to Athens route, and the first national championship race on 10 Mar.1896.

The second authenticated marathon to be held as part of the Pan-Hellenic sports celebrations,acting as an Olympic trial on 24 Mar.1896.

The first women , Stamatis Rovithi, to run the distance on Mar 1896.

The first modern Olympic Games marathon took place with one runner from each of Australia, France, Hungary and the United States, as well as those representing Greece on 10 Apr.1896.

The first marathon to be held outside Greece from Paris to Conflans,France.The winner received 2000 French Francs plus another 2000 Francs on 19 Jul.1896.

The first marathon to be staged in the Western Hemisphere from Stamford,CT to the Columbia Oval, New York, over 25 miles on 20 Sep.1896.

The first Boston marathon from Ashland to Exter Street on 19 Apr.1897.

First Olympic marathon to be held outside Europe at St. Louis on 30 Aug.1904.

First Yonkers,NY marathon on 28 Nov.1907.

First marathon in Great Britain at Coventry over 25 miles on 9 May, 1908.

Olympic Games marathon from Windsor to the White City over a distance of 26 miles 385 yd for the first time on 24 Jul.1908.

First professional marathon in Great Britain over the Olympic course on 10 Oct.1908.

First professional marathon in the United States at Madison Square Garden on 25 Nov.1908.

First marathon in the Australian continent held at Sydney on 12

Apr.1909.

First Polytechnic Harriers'marathon for sporting life trophy from Windsor to Stamford Bridge on 26 May, 1909.

First indoor marathon in Great Britain held at the Royal Albert Hall on 18 Dec.1909.

First professional marathon to be held in South America at Buenos Aires on 24 May 1910.

First Open marathon in Asia over 24 miles as the Japanese Olympic trial on 19 Nov.1911.

Formation of the International Amateur Athletic Federation on 17 Jul.1912.

The fourth I.A.A.F. Congress meeting at Geneva,by which time the World Records Committee had proposed that the standard distance for the Olympic marathon be 26 miles 385 yd. on 27 May 1921.

First Kosice marathon International from 1925 on 28 Oct.1924.

First A.A.U. marathon championship at Boston on 19 Apr.1925.

First A.A.A. championship marathon from Windsor to Stamford Bridge on 30 May 1925.

First British Empire Games'marathon at Hamilton on 21 Aug 1930.

First European Championship marathon at Turin on 9 Sep.1934.

First Mainichi marathon at Osaka on 10 Feb 1946.

First Enschede marathon on 12 Jul 1947.

First Asahi marathon on 7 Dec 1947.

First Asian Games marathon at New Delhi.

First Olympic Games marathon to be held in Australasia (Melbourne) on 1 Dec 1956.

First Olympic marathon to be held at high altitude, at Mexico City on 20 Oct ,1968.

First marathon to be held at the African Games at Lagos.

First London marathon on 29 March,1981.

First World Championship marathons on 14 Aug, 1983.

MARSH, HENRY

U.S.A. (born 15th March,1954) - The unluckiest athlete in his event, he finished first in the 1981 World Cup steeplechase but was disqualified for running around a barrier and in 1983 at the World Championships, he looked certain for the silver medal before falling over the final barrier. He won the 1979 Pan American Games and ran the fastest times in the world in both 1982 and 1983.

MARIN, JOSE

Spain (born 21st Jan.,1950) - He made his name in 1982 becoming the European 20km champion and 50km silver medallist within three days. Again displaying superb form at the World Championships the following year, he placed second in the 50 km event and narrowly failed to take the bronze medal in the 20 km.

MARKOV, KHRISTO

Bulgaria (born 27th Jan.,1965) - World Junior record 1984 and five European Junior record 1983-4. Ten Bulgarian triple jump records 1983-7, the last four also European records. Equalled European indoor long jump best 1985.

MARTI, DEBBIE

U.K. (born 14th May,1968) - An exciting new British female high jumping talent, she jumped 1.88m in 1983 at the age of 15 to exceed anything previously achieved by a British teenager. Competing against girls two and three years her senior at the European Championships that year she performed brilliantly, filling the bronze medal position with her second 1.88m clearance of the season.

MARTIN, LISA

Australia (born 12th May, 1960) - Started as a hurdler, switching to distance running in 1981. Has won six out of twelve marathons to Osaka 1988, 2nd New York 1985-6. Ran Commonwealth half marathon best of 1:09:45 to win Great North Run 1986.

MATCH SCORING

All kinds of track and field meetings are held in many parts of the world.

There are both individual championships and team competitions. There are also matches between two or more teams. There are meetings at all levels, from a school sports day to World Championships. In matches between two teams, whether they are countries or schools, there are usually two competitors from each team entered in each event. The scoring,from first place to fourth, is 5,3,2,1. In the relays it is 5 and 2 for first and second. For three cornered matches , again with two competitors per team, the scoring is 7,5,4,3,2,1 (7,4,2 in the relays).

In international matches, men's and women's events are often scored separately.

MATHIAS, R.B.

U.S.A. (born 17th Nov., 1930) - Mathias was the youngest of all the athletes to have won gold medal in decathlon in 1948 Olympics at Wembley. He was only17 1/2. He broke world record three times and maintained his position till 1952. He won all the ten of the competitions he contested from 1948 to 1956.

MATSON, J.R.

U.S.A. (born 5th March, 1945) - In 1963, Matson , a school student of 18 years , crashed the formidable 60 ft. barrier, created in a period of 45 years. He bettered his titles to 62 ft., 63ft., 64ft., and 65 ft. At the 1964 Olympics he won silver.

MATTHEWS, K.J.

U.K. (21st June,1934) - He participated in five major international 20 kilometers walk test.Of these he won four, the European title in 1962,the Lugano Trophy finals in 1961 and 1963 and Olympic gold medal in 1964.

MC COY, MARK

Guyana (born 10th Dec.,1961) - He was the surprise of Brisbane Commonwealth Games. He bettered 14sec. with a time 13.97 in high hurdles in 1982. In 110m hurdles of World Championships he stood fourth during 1983. He won gold also in 1982 in the same event.

MCDERMOTT, KIRSTY

U.K. (born 6th Aug.,1962) - A poor fourth place in the WAAA Championships 800 metres final in 1982 didn't augur well for her medal chances at that year's Commonwealth Games, but a Welsh 800 metres record of 2:00.56 just before the games seemed to point to something special in Brisbane. Sure enough, she won the 800 metres to become Wales' first female representative to win a Commonwealth Games athletics gold medal.

MC GUIRE, E.M.

U.S.A. (born 3rd June,1944) - In 1963, at the Pan-American Games she won the 100m. in 11.5sec. She also won a gold medal in the 200m. (23.0sec) and silver medals in the 100m and relay at the 1964 Olympic Games.

MCKEAN TOM

U.K. (born 27th Oct.,1963) - Made a great debut in international athletics in 1985, when, in the absence of other top UK 800m runners, he had a string of successes culminating in his win in the European Cup final. He earlier completed a remarkable 34 successive win at 800m. Won medals in both his major races in 1986.

MEADOWBANK STADIUM

Since staging the highly successful 1970 Commonwealth Games, Edinburgh's Meadowbank Stadium has become Britain's secondary athletics venue. That position was underlined when the stadium hosted the 1973 Europa Cup final, the first time the event had come to Britain. It staged the first ever I.A.A.F. permit meeting in June 1983.

MEDALS

In all types of athletics competition successful athletes are invariably awarded medals. The most valued medals are the gold, silver and bronze varieties awarded for first, second and third places, respectively, at major international track and field championships and competitions.

MEETINGS
Gathering of athletes competing in a programme of athletics events held over lone or several days.

MEKONNEN, ABEBE
Ethiopia (born 5th Jan.,1963) - Of his 17 marathons has won five - Rotterdam, Addis Ababa and Montreal 1986, Paris 1987, Tokyo 1988. Nephew of double Olympic champion Abebe Bikila.

MENNEA, PIETRO
Italy (born 28th July,1952) - He retired after winning the Moscow Olympic title in sprinting. Not only did he hold the world record set at altitude for the 200m,but his time of 19.96sec. at sea level was considered to be the best performance ever.He edged Wells out of a second Olympic gold in the 200 metres by 2/100th of a second. He claimed gold in 200 sprints of European Cup during 1975.

MERLENE, OTTEY
Jamaica (born 10th May, 1969) - She won bronze in 200m sprints of 1980 Olympic Games. Won silver in World Championships, 1983. Her marriage deflected her attention from the Olympics and the baby stopped her competing again at top level.

MEYFARTH, ULRIKE
West Germany (born 4th May,1956) - Meyfarth was only sixteen when she became darling of West Germany by winning the Olympic title in 1972 high jump event. She got silver in 1983 World Championships. In European Championships she earned gold in 1982.

MICHEL, DETLEF
East Germany (born 13th Oct.,1955) - The 28 year old gas engineer took advantage by capturing gold in World Championships 1983 in javelin throw.

In European Championships and World Cup 1981, 1983 he won bronze and silver.

MIDDLE DISTANCE RUNNING

It stretches from 800m to 2mi. Olympic and European Championships are staged at 800m and 1500m (120yds. less than a mile). World records are officially recognized at 800m,880yds, 1000m, 1500m, mile, 2000m, 3000m and 2 mi.

With the relentless advance in performance in athletics the 800 metre race now attracts athletes who in the past would have been sprinters. However, it still just makes it into the category of middle distance running. Even more controversy has been raised about the classification of the 5000 metres, but it is now almost agreed by top coaches and athletes that this is no more a long distance but rather a middle distance race. The divisions between sprints and middle distance and between middle distance and long distance have been blurred because of the emergence in recent years of the super-athlete who, although, specializing in, say, the 1500 metres, can hold his own against mere mortals in the 200 metres and is a danger to all who consider themselves 10000 metre specialists. Today's middle distance athlete has both sprinting speed and endurance. His running style is a model of mechanical efficiency, and even in the later stages of a race when fatigue is sapping his strength his skill does not break down.

800 Metres

Experts around the world watched the emergence of

the giant Alberto Juantorena from Cuba in 1976 and predicted a new era for middle distance running. This was the shape of things to come, they decided, huge men with sprinting power who would turn the 800 metres into an extended 400 metres. Then up popped little Sebastian Coe, all 5ft 9 (1/2)in. (177cm) and 123 lb (56kg) of him, and they were forced to reconsider.

800 Metres world record at ten-yearly intervals

1905	1:53.4	Charles Kilpatrick	U.S.A.
1915	1:51.9	Ted Meredith	U.S.A.
1925	1:52.2	Ted Meredith	U.S.A.
1935	1:49.8	Ben Eastman	U.S.A.
1945	1:46.6	Rudolf Harbig	Ger.
1955	1:45.7	Roger Moens	Bel.
1965	1:44.3	Peter Snell	N.Z.
1975	1:44.1	Rick Wohlhuter	U.S.A.
1985	1:41.7	Sebastian Coe	U.K.

One Thousand Metres record at ten-yearly interval

1905	2:35.8	Henri Deloge (Fra) Paris	14 Jul	1902
1915	2:32.3	George Mickler (Ger) Hanover	22 Jun	1913
1925	2:28.5	Sven Lundgen (Swe) Stockholm	27 Sep	1922
1935	2:23.6	Jules Ladoumegue(Fra) Paris	19 Oct	1930
1945	2:21.5	Rudolf Harbig (Ger) Dresden	24 May	1941
1955	2:19.0	Aden Boysen (Nor) Goteborg	30 Aug	1955
	2:19.0	Istvan Rozsaolgyi (Hun) Tata	21 Sept	1955
1965	2:16.2	Jurgen May (GDR) Erfurt	20 Jul	1965
1975	2:13.9	Rick Wohhuter (USA) Oslo	30 Jul	1974
1985	2:12.18	Sebastian Coe(UK) Oslo	11 Jul	1981

MIMOUN, ALAIN

Algeria (born 1921) - Alain Mimoun to give him his full name, ran for France and excelled on track, road and cross-country. He won the World Cross-Country Championships four times, in 1949, 1952,1954 and 1956, and was six times placed in the first three in 11 championships. In the 5000m final of 1952 the world saw one of the best finishing laps ever as Zatopek, trailing Momoun and Herbert Schade (GER), stormed through to win in 14:06.6. Mimoun through to win in 14:06.6. Mimoun was second in 14:07.4.

MINEYEVA, OLGA

U.S.S.R. (born 1st Oct.,1952) - Overshadowed by her record breaking countrywoman Nadezhda Olizarenko in the 1980 Olympic Women's 800 metres final, in which she placed second in a faster time than the previous world record, Mineyeva made no mistake at the European Championships in Athens two years later. There she won the 800 metres in convincing style clocking a fast 1:55.41. Nowadays, with the quick turnover of world class female middle distance runners, it is rare for a girl to win medals at more than one major championships.

MOGENBURG, DIETMAR

West Germany (born 15th Aug., 1961) - The tall architectural student had more reason than most to be angry at the West German boycott of the 1980 Olympics. He was unquestionably the best high jumper in the world. He won gold in European Championships 1982 for high jump and silver and bronze in 1979, 1983 European Cups.

MOIUTAWAKIL, EL NAWAL

Morocco (born 15th April,1962) - First Moroccan and first African woman, apart from South Africans, to win an Olympic gold medal. Second smallest ever Olympic champion. Won six gold medals at the Pan Arab Games in 1985 and four at the 1987 Arab Championships.

MOLLER, LORRAINE

New Zealand (born 1st Jun., 1955) - Won her first eight marathons, before second to Joyce Smith at London in 1982. Of 19 marathons she has now won 12, including Avon 1980, 1982 and 1984; Boston 1982,1984; Osaka 1986-7.

MOCRCROFT, DAVE

U.K. (born 10th Apr.,1953) - One of the most underrated of all world class distance runners, he finally gained just recognition, at the age of 29 when he smashed the 5000 metres world record by a huge 5.79 seconds margin to achieve one of the most remarkable performances ever.Surprisingly, he finished only third in the European Championships 5000 metres that year but won the gold medal in the same event at the Commonwealth Games some weeks later. He was placed third in the European Championships 1500 metres the same season.

MORLEY, SUE

U. K. (born 6th Jan.,1960) - She just missed out on a medal in the women's 400 metres hurdles at the 1982 Commonwealth Games but began to realize her obvious potential in 1983. Breaking 57 seconds for the first time early that year, she reached the World Championships final finishing 7th with a U.K. record of 56.04. Shortly after that she achieved an excellent third place in the women's European Cup final 400 metres hurdles behind two World Championships medallists.

MORROW, B.J.

U.S.A. (born 15th Oct., 1935) - Between 1955 and 1958 he lost only one sprint competition. In the 1956 Olympics he secured three gold medals by winning the 100m and 200m and contributing to the United States relay victory.

MOSES, E.D.

U.S.A. (born 31st Aug., 1955) - Moses is unquestionably an event for the greatest athlete the world has ever seen in terms of dominance over his peers. He won gold in 400m hurdles at Olympic Games in 1976, and another gold in 1983 in World Championships for the same event.

MOTA, ROSA

Portugal (born 29th Jun., 1958) - Has won eight of her eleven marathons, including the European gold in her first marathon in 1982, and again in 1986. She improved her best in each of her first seven marathons and won the first ever Olympic medal by a Portuguese woman.

MUNKELT, THOMAS

East Germany (born 3rd Aug.,1952) - Europe's leading 110 metres hurdler for several years he has compiled an enviable competitive record without ever seriously challenging Frenchman Guy Drut's 1975 European Sprint hurdles record of 13.28. He won three European Cup final wins 1977/79/83 and a World Cup victory in 1977, his greatest successes include European Championships hurdles titles in 1978 and 1982, in between which he became Olympic champion.

MYERS, LE

U.S.A. (born 16th Feb.,1858) - He broke three world records for 100yd, 440yd and 880yd from 1880 to 1888. This has been a marvellous feat. In 1880, he succeeded in winning eight national titles in a week, first the American and then Canadian Championships at 100,200, 440 and 880 yd.

N

NACHAPPA, ASWINI
India (born 21st Oct., 1967) - An `Arjuna Award' winner. She is employed with Vijaya Bank, Bangalore. Started her career as a long jumper. Later started running in 400 m. Presently running 100 m and 200 m. Best performance 11.97 sec in 100 m and 24.07 sec. in 200 m. Has represented the country in the Olympics, Asian Games, World Cup, Asian Track & Field meet and SAF Games.

N.C.A.A.
National Collegiate Athletic Association (USA)

NEDI, DEREJE
Ethiopia (born 10th Oct.,1955) - Started athletics in 1974. Won Frankfurt and Moscow marathons in 1984, Abebe Bikila marathon 1984-1985

NEHEMIAN, RENALDO
U.S.A. (born 24th March, 1959) - Renaldo or 'skeets' as he is known, ran the heart out of the European hurdlers in 1980 but because of the American ban was not allowed to chase what he wanted most, the Olympic title in Moscow with the 12.93 sec. set in Zurich in 1981. Nehemian made his mark at high school, breaking record after record and it was in 1979 that he eliminated the name of Alejandro Casanas of Cuba from the record books when he recorded 13.16sec, only to run even faster, 13 sec flat, when he won the Pan American Games and the Word Cup. He is a useful long jumper as well as a flat 100 and 200 metres runner.

NEUBERT, RAMONA

East Germany (born 26th July,1958) - Totally dominant in the heptathlon, she had broken the world record four times up to the end of 1983. Her highest is 6836 points. Having finished just out of the medals in the Pentathlon at the 1980 Olympic Games, she immediately took to the new event, comfortably winning the European and World heptathlon titles in 1982 and 1983. Her strongest event is long jump.

NEVALA, P.L.

Finland (born 30th Nov.,1940) - In 1963, he secured second position with 283ft.2(1/2)in. and in the world all time list in javelin throw. In 1964 Olympics he won the championship winning 13 (1/2) with 271ft. 2 (1/2)in. He came fourth in the 1966 European Championships.

NEW YORK CITY MARATHON

New York city marathon was created by Fred Lebow, a Romanian refugee working in New York Marathon in 1970. First race was in 1970 on 13 September around the city's Central Park. It became an annual event, and from 1976 the entries surpassing 14,000 with many thousands more disappointed because of the entry limit. New York Marathon demonstrated how a marathon could show off a city to the world. In more recent years the New York race has perhaps been somewhat overshadowed in terms of quality by its great rival, the Chicago Marathon.

NIGHT RUNNING

Most runners have to undertake at least part of their training at night and in winter. This can particularly pose some hazards. The drivers will rarely be on the lookout for runners. Thus the runner has to advertise his presence as vividly as possible to catch the driver's attention. Some training shoes now have reflective material on the heels, and tracksuits and rainsuits can be purchased. Heavy orange or yellow jackets of the type worn by road or rail maintenance workers have excellent visibility, but in practical terms usually make the runner too hot while running. The worst type of clothing to wear while training at night is a black, blue or navy blue tracksuit, which renders the runner virtually invisible to traffic. Runner should run always facing oncoming traffic.

NIHILL, V.P.

U.K. (born 5th Sep., 1939) - In 1962, he won the first national title (the Irish mile) in walking. He won silver in 1964 Olympics 50 km. in 4 hr. 11 min. 31.2 sec. He displayed his exceptional versatility in 1965 by winning national titles.

NIKULIN, IGOR

U.S.S.R. (born 14th Aug.,1960) - He became the youngest ever 80m hammer thrower in 1980. His father Yuriy was fourth in the 1964 Olympics hammer.

NO JUMP/NO THROW

A jump or throw in any of the standard field events which does not satisfy the rules and regulations pertaining to that particular event and does not, therefore, count in the competition.

NORMAN, DECIMA

Australia (born 1915) - Decima holds the record for winning most gold medals by one athlete at a single CG celebration. She won five in 1938 in the 100yards, 660 yards relay, 440 yards relay and long jump. She did not enjoy the Olympic glory, mainly because her best events, the 220 yards and long jump, were not included in the women's programme before the war. She lived with her memories at Albany in the remote south of Western Australia.

NUMBERS

Every competitor during the competition should be supplied with and wear a distinctive number corresponding with his number in the programme. In running races and in all walking events duplicate numbers shall be worn, one on the breast and the other on the back.

NURMI, P.J.

Finland (1897-1973) - He won nine gold medals in seven individual and two team events in three Olympiads and a score of world records over distances ranging from 1500m to 20,000m. He also won a silver medal in 5,000m in 1928. He won silver medals in the 5000m and 3000m steeplechase. By his achievements he nearly became an idol in athletics.

NYLANDER, SVEN

Sweden (born 1 Jan.,1962) - Has a remarkable record of making all major championships finals 1982-7, setting national records in 1982, 1986 and 1987 in these races.

O

OAKES, GARY

U.K. (born 21st Sept.,1958) - One of the smallest international 400 metres hurdlers at 1.77m he excelled in placing third in the 1980 Olympic final clocking a lifetime best of 49.11, the fourth fastest time by a U.K. player.

O'BRIEN, W.P.

U.S.A. (born 28th Jan., 1932) - He revolutionised shot putting and he introduced techniques which bear his name. In 1951 he terminated Jim Fuchs' long supremacy by defeating him for the USA title. In 1952, he won Olympic title and between 1952 and 1956 he won 116 consecutive competitions. In 1953, he broke Fuch's record of 58 ft. 10 (1/4)in. and subsequently carried the record to 59,60,61,62 and 63 ft. He again won the Olympics title in 1956 and also won the Pan-American title in 1955 and 1959 . He has records too of 63 ft 2 1/2)in. 63 ft. 4 in. and 64 ft. 7 (1/2)in.

OERTER, A.A.

U.S.A. (born 19th Sept., 1936) - In discus throwing he won gold medals thrice in 1954, 1960 and 1964 Olympics. He was the first man to exceed 200ft. He further improved his record to 235 ft. 5 (1/2)in.

OFFICIAL

Individual who performs various duties relating to the organization and general running of all types of athletics competition.

OLIZAREKO, NADYEZHDA

U.S.S.R. (born 28th Nov., 1953) - In 800m she won a gold at Moscow

Olympics 1980 and obliterated the world and Olympic records. She earned silver in 1979 World Cup 800m. A year before she won a silver in European Championships again for 800m.

OLYMPIC GAMES

The Olympics are held every four years, and include a great variety of different sports, as well as athletics. The Olympic symbol of five interlocking circles represents the five continents of the world.
The track and field events have been the centre-piece of every Olympic Games since 1896.

Venues	
1896	Athens
1900	Paris
1904	St. Louis
1908	London
1912	Stockholm
1920	Antwerp
1924	Paris
1928	Amsterdam
1932	Los Angeles
1936	Berlin
1940	Not held
1944	Not held
1948	London
1952	Helsinki
1956	Melbourne
1960	Rome
1964	Tokyo
1968	Mexico City
1972	Munich
1976	Montreal
1980	Moscow
1984	Los Angeles
1988	Seoul
1992	Barcelona (to be held)

Olympic Games Gold Medallist (1896-1988)

MEN

100 Metres

GOLD

1896	Thomas Burke (USA)	12.0
1900	Frank Jarvis (USA)	11.0
1904	Archie Hahn (USA)	11.0
1906	Archie Hahn (USA)	11.0
1908	Reginald Walker (SAF)	10.8
1912	Ralph Craig (USA)	10.8
1920	Charles Paddock (USA)	10.8
1924	Harold Abrahams (UK)	10.6
1928	Percy Williams (CAN)	10.8
1932	Eddie Tolan (USA)	10.3
1936	Jesse Owens (USA)	10.3
1948	Harrison Dillard (USA)	10.3
1952	Lindy Remigino (USA)	10.4
1956	Bobby Joe Morow (USA)	10.54
1960	Armin Hary (GER)	10.2
1964	Bob Hayes (USA)	10.0
1968	James Hines (USA)	9.9
1972	Valeriy Borzov (URS)	10.14
1976	Hasely Crawford (TRI)	10.06
1980	Allan Wells (UK)	10.25
1984	Carl Lewis (USA)	9.99
1988	Carl Lewis (USA)	9.92

SILVER

1896	Hofmann (GER)	12.2
1900	Tewksbury (USA)	11.1
1904	Cartmell (USA)	11.2
1908	Rector (USA)	10.9
1912	Meyer (USA)	10.9
1920	Kirksey (USA)	10.8
1924	Scholz (USA)	10.7

1928	London (UK)	10.9
1932	Metcalfe (USA)	10.3
1936	Metcalfe (USA)	10.4
1948	Ewell (USA)	10.4
1952	Mckenley (JAM)	10.4
1956	Baker (USA)	10.5
1960	Sime (USA)	10.2
1964	Figuerola (CUB)	10.2
1968	Miller (JAM)	10.0
1972	Taylor (USA)	10.24
1976	Quarrie (JAM)	10.07
1980	Leonard (CUB)	10.25
1984	Graddy (USA)	10.19
1988	Christie (UK)	9.97

BRONZE

1896	Szokolyi (HUN)	12.6
1900	Rowley (AUS)	11.2
1904	Hogenson (USA)	11.2
1908	Kerr (CAN)	11.0
1912	Lippincott (USA)	10.9
1920	Edward (UK)	9.97
1924	Porritt (NZL)	10.8
1928	Lammers (GER)	10.9
1932	Jonath (GER)	10.4
1936	Osendarp (HOL)	10.5
1948	LaBeach (PAN)	10.4
1952	McD.Bailey (UK)	10.4
1956	Hogan (AUS)	10.6
1960	Radford (UK)	10.3
1964	Jeromel (CAN)	10.2
1968	Greene (USA)	10.0
1972	Miller (JAM)	10.33
1976	Borzov (URS)	10.14
1980	Petrov (BUL)	10.39
1984	Johnson (CAN)	10.22
1988	C.Smith (USA)	9.99

200 Metres

GOLD

1900	Walter Tewksbury (USA)	22.2
1904	Archie Hahn (USA)	21.6
1908	Robert Kerr (CAN)	22.6
1912	Ralph Craig (USA)	21.7
1920	Allen Woodring (USA)	22.0
1924	Jackson Scholz (USA)	21.6
1928	Percy Williams (CAN)	21.8
1932	Eddie Tolan (USA)	21.2
1936	Jesse Owens (USA)	20.7
1948	Mel Patton (USA)	21.1
1952	Andrew Stanfield (USA)	20.7
1956	Bobby Joe Morrow (USA)	20.6
1960	Livio Berutti (ITA)	20.5
1964	Henry Carr (USA)	20.3
1968	Tommie Smith (USA)	19.8
1972	Valeriy Borzov (URS)	20.00
1976	Don Quarrie (JAM)	20.23
1980	Pietro Mennea (ITA)	20.19
1984	Carl Lewis (USA)	19.80
1988	Deloach (USA)	19.75

SILVER

1900	Pitchard (IND)	22.8
1904	Cartmell (USA)	21.9
1908	Cloughen (USA)	22.6
1912	Lippincott (USA)	21.8
1920	Paddock (USA)	22.1
1924	Paddock (USA)	22.7
1928	Rangeley (UK)	21.9
1932	Simpson (USA)	21.4
1936	Robinson (USA)	21.1
1948	Ewell (USA)	21.1
1952	Baker (USA)	20.8
1956	Stanfield (USA)	20.7
1960	Carney (USA)	20.6

1964	Drayton (USA)	20.5
1968	Norman (AUS)	20.0
1972	Black (USA)	20.19
1976	Hampton (USA)	20.29
1980	Wells (UK)	20.21
1984	Baptiste (USA)	19.79
1988	Carl Lewis (USA)	19.79

BRONZE

1900	Rowley (AUS)	22.9
1904	Hogenson (USA)	22.8
1908	Cartmell (USA)	22.7
1912	Applegarth (UK)	22.0
1920	Edward (UK)	22.2
1924	Liddell (UK)	21.9
1928	Kornig (GER)	21.9
1932	Matcalfe (USA)	21.5
1936	Osendarp (HOL)	21.3
1948	LaBeach (PAN)	21.2
1952	Gathers (USA)	20.8
1956	Baker (USA)	20.9
1960	Seye (FRA)	20.7
1964	Roberts (TRI)	20.6
1968	Carlos (USA)	20.0
1972	Mennea (ITA)	20.30
1976	Evans (USA)	20.43
1980	Quarrie (JAM)	20.29
1984	Jefferson (USA)	20.26
1988	DA Silva (BRA)	20.04

400 Metres

GOLD

1896	Thomas Burke (USA)	54.2
1900	Maxwell Long (USA)	49.4
1904	Harry Hillman (USA)	49.2
1906	Paul Pilgrrim (USA)	53.2
1908	Wyndham Halswelle (UK) 50.0	

1912	Charles Reidpath (USA)	48.2
1920	Bevil Rudd (SAF)	49.6
1924	Eric Liddell (GBR)	47.6
1928	Ray Barbuti (USA)	47.8
1932	William Carr (USA)	46.2
1936	Archie Williams (USA)	46.5
1948	Arthur Wint (JAM)	46.2
1952	George Rhoden (JAM)	45.9
1956	Charles Jenkins (USA)	46.7
1960	Otis Davis (USA)	44.9
1964	Mike Larrabee (USA)	45.1
1968	Lee Evans (USA)	43.8
1972	Vince Mathews (USA)	44.66
1976	Alberto Juantorena (CUB)	44.26
1980	Viktor Markin (URS)	44.60
1984	Alonzo Babers (USA)	44.27
1988	Carl Lewis (USA)	43.87

SILVER

1896	Jamison (USA)	54.5
1900	Holland (USA)	49.6
1904	Waller (USA)	49.9
1908	Halswelle only finalist	
1912	Braun (GER)	48.3
1920	Butler (UK)	49.9
1924	Fitch (USA)	48.4
1928	Ball (CAN)	48.0
1932	Eastman (USA)	46.4
1936	Brown (UK)	46.7
1948	McKenley (JAM)	46.4
1952	McKenley (JAM)	45.9
1956	Haas (FRG)	46.8
1960	Kaufmann (FRG)	44.9
1964	Mottley (TRI)	45.2
1968	James (USA)	43.9
1972	Collett (USA)	44.80
1976	Newhouse (USA)	44.40

1980	Mitchell (AUS)	44.84
1984	Tiacoh (CIV)	44.45
1988	Reynolds (USA)	43.93

BRONZE

1896	Hofmann (GER)	56.0
1900	Schulz (DEN)	50.1
1904	Groman (USA)	50.0
1908	Halswelle only finalist	--
1912	Lindberg (USA)	48.4
1920	Engdahl (SWE)	49.9
1924	Butler (UK)	48.6
1928	Biichner (GER)	48.2
1932	Wilson (CAN)	47.7
1936	LuValle (USA)	46.8
1948	Whitfield (USA)	46.9
1952	Matson (USA)	46.8
1956	Hellsten (FIN)	47.0
	Ignatyev (URS)	47.0
1960	Spence (SA)	45.5
1964	Badenski (POL)	45.6
1968	Freeman (USA)	44.4
1972	Sang (KEN)	44.92
1976	Frazier (USA)	44.95
1980	Schaffer (GDR)	44.87
1984	Mckay (USA)	44.71
1988	Everett (USA)	---

800 metres

GOLD

1896	Edwin Flack (AUS)	2:11.0
1900	Alfred Tyson (UK)	2:01.2
1904	James Lightbody (USA)	1:56.0
1906	Paul Pilgrim (USA)	2:01.5
1908	Mel Sheppard (USA)	1:52.8
1912	James Meredith (USA)	1:51.9
1920	Albert Hill (UK)	1:53.4

1924	Doughlas Lowe (UK)	1:52.4
1928	Doughlas Lowe (UK)	1:51.8
1932	Thomas Hampson (UK)	1:49.7
1936	John Woodruff (USA)	1:52.9
1948	Mal Whitfield (USA)	1:49.2
1952	Mal Whitfield (USA)	1:49.2
1956	Tom Courtney (USA)	1:47.7
1960	Peter Snell (NZL)	1:46.3
1964	Peter Snell (NZL)	1:45.1
1968	Ralph Doubell (AUS)	1:44.3
1972	DaveWottle (USA)	1:45.9
1976	Alberto Juantorena (CUB)	1:43.5
1980	Steve Ovett (UK)	1:45.4
1984	Joaquim Cruz (BRA)	1:43.00
1988	Ereng (KEN)	1:43.45

SILVER

1896	Dani (HUN)	2:11.8
1900	Cregan (USA)	2:03.0
1904	Valentine (USA)	1:56.3
1908	Lunghi (ITA)	1:54.2
1912	Sheppard (USA)	1:52.0
1920	Eby (USA)	1:53.6
1924	P.Martin (SWZ)	1:52.6
1928	Bylehn (SWE)	1:52.8
1932	Wilson (CAN)	1:49.9
1936	Lanzi (ITA)	1:53.3
1948	Wint (JAM)	1:49.5
1952	Wint (JAM)	1:49.4
1956	Johnson (UK)	1:47.8
1960	Moens (BEL)	1:46.5
1964	Crothers (CAN)	1:45.6
1968	Kiprugut (KEN)	1:44.5
1972	Arzhanov (SU)	1:45.9
1976	Van Damme (BEL)	1:43.9
1980	Coe (UK)	1:45.9
1984	Coe (UK)	1:43.64
1988	Cruz (BRA)	1:43.90

BRONZE

1896	Golemis (GER)	2:11.9
1900	Hall (USA)	2:03.08
1904	Breitkreutz (USA)	1:56.4
1908	Braun (GER)	1:55.2
1912	Davenport (USA)	1:52.0
1920	Rudd (SA)	1:54.0
1924	Enck (USA)	1:53.0
1928	Engelhard (GER)	1:53.2
1932	Edwards (CAN)	1:51.5
1936	Edwards (CAN)	1:53.6
1948	Hansenne (FRA)	1:49.7
1952	Ulzheimer (FRG)	1:49.7
1956	Boysen (NOR)	1:48.1
1960	Kerrr (JAM)	1:47.1
1964	Kiprugut (KEN)	1:45.9
1968	Farrell (USA)	1:45.4
1972	Boit (KEN)	1:46.0
1976	Wohlhuter (USA)	1:44.1
1980	Kirov (URS)	1:46.0
1984	Jones (USA)	1:43.83
1988	Aouita (MOR)	1:44.6

1500 Metres

GOLD

1896	Edwin Flack (AUS)	4:33.2
1900	Charles Bennett (UK)	4:06.2
1904	James Lightbody (USA)	4:05.4
1906	James Lightbody (USA)	4:12.06
1908	Mel Sheppard (USA)	4:03.4
1912	Arnold Jackson (UK)	3:56.8
1920	Albert Hill (UK)	4:01.8
1924	Paavo Nurmi (FIN)	3:53.6
1928	Harri Larva (FIN)	3:53.2
1932	Luigi Beccali (ITA)	3:51.2
1936	Jack Lovelock (NZL)	3:47.8
1948	Henry Eriksson (SWE)	3:49.8

1952	Josef Barthel (LUX)	3:45.1
1956	Ron Delany (IRL)	3:41.2
1960	Herb Elliott (AUS)	3:35.6
1964	Peter Snell (NZL)	3:38.1
1968	Kipchoge Keino (KEN)	3:34.9
1972	Pekka Vasala (FIN)	3:36.3
1976	John Walker (NZL)	3:39.2
1980	Sebastian Coe (UK)	3:38.4
1984	Sebastian Coe (UK)	3:32.53
1988	Rono (KEN)	3:35.96

SILVER

1896	Blake (USA)	4:34.0
1900	Deloge (FRA)	4:06.6
1904	Verner (USA)	4:06.8
1908	Wilson (UK)	4:03.6
1912	Kiviat (USA)	3:56.9
1920	Baker (UK)	4:02.4
1924	Scharer (SUI)	3:55.0
1928	Ladoumegue (FRA)	3:53.8
1932	Cornes (UK)	3:52.6
1936	Cunningham (USA)	3:48.4
1948	Strand (SWE)	3:50.4
1952	McMillen (USA)	3:45.2
1956	Richtzenhain (UK)	3:42.0
1960	Jazy (FRA)	3:38.4
1964	Odlozil (TCH)	3:39.6
1968	Ryun (USA)	3:37.8
1972	Keino (KEN)	3:36.8
1976	Van Damme (BEL)	3:39.3
1980	Straub (GDR)	3:38.8
1984	Cram (UK)	3:33.40
1988	Elliott (UK)	3:36.15

BRONZE

1896	Lermusiaux (FRA)	4:36.0

1900	Bray (USA)	4:07.2
1904	Hearn (USA)	4:06.1
1908	Hallows (UK)	4:04.0
1912	Taber (USA)	3:56.9
1920	Shields (USA)	4:03.1
1924	Stallard (UK)	3:55.6
1928	Purje (FIN)	3:56.4
1932	Edwards (CAN)	3:52.8
1936	Beccali (ITA)	3:49.2
1948	Slykhuis (HOL)	3:50.4
1952	Lueg (FRG)	3:45.4
1956	Landy (AUS)	3:42.0
1960	Rozsavolgyi (HUN)	3:39.2
1964	Davies (NZL)	3:39.6
1968	Tummler (FRG)	3:39.0
1972	Dixon (NZL)	3:37.5
1976	Wellmann (FRG)	3:39.3
1980	Ovett (UK)	3:39.0
1984	Abascal (ESP)	3:34.0
1988	Herold (GDR)	3:36.21

5000 Metres
GOLD

1912	Hannes Kolehmainen (FIN)	14:36.6
1920	Joseph Guillemot (FRA)	14:55.6
1924	Paavo Nurmi (FIN)	14:31.2
1928	Ville Ritola (FIN)	14:38.0
1932	Lauri Lehtinen (FIN)	14:30.0
1936	Gunnar Hockert (FIN)	14:22.2
1948	Gaston Rieff (BEL)	14:17.6
1952	Emil Zatopek (TCH)	14:06.6
1956	Vladimir Kuts (URS)	13:39.6
1960	Murray Halberg (NZL)	13:43.4
1964	Bob Schul (USA)	13:48.8
1968	Mohamed Gammoudi (TUN)	14:05.0
1972	Lasse Viren (FIN)	13:26.4
1976	Lasse Viren (FIN)	13:24.8

1980	Miruts Yifter (ETH)	13:21.0
1984	Said Aouita (MAR)	13:05.59
1988	Ngugi(KEN)	13:11.70

SILVER

1912	Bouin (FRA)	14:36.7
1920	Nurmi (FIN)	15:00.0
1924	Ritola (FIN)	14:31.4
1928	Nurmi (FIN)	14.40.0
1932	Hill (USA)	14:30.0
1936	Lehtinen (FIN)	14:25.8
1948	Zatopek (TCH)	14:17.8
1952	Mimoun (FRA)	14:07.4
1956	Pirie (UK)	13:50.6
1960	Grodotzki (UK)	13:44.6
1964	Norpoth (FRG)	13:49.6
1968	Keino (KEN)	14:05.2
1972	Gammoudi (TUN)	13:27.4
1976	Quaz (NZL)	13:25.2
1980	Nyambui (TAN)	13:21.6
1984	Ryffel (SUI)	13:07.4
1988	Baumann (FRG)	13:15.52

BRONZE

1912	Hutson (UK)	15:07.6
1920	Backman (SWE)	15:13.0
1924	Wide (SWE)	15:01.8
1928	Wide (SWE)	14:41.2
1932	Virtanen (FIN)	14.44.0
1936	Jonsson (SWE)	14:29.0
1948	Slykhuis (HOL)	14:26.8
1952	Schade (FRG)	14:08.6
1956	Ibbotson (UK)	13:54.4
1960	Zimny (POL)	13:44.8
1964	Dellinger (USA)	13:49.8
1968	Temu (KEN)	14:06.4
1972	I.Stewart (UK)	13:27.6

1976	Hidenbrand (FRG)	13:25.4
1980	Maaninka (FIN)	13:22.0
1984	Leitao (POR)	13:09.2
1988	Kunze (GDR)	13:15.73

10 000 Metres

GOLD

1912	Kolehmainen (FIN)	31:20.8
1920	Nurmi (FIN)	31:45.8
1924	Ritola (FIN)	30:23.2
1928	Nurmi (FIN)	30:18.8
1932	Kusocinski (POL)	30:11.4
1936	Salminen (FIN)	30:15.4
1948	Zatopek (TCH)	29:59.6
1952	Zatopek (TCH)	29:17.0
1956	Kuts (URS)	28:45.6
1960	Bolotnikov (URS)	28:32.2
1964	Mills (USA)	28:24.4
1968	Temu (KEN)	29:27.4
1972	Viren (FIN)	27:38.2
1976	Viren (FIN)	27:45.2
1980	Yifter (ETH)	27:42.7
1984	Cova (ITA)	27:47.5
1988	Boutaib (MAR)	27:21.46

SILVER

1912	Tewanima (USA)	32:06.6
1920	Guillemot (FRA)	31:47.2
1924	Wide (SWE)	30:55.2
1928	Ritola (FIN)	30:19.4
1932	Isohollo (FIN)	30:12.6
1936	Askola (FIN)	30.12.6
1948	Mimoun (FRA)	30:47.4
1952	Mimoun (FRA)	29:32.8
1956	Kovacs (HUN)	28:52.2
1960	Grodotzki (GDR)	28:37.0
1964	Gammoudi (TUN)	28:24.8

1968	Wolde (ETH)	29:28.0
1972	Puttemans (BEL)	27:39.6
1976	Lopes (POR)	27:45.2
1980	Maaninka (FIN)	27:44.3
1984	Mcleod (UK)	28:06.2
1988	Antibo (ITA)	27:23.55

BRONZE

1912	Stenroos (FIN)	32:21.8
1920	Wilson (UK)	31:50.8
1924	Berg (FIN)	31:43.0
1928	Wide (SWE)	31:00.8
1932	Virtanen (FIN)	30:35.0
1936	Isohollo (FIN)	30:20.2
1948	Albertsson (SWE)	30:53.6
1952	Anufriyev (URS)	29:48.2
1956	Lawrence (AUS)	28:53.6
1960	Power (AUS)	28:38.2
1964	Clarke (AUS)	28:38.2
1968	Gammoudi (TUN)	29:34.2
1972	Yifter (ETH)	27:41.0
1976	Foster (UK)	27:54.9
1980	Kedir (ETH)	27:44.7
1984	Mysocki (KEN)	28:06.46
1988	Kimeli (KN)	27:25.16

Marathon

GOLD

1896	Spyridon Louis (GRE)	2h 58:50
1900	Michel Theato (FRA)	2h 59:45
1904	Thomas Hicks (USA)	3h 28:35
1906	William Sherring (CAN)	2h 51:23.6
1908	John Hayes (USA)	2h 55:18.4
1912	Kenneth McArthur (SAF)	2h 36:50.8
1920	Hannes Kolehmainen (FIN)	2h 41:22.6
1924	Albin Stenroos (FIN)	2h 41:22.6
1928	Mohammed El Quafi (FRA)	2h 32:57

1932	Juan Carlos Zabala (ARG)	2h 31:36
1936	Kitei Son (JPN)	2h 29:19.2
1948	Delfo Carera (ARG)	2h 34:51.6
1952	Emil Zatopek (TCH)	2h 23:03.2
1956	Alain Mimoun (FRA)	2h 25:00
1960	Abebe Bikila (ETH)	2h 15:16.2
1964	Abebe Bikila (ETH)	2h 12:11.2
1968	Mamo Wolde (ETH)	2h 20:26.4
1972	Frank Shorter (USA)	2h 12:19.8
1976	Waldemar Cierpinski (GDR)	2h 09:55.0
1980	Waldemar Cierpinski (GDR)	2h 11:03
1984	Carlos Lopes (POR)	2h 09:21
1988	Bordin (ITA)	2h 10:32

SILVER

1896	Vasilakos (GER)	3h 06:3
1900	Champion (FRA)	3h 04:17
1904	Corey (USA)	3h 34:52
1908	Hefferon (SA)	2h 56:06
1912	Gitsham (SA)	2h 37:52
1920	Lossman (EST)	2h 32:49
1924	Bertini (ITA)	2h 47:20
1928	Plaza (CHI)	2h 33:23
1932	Ferris (UK)	2h 31:55
1936	Harper (UK)	2h 31:24
1948	Richards (UK)	2h 35:08
1952	Gorno (ARG)	2h 25:35
1956	Mihalic (YUG)	2h 26:32
1960	Rhadi (MOR)	2h 15:42
1964	Heatley (UK)	2h 16:20
1968	Kimihara (JAP)	2h 23:31
1972	Lismont (BEL)	2h 14:32
1976	Shorter (USA)	2h 10:46
1980	Nijboer (HOL)	2h 11:20
1984	Treacy (IRL)	2h 09:56
1988	Wakihuru (KEN)	2h 10:47

BRONZE

1896	Kellner (HUN)	3h 06:35
1900	Fast (SWE)	3h 37:14
1904	Newton (USA)	3h 47:33
1908	Foshaw (USA)	2h 57:11
1912	Strobino (USA)	2h 38:43
1920	Arri (ITA)	2h 36:33
1924	DeMar (USA)	2h 48:14
1928	Marttelin (FIN)	2h 35:02
1932	Toivonen (FIN)	2h 32:12
1936	Nan (JAP)	2h 31:42
1948	Gailly (BEL)	2h 35:34
1952	Jansson (SWE)	2h 26:07
1956	Karvonen (FIN)	2h 27:47
1960	Magee (NZL)	2h 17:19
1964	Tsuburaya (JAP)	2h 16:23
1968	Ryan (NZL)	2h 23:45
1972	Wolde (ETH)	2h 15:09
1976	Lismont (BEL)	2h 15:09
1980	Dzhumanazarov (URS)	2h 11:35
1984	Spedding (UK)	2h 09:58
1988	Saleh (DJI)	2h 10:59

3000 Metres Steeplechase

GOLD

1900	George Orton (CAN)	7:34.4
1902	John Rimmer (UK)	12:58.4
1904	James Lightbody (USA)	7:39.6
1908	Arthur Russell (UK)	10:47.8
1912	Not contested	
1920	Percy Hodge (UK)	10:00.4
1924	Ville Ritola (FIN)	9:33.6
1928	Toivo Loukola (FIN)	9:21.8
1932	Volmari Iso Hollo (FIN)	10:33.4
1936	Volmari Iso Hollo (FIN)	9:03.8
1948	Tore Sjostrand (SWE)	9:04.6
1952	Horace Ashenfelter (USA)	8:45.4

1956	Chris Brasher (UK)	8:41.2
1960	Zdzislaw Krzyszkowiak (POL)	8:34.2
1964	Gaston Roelants (BEL)	8:30.8
1968	Amos Biwott (KEN)	8:51.0
1972	Kipchoge Keino (KEN)	8:23.6
1976	Anders Garderud (SWE)	8:08.0
1980	Bronislaw Malinowski (POL)	8:09.7
1984	Julius Korir (KEN)	8:11.80

SILVER

1900	Robinson (UK)	7:38.0
1904	Daly (UK)	7:40.6
1908	Robertson (UK)	10:48.4
1912	Not contested	
1920	Flynn (USA)	10:05.4
1924	Katz (FIN)	9:44.0
1928	Nurmi (FIN)	9:31.2
1932	Evenson (UK)	10:46.0
1936	Tuominen (FIN)	9:06.8
1948	Elmsater (SWE)	9:08.2
1952	Kazantsev (URS)	8:36.4
1956	Rozsnyoi (HUN)	8:43.6
1960	Sokolov (URS)	8:36.4
1964	Herriott (UK)	8:32.4
1968	Kogo (KEN)	8:51.6
1972	Jipcho (KEN)	8:24.6
1976	Malinowski (POL)	8:09.2
1980	Bayi (TAN)	8:12.5
1984	Mahmoud (FRA)	8:13.31
1988	Koech (KEN)	8:06.79

BRONZE

1900	Chastaniee (FRA)	--
1904	Newton (USA)	--
1908	Eisele (USA)	--
1912	Not contested	--
1920	Ambrosini (ITA)	--

1924	Bontemps (FRA)	9:45.2
1928	Andersen (FIN)	9:35.6
1932	McCluskey (USA)	10:46.2
1936	Dompert (UK)	9:07.2
1948	Hagstron (SWE)	9:11.8
1952	Disley (UK)	8:51.8
1956	Larsen (NOR)	8:44.0
1960	Rzhishchin (URS)	8:42.2
1964	Belyayev (URS)	8:33.8
1968	Young (USA)	8:51.8
1972	Kantanen (FIN)	8:24.8
1976	Baumgartl (GDR)	8:10.4
1980	Tura (ETH)	8:13.6
1984	Diemer (USA)	8:14.0
1988	Rowland (UK)	8:07.96

110 Metres Hurdles

GOLD

1896	Thomas Curtis (USA)	17.6
1900	Alvin Kraenziein (USA)	15.4
1904	Frederick Schule (USA)	16.0
1906	Robert Leavitt (USA)	16.2
1908	Forrest Smithson (USA)	15.0
1912	Frederick Kelly (USA)	15.1
1920	Earl Thomson (CAN)	14.8
1924	Daniel Kinsey (USA)	15.0
1928	Sydney Atkinson (SAF)	14.8
1932	George Saling (USA)	14.6
1936	Forest Towns (USA)	14.2
1948	William Porter (USA)	13.9
1952	Harrison Dilard (USA)	13.7
1956	Lee Calhoun (USA)	13.5
1960	Lee Calhoun (USA)	13.8
1964	Hayes Jones (USA)	13.6
1968	Willie Davenport (USA)	13.3
1972	Rod Milburn (USA)	13.24
1976	Guy Drutn(FRA)	13.30

1980	Thomas Munkelt (GDR)	13.39
1984	Roger Kingdom (USA)	13.20
1988	Roger Kingdom (USA)	12.98

SILVER

1896	Goulding (UK)	17.7
1900	McLean (USA)	15.5
1904	Schideler (USA)	16.3
1908	Garrels (USA)	15.7
1912	Wendell (USA)	15.2
1920	Barron (USA)	15.1
1924	Atkinson (SA)	15.0
1928	Anderson (USA)	14.8
1932	Beard (USA)	14.7
1936	Finlay (UK)	14.4
1948	Scott (USA)	14.1
1952	J.Davis (USA)	13.7
1956	J. Davis (USA)	13.5
1960	May (USA)	13.8
1964	Lindgren (USA)	13.7
1968	Hall (USA)	13.4
1972	Drut (FRA)	13.34
1976	Casanas (CUB)	13.33
1980	Casanas (CUB)	13.40
1984	Foster (USA)	13.23
1988	Jackson (UK)	13.28

BRONZE

1896	--	--
1900	Moloney (USA)	--
1904	Ashburner (USA)	16.4
1908	Shaw (USA)	--
1912	Hawkins (USA)	15.3
1920	Murray (USA)	15.2
1924	Pettersson (SWE)	15.4
1928	Collier (USA)	14.9
1932	Finlay (UK)	14.8

1936	Pollard (USA)	14.4
1948	Dixon (USA)	14.1
1952	Barnard (USA)	14.1
1956	Shankle (USA)	14.1
1960	H.Jones (USA)	14.0
1964	Mikhailov (URS)	13.7
1968	Ottoz (ITA)	13.4
1972	Hill (USA)	13.48
1976	Davenport (USA)	13.38
1980	Puchkov (URS)	13.44
1984	Bryggare (FIN)	13.40
1988	Campbell (USA)	13.38

400 Metres Hurdles

GOLD

1900	Walter Tewksbury (USA)	57.6
1904	Harry Hillman (USA)	53.0
1908	Charles Bacon (USA)	55.0
1912	Not contested	
1920	Frank Loomis (USA)	54.0
1924	Morgan Taylor (USA)	52.6
1928	Lord Burghley (UK)	53.4
1932	Bob Tisdall (IRL)	51.7
1936	Glenn Hardin (USA)	52.4
1948	Roy Cochran (USA)	51.1
1952	Charlie Moore (USA)	50.8
1956	Glenn Davis (USA)	50.1
1960	Glenn Davis (USA)	49.3
1964	Rex Cawley (USA)	49.6
1968	David Hemery (UK)	48.1
1972	John Akii Bua (UGA)	47.82
1976	Edwin Moses (USA)	47.64
1980	Volker Beck (GDR)	48.70
1984	Edwin Moses (USA)	47.75
1988	Phillips (USA)	47.19

SILVER

1900	Tauzin (FRA)	58.3
1904	Waller (USA)	53.2
1908	Hillman (USA)	55.3
1912 Not contested		
1920	Norton (USA)	55.3
1924	Vilen (FIN)	53.8
1928	Cuhel (USA)	53.6
1932	Hardin (USA)	51.9
1936	Loaring (CAN)	52.7
1948	White (CEY)	51.8
1952	Lituyev (URS)	51.3
1956	Southern (USA)	50.8
1960	Cushman (USA)	49.6
1964	Coopr (UK)	50.1
1968	Hennige (FRG)	49.0
1972	Mann (USA)	48.51
1976	Shine (USA)	48.69
1980	Arkhipyenko (URS)	48.86
1984	Harris (USA)	48.13
1988	Dia Ba (SEN)	47.23

BRONZE

1900	Orton (CAN)	--
1904	Poage (USA)	--
1908	Tremeer (UK)	57.0
1912 Not contested		
1920	Desch (USA)	54.5
1924	Riley (USA)	54.2
1928	Taylor (USA)	53.6
1932	Taylor (USA)	52.0
1936	White (PHI)	52.8
1948	R.Larsson (SWE)	52.2
1952	Holland (NZL)	52.2
1956	Culbreath (USA)	51.6
1960	Howard (USA)	49.7
1964	Morale (ITA)	50.1

1968	Sherwood (UK)	49.0
1972	Hemery (UK)	48.52
1976	Gavrilyenko (URS)	49.45
1980	Oakes (UK)	49.11
1984	Schmid (FRG)	48.19
1988	Moses (USA)	47.56

4x100 Metres Relay
GOLD

1912	Great Britain	42.4
1920	United States	42.2
1924	United States	41.0
1928	United States	41.0
1932	United States	40.0
1936	United States	39.8
1948	United States	40.6
1952	United States	40.1
1956	United States	39.5
1960	Germany	39.5
1964	United States	39.0
1968	United States	38.2
1972	United States	38.19
1976	United States	38.33
1980	Soviet Union	38.26
1984	United States	37.83
1988	Soviet Union	38.19

SILVER

1912	Sweden	42.6
1920	France	42.6
1924	UK	41.2
1928	Germany	41.2
1932	Germany	40.9
1936	Italy	41.1
1948	UK	41.3
1952	USSR	40.3
1956	USSR	39.8

1960	USSR	40.1
1964	Poland	38.3
1968	Cuba	38.3
1972	USSR	38.50
1976	Germany	36.66
1980	Poland	38.33
1984	Jamaica	38.62
1988	UK	38.28

BRONZE

1912	--	--
1920	Sweden	42.9
1924	Holland	41.8
1928	UK	41.8
1932	Italy	41.2
1936	Germany	41.2
1948	Italy	41.5
1952	Hungary	40.5
1956	Germany	40.3
1960	UK	40.2
1964	France	39.3
1968	France	38.4
1972	FRG	38.79
1976	USSR	38.78
1980	France	38.53
1984	Canada	38.70
1988	France	38.40

4 x400 Metres Relay

GOLD

1908	United States	3:29.4
1912	United States	3:16.6
1920	Great Britain	3:22.2
1924	United States	3:16.0
1928	United States	3:14.2
1932	United States	3:08.2
1936	Great Britain	3:09.0

1948	United States	3:10.4
1952	Jamaica	3:03.9
1956	United States	3:04.8
1960	United States	3:02.2
1964	United States	3:00.7
1968	United States	2:56.1
1972	Kenya	2:59.83
1976	United States	2:58.65
1980	Soviet Union	3:01.08
1984	United States	2:57.91
1988	United States	2:56.16

SILVER

1908	GER	- -
1912	FRA	3:20.7
1920	SA	3:24.2
1924	SWE	3:17.0
1928	GER	3:14.8
1932	UK	3:11.2
1936	USA	3:11.0
1948	FRA	3:14.8
1952	USA	3:04.0
1956	AUS	3:06.2
1960	FRG	3:02.7
1964	UK	3:01.6
1968	KEN	2:59.6
1972	UK	3:00.5
1976	POL	3:01.4
1980	GDR	3:01.3
1984	UK	2:59.13
1988	JAM	3:00.30

BRONZE

1908	HUN	- -
1912	UK	3:23.2
1920	FRA	3:24.8
1924	UK	3:17.4

1928	CAN	3:15.4
1932	CAN	3:12.8
1936	GER	3:11.8
1948	SWE	3:16.0
1952	GER	3:06.6
1956	UK	3:07.1
1960	W.INDIES	3:04 0
1964	TRI	3:01.7
1968	TRI	3:00.5
1972	FRA	3:00.7
1976	FRG	3:02.0
1980	ITA	3:04.3
1984	NGR	2:59.32
1988	FRG	3:00.56

20 000 Metres Road Walk

GOLD

1956	Leonid Spirin (URS)	1h 31:27.4
1960	Vladimir Golubnichiy (URS)	1h 34:07.2
1964	Ken Matthews (UK)	1h 29:34.0
1968	Vladimir Golubnichiy (URS)	1h 33:58.4
1972	Peter Frenkel (GDR)	1h 26:42.4
1976	Daniel Bautista (MEX)	1h 24:40.6
1980	Maurizio Damilano (ITA)	1h 23:35.5
1984	Ernesto Canto (MEX)	1h 23:13
1988	Pribilenic (TCH)	1h 19:57

SILVER

1956	Mikenas (URS)	1h 32:03
1960	Freeman (AUS)	1h 34:17
1964	Lindner (GDR)	1h 31:14
1968	Pedraza (MEX)	1h 34:00
1972	Golubnichiy (URS)	1h 26:56
1976	Reimann (GDR)	1h 25:14
1980	Pochinchuk (URS)	1h 24:46
1984	Gonzalez (MEX)	1h 23:20
1988	Weigel (GDR)	1h 19:60

BRONZE

1956	Junk (URS)	1h 32:12
1960	Vickers (UK)	1h 32:12
1964	Golubnichiy (URS)	1h 32:00
1968	Smaga (URS)	1h 34:04
1972	Reimann (GDR)	1h 27:17
1976	Frenkel (GDR)	1h 25:30
1980	Wieser (GDR)	1h 25:59
1984	Damilano (ITA)	1h 23:26
1988	Damilano (I TA)	1h 20:14

50 000 Metres Road Walk

GOLD

1932	Thomas Green (UK)	4h 50:10
1936	Harold Whitlock (UK)	4h 30:41.1
1948	John Ljunggren (SWE)	4h 41:52
1952	Giuseppe Dordoni (ITA)	4h 28:07.8
1956	Norman Read (NZL)	4h 30:42.8
1960	Don Thompson (UK)	4h 25:30.0
1964	Abdon Pamich (ITA)	4h 11:12.4
1968	Christoph Hohne (GDR)	4h 20:13.6
1972	Bernd Kannenberg (FRG)	3h 56:11.6
1976	Not contested	
1980	Hertwig Gauder (GDR)	3h 49:24
1984	Raul Gonzalez (MEX)	3h 47:26
1988	Ivanenko (URS)	3h 28:29

SILVER

1932	Dalins (LAT)	4h 57:20
1936	Schwab (SUI)	4h 32:10
1948	Godel (SUI)	4h 48:17
1952	Dolezal (TCH)	4H 30:18
1956	Maskinskov (URS)	4h 32:57
1960	Ljunggren (SWE)	4h 25:47
1964	Nihill (UK)	4h 11:32
1968	Kiss (HUN)	4h 30:17
1972	Soldatyenko (URS)	3h 58:24

1976	Not contested	
1980	Llopart (ESP)	3h 51:25
1984	Gustafsson (SWE)	3h 53:19
1988	Weigel (GDR)	3h 38:56

BRONZE

1932	Frigerio	4h 59:06
1936	Bubenko (LAT)	4h 32:43
1948	Lloyd-Johnson (UK)	4h 48:31
1952	Roka (HUN)	4h 31:28
1956	Ljunggren (SWE)	4h 35:02
1960	Pamich (ITA)	4h 27:56
1964	Pettersson (SWE)	4h 14:18
1968	Young (USA)	4h 31:56
1972	Young (USA)	4h 00:46
1976	Not contested	
1980	Ivchenko (URS)	3h 56:32
1984	Bellucci (ITA)	3h 53:45
1988	Gauder (GDR)	3h 39:45

High Jump

GOLD

1896	Ellery Clark (USA)	1.81m
1900	Irving Baxter (USA)	1.90m
1904	Samuel Jones (USA)	1.80m
1906	Con Leahy (UK)	1.77m
1908	Harry Porter (USA)	1.905m
1912	Alma Richards (USA)	1.93m
1920	Richmond Landon (USA)	1.94m
1924	Harold Osborn (USA)	1.98m
1928	Robert King(USA)	1.94m
1932	Duncan McNaughton (CAN)	1.97m
1936	Cornelius Johnson (USA)	2.03m
1948	John Winter (AUS)	1.98m
1952	Walt Davis (USA)	2.04m
1956	Charlie Dumas (USA)	2.12m
1960	Robert Shavlakadze (URS)	2.16m

1964	Valeriy Brumel (URS)	2.18m
1968	Dick Fosbury (USA)	2.24m
1972	Yuriy Tarmak (URS)	2.23m
1976	Jacek Wszola (POL)	2.25m
1980	Gerd Wessig (GDR)	2.36m
1984	Dietmar Mogenburg (FRG)	2.35m
1988	Avdeyenko (URS)	2.38m

SILVER

1896	Connolly (USA)	1.65m
1900	P.Leahy (UK)	1.78m
1904	Serviss (USA)	1.77m
1908	C.Leahy (UK)	1.88m
	Somody (HUN)	1.88m
	G. Andre (FRA)	1.88m
1912	Liesche (GER)	1.91m
1920	Muller (USA)	1.90m
1924	Brown (USA)	1.95m
1928	Hedges (USA)	1.91m
1932	Van Osdel (USA)	1.97m
1936	Albritton (USA)	2.00m
1948	Paulson (USA)	1.95m
1952	Wiesner (USA)	2.01m
1956	Porter (AUS)	2.10m
1960	Brumel (URS)	2.16m
1964	Thomas (USA)	2.18m
1968	Caruthers (USA)	2.22m
1972	Junge (GDR)	2.21m
1976	Joy (CAN)	2.23m
1980	Wszola (POL)	2.31m
1984	Sjoberg (SWE)	2.33m
1988	Conway (USA)	2.36m

BRONZE

1896	Garrett (USA)	1.65m
1900	Gonczy (HUN)	1.75m
1904	Weinstein (GER)	1.77m

1908	--	--
1912	Horine (USA)	1.89m
1920	Ekelund (SWE)	1.90m
1924	Lewden (FRA)	1.92m
1928	Menard (FRA)	1.91m
1932	Toribio (PHI)	1.97m
1936	Thurber (USA)	2.00m
1948	Stanich (USA)	1.95m
1952	Conceicao (BRA)	1.98m
1956	Kashkarov (URS)	2.08m
1960	Thomas (USA)	2.14m
1964	Rambo (USA)	2.16m
1968	Gavrilov (URS)	2.20m
1972	Stones (USA)	2.21m
1976	Stones (USA)	2.21m
1980	Freimuth (GDR)	2.31m
1984	Zhu (CHN)	2.31m
1988	Povarnitsyn (URS)	2.36m
	Sjoberg (SWE)	2.36m

Pole Vault
GOLD

1896	William Hoyt (USA)	3.30m
1900	Irving Baxter (USA)	3.30m
1904	Charles Dvorak (USA)	3.50m
1906	Fernand Gonder (FRA)	3.40m
1908	Edward Cooke (USA)	3.70m
	Alfred Gilbert (USA)	3.70m
1912	Frank Foss (USA)	4.09m
1920	Frank Foss (USA)	4.09m
1924	Lee Barnes (USA)	3.95m
1928	Sabin Carr (USA)	4.20m
1932	William Miller (USA)	4.31m
1936	Earle Meadows (USA)	4.35m
1948	Guinn Smith (USA)	4.30m
1952	Bob Richard (USA)	4.55m
1956	Bob Richards (USA)	4.56m

1960	Don Bragg (USA)	4.70m
1964	Fred Hansen(USA)	5.10m
1968	Bob Seagren (USA)	5.40m
1972	Wolfgang Nordwig (GDR)	5.50m
1976	Tadeusz Slusarski (POL)	5.50m
1980	Wladislaw Kozakiewicz (POL)	5.78m
1984	Pierre Quinon (FRA)	5.75m
1988	Bubka (URS)	5.90m

SILVER

1896	Tyler (USA)	3.25m
1900	Colkett (USA)	3.25m
1904	Damse (USA)	3.43m
1908	--	
1912	Nelson (USA)	3.85m
	Wright (USA)	3.85m
1920	Petersen (DEN)	3.70m
1924	Graham (USA)	3.95m
1928	Droegemuller (USA)	4.10m
1932	Nishida (JAP)	4.30m
1936	Nishida (JAP)	4.25m
1948	Kataja (FIN)	4.20m
1952	Las (USA)	4.50m
1956	Gutowski (USA)	4.53m
1960	Morris (USA)	4.60m
1964	Reinhardt (FRG)	5.05m
1968	Schiprowski (FRG)	5.40m
1972	Seagren (USA)	5.40m
1976	Kallimoaki (FIN)	5.50m
1980	Volkov (URS)	5.65m
	Slusarski (POL)	5.65m
1984	Tully (USA)	5.65m
1988	Gataulline (URS)	5.85m

BRONZE

1896	Damaskos (GER)	2.85m
1900	Andersen (NOR)	3.20m

1904	Wilkins (USA)	3.43m
1908	Jacobs (USA)	3.58m
	Archibald (CAN)	3.58m
	Soderstrom (SWE)	3.58m
1912	--	--
1920	Mysers (USA)	3.60m
1924	Brooker (USA)	3.90m
1928	McGinnis (USA)	3.95m
1932	Jefferson(USA)	4.20m
1936	Oe(JAP)	4.25m
1948	Richards (USA)	4.20m
1952	Lundberg (SWE)	4.40m
1956	Roubanis (GRE)	4.50m
1960	Landstrom(FIN)	4.55m
1964	Lehnertz(FRG)	5.00m
1968	Nordwig(GDR)	5.40m
1972	J.Johnson (USA)	5.35m
1976	Roberts (USA)	5.50m
1980	--	--
1984	Bell (USA)	5.60m
	Vigneron (FRA)	5.60m
1988	Yegorov (URS)	5.80m

Long Jump
GOLD

1896	Ellery Clark (USA)	6.35m
1900	Alvin Kraenzlein (USA)	7.18m
1904	Myer Prinstein (USA)	7.34m
1906	Myer Prinstein (USA)	7.20m
1908	Francis Irons (USA)	7.48m
1912	Albert Gutterson (USA)	7.60m
1920	William Pettersson (SWE)	7.15m
1924	William DeHart Hubbard (USA)	7.44m
1928	Edward Hamm (USA)	7.73m
1932	Ed Gordon (USA)	7.63m
1936	Jesse Owens (USA)	8.06m
1948	Willie Steele (USA)	7.82m

1952	Jerome Biffle (USA)	7.57m
1956	Greg Bell (USA)	7.83m
1960	Ralph Boston (USA)	8.12m
1964	Lynn Davies (UK)	8.07m
1968	Bob Beamon (USA)	8.90m
1972	Randy Williams (USA)	8.24m
1976	Arnie Robinson (USA)	8.35m
1980	Lutz Dombrowski (GDR)	8.54m
1984	Carl Lewis (USA)	8.54m
1988	Carl Lewis (USA)	8.72m

SILVER

1896	Garrett (USA)	6.18m
1900	Prinstein (USA)	7.17m
1904	Frank (USA)	6.89m
1908	Kelly (USA)	7.09m
1912	Bricker (CAN)	7.21m
1920	Johnson (USA)	7.09m
1924	Ed Gourdin(USA)	7.27m
1928	Cator (HAI)	7.58m
1932	Redd (USA)	7.60m
1936	Long (GER)	7.87m
1948	Bruce (AUS)	7.55m
1952	Meredith Gourdine (USA)	7.53m
1956	Bennett (USA)	7.68m
1960	Robertson (USA)	8.11m
1964	Boston (USA)	8.03m
1968	Beer (GDR)	8.19m
1972	Baumgartner (FRG)	8.18m
1976	R.Williams (USA)	8.11m
1980	Paschek (GDR)	8.21m
1984	Honey (AUS)	8.24m
1988	Powell (USA)	8.49m

BRONZE

1896	Connolly (USA)	6.11m
1900	P. Leahy (UK)	6.95m

1904	Stangland (USA)	6.88m
1908	Bricker (CAN)	7.08m
1912	Aberg (SWE)	7.18m
1920	Abrahamsson (SWE)	7.08m
1924	Hansen (NOR)	7.26m
1928	Bates (USA)	7.40m
1932	Nambu (JAP)	7.45m
1936	Tajima (JAP)	7.74m
1948	Douglas (USA)	7.54m
1952	Foldessy (HUN)	7.30m
1956	Valkama (FIN)	7.48m
1960	Ter-Ovanesyan (URS)	8.04m
1964	Ter-Ovanesyan (URS)	7.99m
1968	Boston (USA)	8.16m
1972	Robinson (USA)	8.03m
1976	Wartenberg(GDR)	8.02m
1980	Podluzhniy (URS)	8.18m
1984	Evangelisti (ITA)	8.24m
1988	Myricks (USA)	8.27m

Triple Jump
GOLD

1896	James Connolly (USA)	13.71m
1900	Myer Prinstein (USA)	14.47m
1904	Myer Prinstein (USA)	14.35m
1906	Peter O'Conor (UK)	14.07m
1908	Tim Ahearne (UK)	14.91m
1912	Gustaf Lindblom (SWE)	14.76m
1920	Vilho Tuulos (FIN)	14.50m
1924	Anthony Winter (AUS)	15.52m
1928	Mikio Oda (JPN)	15.21m
1932	Chuhei Nambu (JPN)	15.72m
1936	Naoto Tajima (JPN)	16.00m
1948	Arne Ahman(SWE)	15.40m
1952	Adhemar Ferreira da Silva (BRA)	16.22m
1956	Adhemar Ferreira da Silva (BRA)	16.35m
1960	Jozef Schmidt (POL)	16.81m

1964	Jozef Schmidt (POL)	16.85m
1968	Viktor Saneyev (URS)	17.39m
1972	Viktor Saneyev (URS)	17.29m
1976	Viktor Saneyev (URS)	17.35m
1980	Jaak Uudmae (URS)	17.35m
1984	Al Joyner (USA)	17.26m
1988	Markov (BUL)	17.61m

SILVER

1896	Tuffefre (FRA)	12.70
1900	Connolly (USA)	13.97
1904	Englehardt (USA)	13.90
1908	MacDonald (CAN)	14.76
1912	Aberg (SWE)	14.51
1920	Jansson (SWE)	14.48
1924	Brunetto (ARG)	15.42
1928	Casey (USA)	15.17
1932	Svensson (SWE)	15.32
1936	Harada (JAP)	15.66
1948	Avery (AUS)	15.36
1952	Shcheerbakov(URS)	15.98
1956	Einarsson (ICE)	16.26
1960	Goryayev (URS)	16.63
1964	Fedosyeyev (URS)	16.58
1968	Prudencio (BRA)	17.27
1972	Drehmel (GDR)	17.31
1976	Butts (USA)	17.18
1980	sanyeyev (USA)	17.18
1984	Conley (USA)	17.18
1988	Lapchine (URS	17.52

BRONZE

1896	Persakis (GRE)	12.52
1900	Sheldon (USA)	13.64
1904	Stangland (USA)	13.36
1908	Larsen (NOR)	14.39
1912	Almlof (SWE)	14.17

1920	Almlof (SWE)	14.27
1924	Tuulos (FIN)	15.37
1928	Tuulos (FIN)	15.11
1932	Oshima (JAP)	15.12
1936	Metcalfe (AIS)	15.50
1948	Seerialp (TUR)	15.02
1952	Devonish (VEN)	15.52
1956	Kreyer (URS)	16.02
1960	Kreyer (URS)	16.432
1964	Kravchenko (URS)	16.57
1968	Gentile (ITA)	17.22
1972	Predencio (BRA)	17.05
1976	de Oliveria (BRA)	16.90
1980	de Oliveria (BRA)	17.22
1984	Conner (UK)	16.87
1988	Kovalenko (URS)	17.42

Shot Put

GOLD

1896	Robert Garrett (USA)	11.22m
1900	Richard Sheldon (USA)	14.10m
1904	Ralph Rose (USA)	14.80m
1906	Martin Sheridan (USA)	12.32m
1908	Ralph Rose (USA)	14.80m
1912	Patrick McDonald (USA)	15.34m
1920	Ville Porhola (FIN)	14.81m
1924	Clarence Houser (USA)	14.99m
1928	John Kuck (USA)	15.87m
1932	Leo Sexton (USA)	16.00m
1936	Hans Woellke (GDR)	16.20m
1948	Wilbur Thompson(USA)	17.12m
1952	Parry O'Brien (USA)	17.41m
1956	Parry O'Brien (USA)	18.57m
1960	Bill Nieder (USA)	19.68m
1964	Dallas Long (USA)	20.33m
1968	Randy Matson (USA)	20.54m
1972	Wladyslaw Komar (POL)	21.18m

1976	Udo Beyer (GDR)	21.05m
1980	Vladimir Kiselyev (URS)	21.35m
1984	Alessandro Andrei (ITA)	21.26m
1988	Timmermann (GDR)	22.47m

SILVER

1896	Gouskos (GRE)	11.20
1900	Mc Cracken (USA)	12.85
1904	Coe (USA)	14.40
1908	Horgan (GBR)	13.62
1912	Rose (USA)	15.25
1920	Niklander (FIN)	14.15
1924	Hartranft (USA)	14.89
1928	Brix (USA)	15.75
1932	Rothert (USA)	15.67
1936	Barlund (FIN)	16.12
1948	Delaney (USA)	16.68
1952	Hooper (USA)	17.39
1956	Nieder (USA)	18.18
1960	O'Brien (USA)	19.11
1964	Matson (USA)	20.20
1968	Woods (USA)	20.12
1972	Woods (USA)	21.17
1976	Mironov (URS)	21.03
1980	Barishnikov (URS)	21.08
1984	Carter (USA)	21.09
1988	Barnes (USA)	22.39

BRONZE

1896	Papasideris (GRE)	10.36
1900	Garrett (USA)	12.37
1904	L. Feuerbach (USA)	13.18
1908	Garrels (USA)	13.18
1912	Whitney (USA)	13.93
1920	Liversedge (USA)	14.15
1924	Hills (USA)	14.64
1928	Hirschfeld (GER)	15.66

1932	Douda (TCH)	15.61
1936	Stock (GER)	15.66
1948	Fuchs (USA)	16.42
1952	Fuchs (USA)	17.06
1956	Skobla (TCH)	17.65
1960	Long (USA)	19.01
1964	Varju (HUN)	19.39
1968	Gushchin (URS)	20.09
1972	Briesenick (GDR)	21.14
1976	Barishnikov (URS)	21.00
1980	Beyer (GDR)	21.06
1984	Laut (USA)	20.97
1988	Guenthoer (SUI)	21.99

Discus

GOLD

1896	Robert Garrett (USA)	29.15m
1900	Rudolf Bauer (HUN)	36.04m
1904	Martin Sheridan (USA)	39.28m
1906	Martin Sheridan (USA)	41.46m
1908	Martin Sheridan (USA)	40.89m
1912	Armas Taipale (FIN)	45.21m
1920	Elmer Niklander (FIN)	44.68m
1924	Clarence Houser (USA)	46.15m
1928	Clarence Houser (USA)	47.32m
1932	John Anderson (USA)	49.49m
1936	Ken Carpenter (USA)	50.48m
1948	Adolfo Consolini (ITA)	52.78m
1952	Sim Iness (USA)	55.03m
1956	Al Oerter (USA)	56.36m
1960	Al Oerter (USA)	59.18m
1964	Al Oerter (USA)	61.00m
1968	Al Oerter (USA)	64.78m
1972	Ludvik Danes (TCH)	64.40m
1976	Mac Wilkins (USA)	67.50m
1980	Viktor Rashchupkin (URS)	66.64m
1984	Rolf Danneberg (FRG)	66.60m
1988	Schult (GDR)	68.82

SILVER

1896	Paraskevopoulos (GRE)	28.95
1900	Janda-Suk (BOH)	35.25
1904	Rose (USA)	39.28
1908	Giffin (USA)	40.70
1912	Byrd (USA)	42.32
1920	Taipale (FIN)	44.19
1924	Nittymaa (FIN)	44.95
1928	Kivi (FIN)	47.23
1932	Laborde (USA)	48.47
1936	Dunn (USA)	49.36
1948	Tosi (ITA)	51.78
1952	Consolini (ITA)	53.78
1956	Gordien (USA)	54.81
1960	Babka (USA)	58.02
1964	Danek (TCH)	60.52
1968	Milde (GDR)	63.08
1972	Silvester (USA)	63.50
1976	Schmidt (GDR)	66.22
1980	Bugar (TCH)	66.38
1984	Wikins (USA)	66.30
1988	Ubarts (URS)	67.48

BRONZE

1896	Versis (GRE)	28.78
1900	Sheldon (USA)	34.60
1904	Georgantas (GRE)	37.68
1908	H. Jorr (USA)	39.44
1912	Duncan (USA)	42.28
1920	Pope (USA)	42.13
1924	Lieb (USA)	44.83
1928	Corson (USA)	47.10
1932	Winter (FRA)	47.85
1936	Oberweger (ITA)	49.23
1948	Gordien (USA)	50.77
1952	Dillion (USA)	53.28
1956	Koch (USA)	54.40

1960	Cochran (USA)	57.16
1964	Weill (USA)	59.49
1968	Danek (TCH)	62.92
1972	Bruch (WE)	63.40
1976	Powell (USA)	65.70
1980	Delis (CUB)	66.32
1984	Powell (USA)	65.46
1988	Danneberg (FRG)	67.38

Hammer

GOLD

1900	John Flanagan (USA)	49.73m
1904	John Flanagan (USA)	51.23m
1908	John Flanagan (USA)	51.92m
1912	Matt McGrath (USA)	54.74m
1920	Patrick Ryan (USA)	52.87m
1924	Fred Tootell (USA)	53.29m
1928	Patrick O'Callaghan (IRL)	51.39m
1932	Patrick O'Callaghan(IRL)	53.92m
1936	Karl Hein (GER)	56.49m
1948	Imre Nemeth (HUN)	56.07m
1952	Jozsef Csermak (HUN)	60.34m
1956	Harold Connolly (USA)	63.19m
1960	Vasiliy Rudenkov (URS)	67.10m
1964	Romuald Klim (URS)	69.74m
1968	Gyula Zsivotzky (HUN)	73.36m
1972	Anatoliy Bondarchuk (URS)	75.50m
1976	Yuriy Sedykh (URS)	77.52m
1980	Yuriy Sedykh (URS)	81.80m
1984	Juha Tiainen (FIN)	78.08m
1988	Litvinov (URS)	84.80m

SILVER

1896	Not contested	
1900	Hare (USA)	49.13
1904	De Witt (USA)	50.26
1908	Mc Grath (USA)	51.18

1912	Gillis (CAN)	48.39
1920	Lind (SWE)	48.43
1924	Mc Grath (USA)	50.84
1928	Skiold (SWE)	51.29
1932	Porhola (FIN)	52.27
1936	Blask (GER)	55.04
1948	Gubijan (YUG)	54.27
1952	Storch (GER)	58.86
1956	Krivonosov (URS)	63.03
1960	Zsivotzky (HUN)	65.79
1964	Zsivotzky (HUN)	69.09
1968	Klim (URS)	73.28
1972	Sachse (GDR)	74.96
1976	Spiridonov (URS)	76.08
1980	Litvinov (URS)	80.64
1984	Riehm (FRG)	77.98
1988	Sedykh (URS)	83.76

BRONZE

1896	Not contested	
1900	Mc Cracken (USA)	42.46
1904	Rose (USA)	45.73
1908	Walsh (USA)	48.50
1912	Childs (USA)	48.17
1920	Bennet (USA)	48.25
1924	Nokes (UK)	48.87
1928	Black (USA)	49.03
1932	Zaremba (USA)	50.33
1936	Warngard (SWE)	54.83
1948	R. Bennett (USA)	53.73
1952	I. Nemeth (HUN)	57.74
1956	Samotsvyetov (URS)	62.56
1960	Rut (POL)	65.64
1964	Uwe Beyer (FRG)	68.09
1968	Lovasz (HUN)	69.78
1972	Khmyelesvkiy (URS)	74.04
1976	Bondarchuk (URS)	75.48

1980	Tamm (URS)	78.96
1984	Ploghaus (FRG)	76.68
1988	Tamm (URS)	81.16

Javelin

GOLD

1904	Erik Lemming (SWE)	53.90m
1908	Erik Lemming (SWE)	54.82m
1912	Erik Lemming (SWE)	60.64m
1920	Jonni Myyra (FIN)	65.78m
1924	Jonni Myyra (FIN)	62.96m
1928	Erik Lundkvist (SWE)	66.60m
1932	Matti Jarvinen (FIN)	72.71m
1936	Gerhard Stock (GER)	71.84m
1948	Tapio Rautavara (FIN)	69.77m
1952	CyrusYoung (USA)	73.78m
1956	Egil Danielsen (NOR)	85.71m
1960	Viktor Tsibulenko (URS)	84.64m
1964	Pauli Nevala (FIN)	82.66m
1968	Janis Lusis (URS)	90.10m
1972	Klaus Wolfermann (FRG)	90.48m
1976	Miklos Nemeth (HUN)	94.58m
1980	Dainis Kula (URS)	91.20m
1984	Arto Harkonen (FIN)	86.76m
1988	Korjus (FIN)	84.28

SILVER

1904	--	--
1908	Halse (NOR)	50.57
1912	Saristo (FIN)	58.66
1920	Peltonen (FIN)	64.50
1924	Lindstrom (SWE)	60.92
1928	Szepes (HUN)	65.26
1932	Sippala (FIN)	69.80
1936	Nikkanen (FIN)	70.77
1948	Seymour (USA)	67.56
1952	Miller (USA)	72.46

1956	Sidlo (POL)	79.98
1960	Kruger (GDR)	79.36
1964	Kulcsar (HUN)	82.32
1968	Kinnunen (FIN)	88.58
1972	Lusis (URS)	90.46
1976	Siitonen (FIN)	87.92
1980	Makarov (URS)	89.64
1984	Ottley (UK)	85.74
1988	Zelezny (TCH)	84.12

BRONZE

1908	Nilsson (SWE)	47.10
1912	Koczan (HUN)	5.50
1920	Johansson (FIN)	63.09
1924	Oberst (USA)	58.35
1928	Sunde (NOR)	63.97
1932	Penttila (FIN)	68.70
1936	Toivonen (FIN)	70.72
1948	Varszegi (HUN)	67.03
1952	Hyytiainen (FIN)	71.89
1956	Tsibulenko (URS)	79.50
1960	Kulcsafr (HUN)	78.57
1964	Lusis (URS)	80.57
1968	Kulcsar (HUN)	87.06
1972	Schmidt (USA)	84.42
1976	Megelea (ROM)	87.16
1980	Hanisch (GDR)	86.72
1984	Eldebrink (SWE	83.72
1988	Raty (FIN)	83.26

Decathlon

GOLD

1904	Thomas Kiely (UK)	6036pts.
1912	Hugo Wieslander (SWE)	6162pts.
1920	Helge Lovland (NOR)	5970pts.
1924	Harold Osborn (USA)	6668pts.
1928	Paavo Yrjola (FIN)	6774pts.

1932	Jim Bausch (USA)	6986pts.
1936	Glenn Morris (USA)	7421pts.
1948	Bob Mathias (USA)	6826pts.
1952	Bob Mathias (USA)	7731pts.
1956	Milt Campbell (USA)	7708pts.
1960	Rafer Johnson (USA)	8001pts.
1964	Willi Holdorf (GER)	7887pts.
1968	Bill Toomey(USA)	8193pts.
1972	Nikolai Avilov (URS)	8454pts.
1976	Bruce Jenner (USA)	8617pts.
1980	Daley Thompson (UK)	8495pts.
1984	Daley Thompson (UK)	8798pts.
1988	Schenk (GDR)	2448pts.

SILVER

1912	Wieslander(SWE)	7724/6161
1920	Hamilton (USA)	6770/5912
1924	Norton (USA)	7350/6340
1928	Jarvinen(FIN)	7931/6815
1932	Javinen (FIN)	8292/7038
1936	Clark (USA)	7601/7226
1948	Heinrich (FRA)	6974/6740
1952	Campbell (USA)	6975/7132
1956	Johnson (USA)	7587/7568
1960	Yang (TPE)	8334/7930
1964	Aun (URS)	7842
1968	Walde (FRG)	8111
1972	Litvinyenko (URS)	8035
1976	Kratschmer(FRG)	8411
1980	Kustsenko(URS)	8331
1984	Hingsen (FRG)	8673
1988	Voss (GDR)	8399

BRONZE

1912	Lomberg (SWE)	7413/5943
1920	Olsson (SWE)	6579/5825
1924	Klumberg (EST)	7329/6260

1928	Doherty (USA)	7706/6593
1932	Eberle (GER)	8030/6830
1936	Parker (USA)	7275/6918
1948	Simmons (USA)	6950/6711
1952	Simmons (USA)	6788/7069
1956	Kuznyetsov (URS)	7465/7461
1960	Kuznyetsov (URS)	7809/7624
1964	Walde (FRG)	7809
1968	Bendlin (FRG)	8064
1972	Katus (POL)	7984
1976	Avilov (URS)	8369
1980	Zhelanov (URS)	8135
1984	Wentz (FRG)	8412
1988	Steen (CAN)	8328

TRACK AND FIELD (Women)

100 Metres

GOLD

1928	Elizabeth Robinson (USA)	12.2
1932	Stanislawa Walasiewics (POL)	11.9
1936	Helen Stephens (USA)	11.5
1948	Fanny Blankers Koen (HOL)	11.9
1952	Marjorie Jackson (AUS)	11.5
1956	Betty Cuthbert (AUS)	11.5
1960	Wilma Rudolph (USA)	11.0
1964	Wyomia Tyus (USA)	11.4
1968	Wyomia Tyus (USA)	11.0
1972	Renate Stecher (GDR)	11.07
1976	Annegret Richter (FRG)	11.08
1980	Ludmila Kondratyeva (URS)	11.06
1984	Evelyn Ashford (USA)	10.97
1988	Joyner (USA)	10.54

SILVER

1928	Rosenfeld (CAN)	12.3
1932	Strike (CAN)	11.9

1936	Walasiewicz (POL)	11.7
1948	Manley (GBR)	12.2
1952	Hasenjager (SA)	11.8
1956	Stubnick (GDR)	11.7
1960	Hyman (GBR)	11.3
1964	Mc Guire (USA)	11.6
1968	Ferrell (USA)	11.11
1972	Boyle (AUS)	11.23
1976	Stecher (GDR)	11.13
1980	Gohr (GDR)	11.07
1984	Brown (USA)	11.13
1988	Ashford (USA)	10.83

BRONZE

1928	E. Smith (CAN)	12.3
1932	Von Bremen (USA)	12.0
1936	Krauss (GER)	11.9
1948	Strickland (AUS)	12.2
1952	Strickland (AUS)	11.9
1956	Matthews (AUS)	11.7
1960	Leone (ITA)	11.31
1964	Klobukowska (POL)	11.6
1968	Szewinska (POL)	11.1
1972	Chivas (CUB)	11.24
1976	Helten (FRG)	11.17
1980	Auerswald (GDR)	11.14
1984	Ottey-Page (JAM)	11.16
1988	Drechsler (GDR)	10.85

200 Metres

GOLD

1948	Fanny Blankers Koen (HOL)	24.4
1952	Marjorie Jackson (AUS)	23.7
1956	Betty Cuthbert (AUS)	23.4
1960	Wilma Rudolph (USA)	24.0
1964	Edith Maguire (USA)	23.0
1968	Irena Szewinska (POL)	22.5

1972	Renate Stecher (GDR)	22.40
1976	Barbel Eckert (GDR)	22.37
1980	Barbel Wockel (GDR)	22.03
1984	Valerie Brisco-Hooks (USA)	21.81
1988	Joyner (USA)	21.34

SILVER

1948	Williamson (UK)	25.1
1952	Brouwer (HOL)	24.2
1956	Stibnick (GDR)	23.7
1960	Heine (GER)	24.2
1964	Szewinska (POL)	23.1
1968	Boyle (AUS)	22.7
1972	Boyle (AUS)	22.45
1976	Richter (FRG)	22.39
1980	Bochina (URS)	22.19
1984	Griffith (USA)	22.04
1988	Jackson (JAM)	21.72

BRONZE

1948	Petterson (USA)	25.2
1952	Khnikina (URS)	24.2
1956	Matthews (AUS)	23.8
1960	Hyman (UK)	24.7
1964	Black (AUS)	23.1
1968	Lamy (AUS)	22.8
1972	Szewinska (POL)	22.74
1976	Stecher (GDR)	22.47
1980	Ottey (JAM)	22.20
1984	Ottey (JAM)	22.09
1988	Drechsler (GDR)	21.95

400 Metres

GOLD

1964	Betty Cuthbert (AUS)	52.0
1968	Colette Besson (FRA)	52.0
1972	Monika Zehrt (GDR)	51.08

1976	Irena Szewinska (POL)	49.29
1980	Marita Koch (GDR)	48.88
1984	Valerie Brisco-Hooks (USA)	48.83
1988	Bryzgina (URS)	48.65

SILVER

1964	Packer (UK)	52.2
1968	Board (UK)	52.1
1972	Wilden (FRG)	51.21
1976	Brehmer (GDR)	50.51
1980	Kratochvilova (TCH)	49.46
1984	Cheeseborough (USA)	49.05
1988	Mueller (GDR)	4945

BRONZE

1964	Amoore (AUS)	53.4
1968	Pechenkina (URS)	52.2
1972	Hammond (USA)	51.64
1976	Streidt (GDR)	50.55
1980	Lathan (GDR)	49.66
1984	Cook (GBR)	49.42
1988	Nazarova (URS)	49.90

800 Metres

GOLD

1928	Lina Radke (GER)	2:16.8
1932	Not contested	
1936	Not contested	
1948	Not contested	
1952	Not contested	
1958	Not contested	
1960	Ludmila Shevtsova (URS)	2:04.3
1964	Ann Packer (GBR)	2:01.1
1968	Madeline Manning (USA)	2:00.0
1972	Hildegard Falck (FRG)	1:58.6
1976	Tatyana Kazankina (URS)	1:54.9
1980	Nadyezda Olizarenko (URS)	1:53.5

1984	Doina Melinte (ROM)	1:57.6
1988	Wodars (GDR)	1:56.10

SILVER

1928	Hitomi (JAP)	2:17.6
1932	Not contested	
1936	Not contested	
1948	Not contested	
1952	Not contested	
1956	Not contested	
1960	Jones (AUS)	2:04.4
1964	Dupureur (FRA)	2:01.9
1968	Sailai (ROM)	2:02.5
1972	Sbaite (URS)	1:58.7
1976	Shtereva (BUL)	1:55.4
1980	Mineyeva (URS)	1:54.9
1984	Gallagher (USA)	1:58.6
1988	Wachtel (GDR)	1:56.64

BRONZE

1928	Gentzel (SWE)	2:17.8
1932	Not contested	
1936	Not contested	
1948	Not contested	
1952	Not contested	
1956	Not contested	
1960	Donath (GDR)	2:05.6
1964	Chamberlain (NZL)	2:02.8
1968	Gommers (HOL)	2:02.6
1972	Hoffmeister (GDR)	1:59.2
1976	Zinn (GDR)	1:55.6
1980	Providokhina (URS)	1:55.5
1984	Lovin (ROM)	1:58.8
1988	Gallagher (USA)	1:56.91

1500 Metres

GOLD

1972	Ludmila Bragina (URS)	4:01.4
1976	Tatyana Kazankina (URS)	4:05.6
1980	Tatyana Kazankina (URS)	1:54.9
1984	Gabriella Doria (ITA)	4:03.25
1988	Ivan (ROM)	3:53.96

SILVER

1972	Hoffmeister (GDR)	4:02.8
1976	Hoffmeister (GDR)	4:06.0
1980	Wartenberg (GDR)	3:57.8
1984	Melinte (ROM)	4:03.7
1988	Baikauskaite (URS)	4:00.24

BRONZE

1972	Pigni- Cacchi (ITA)	4:02.9
1976	Klapezynski (GDR)	4:06.1
1980	Olizaryenko (URS)	3:59.6
1984	Maricica Puica (ROM)	4:04.1
1988	Samolenko (URS)	4:00.30

3000 Metres

GOLD

1984	Maricica Puica (ROM)	8:35.96
1988	Samolenko (URS)	8:26.53

SILVER

1984	Wendy Sly(UK)	8:39.47
1988	Ivan (Rom)	8:27.15

BRONZE

1984	Lynn Williams (CAN)	8:42.17
1988	Murray (UK)	8:29.2

Marathon

GOLD

1984	Joan Benoit (USA)	2h 24:52
1988	Mota (POR)	2h 25:40

SILVER

1984	Waitz (NOR)	2h 26:18
1988	Martin (AUS)	2h 25:53

BRONZE

1984	Mota (POR)	2h 26:57
1988	Doere (GDR)	2h 25:53

100 Metres Hurdles

GOLD

1932	Mildred Didrikson (USA)	11.7
1936	Trebisonda Valla (ITA)	11.7
1948	Fanny Blankers Koen (HOL)	11.2
1952	Shirley de la Hunty (AUS)	10.9
1956	Shirley de la Hunty (AUS)	10.7
1960	Irina Press (URS)	10.8
1964	Karin Balzer (GER)	10.5
1968	Maureen Caird (AUS)	10.3
1972	Annelie Ehrhardt (GDR)	12.59
1976	Johanna Schaller (GDR)	12.77
1980	Vera Komisova (URS)	12.56
1984	Benita Fitzgerald Brown (USA)	12.84
1988	Donkova (BUL)	12.38

SILVER

1932	Hall (USA)	11.7
1936	Steuer (GER)	11.7
1948	Gardner (UK)	11.2
1952	Golubnichaya (URS)	11.1
1956	Birkemeyer (GDR)	10.9
1960	Quinton (UK)	10.9
1964	Ciepla (POL)	10.5

1968	Ryan-Kilborn (AUS)	10.4
1972	Bufanu (ROM)	12.84
1976	Anisimova (URS)	12.78
1980	Klier-Schaller (GDR)	12.63
1984	Strong (UK)	12.88
1988	Siebert (GDR)	12.61

BRONZE

1932	Clark (SA)	11.8
1936	Taylor (CAN)	11.7
	Testoni (ITA)	11.7
1948	Strickland (AUS)	11.4
1952	Sander (GER)	11.1
1956	Thrower (AIS)	11.0
1960	Birkemeyer (GDR)	11.0
1964	Ryan (AUS)	10.5
1968	Chi Cheng (TPE)	10.4
1972	Balzer (GDR)	12.90
1976	Lebedyeva (URS)	12.80
1980	Langer(POL)	12.65
1984	Turner (USA)	13.06
1988	Zackiewicz (FRG)	12.75

400 Metres Hurdles

GOLD

1984	Nawal El Moutawakel (MAR)	54.61
1988	Flintoff-King (AUS)	53.17

SILVER

1984	Brown (USA)	55.20
1988	Ledovskaia (URS)	53.18

BRONZE

1984	Cojocaru (ROM)	55.41
1988	Fiedler (GDR)	53.63

4x100 Metres Relay

GOLD

1928	Canada	48.4
1932	USA	47.0
1936	USA	46.9
1948	The Netherlands	47.5
1952	USA	45.9
1956	Australia	44.5
1960	USA	44.5
1964	Poland	43.6
1968	USA	42.8
1972	FRG	42.81
1976	GDR	42.55
1980	GDR	41.60
1984	USA	41.65
1988	USA	41.98

SILVER

1928	USA	48.8
1932	CAN	47.0
1936	UK	47.6
1948	AUS	47.6
1952	GER	45.9
1956	UK	44.7
1960	FRG	44.8
1964	USA	43.9
1968	CUB	43.3
1972	GDR	42.95
1976	FRG	42.95
1980	URS	42.10
1984	CAN	42.77
1988	GDR	42.09

BRONZE

1928	GER	49.0
1932	UK	47.6
1936	CAN	47.8

1948	CAN	47.8
1952	UK	46.2
1956	USA	44.9
1960	POL	45.0
1964	UK	44.0
1968	URS	43.4
1972	CUB	43.36
1976	URS	43.09
1980	UK	42.43
1984	UK	43.11
1988	URS	42.75

4x400 Metres Relay

GOLD

1972	GDR	3:22.95
1976	GDR	3:19.23
1980	SRS	3:20.12
1984	USA	3:18.29
1988	URS	3:15.18

SILVER

1972	USA	3:25.2
1976	USA	3:22.8
1980	GDR	3:20.4
1984	CAN	3:21.21
1988	USA	3:15.51

BRONZE

1972	FRG	3:26.6
1976	URS	3:24.2
1980	GBR	3:27.5
1984	FRG	3:22.9
1988	GDR	3:18.29

High Jump

GOLD

1928	Ethel Catherwood (CAN)	1.59m

1932	Jean Shiley (USA)	1.65m
1936	Ibolya Csak (HUN)	1.60m
1948	Alice Coachman (USA)	1.68m
1952	Esther Brand (SAF)	1.67m
1956	Mildred McDaniel (USA)	1.76m
1960	Iolanda Balas (ROM)	1.85m
1964	Iolanda Balas (ROM)	1.90m
1968	Miloslava Rezkova (TCH)	1.82m
1972	Ulrike Meyfarth (FRG)	1.92m
1976	Rosemarie Ackermann (GDR)	1.93m
1980	Sara Simeoni (ITA)	1.97m
1984	Anisoara Stanciu (ROM)	6.96m
1988	Ritter (USA)	2.03m

SILVER

1928	Gisolf (HOL)	1.56
1932	Didrikson (USA)	1.65
1936	Dorothy Odam (UK)	1.60
1948	Dorothy Tyler (UK)	1.68
1952	Lerwill (UK)	1.65
1956	Pisaryeva (URS)	1.67
	Hopkins (UK)	1.67
1960	Jozwiakowska (POL)	1.71
	Shirley (UK)	1.71
1964	Brown (AUS)	1.80
1968	Okorokova (URS)	1.80
1972	Blagoyeva (BUL)	1.88
1976	Simeoni (ITA)	1.91
1980	Kielan (POL)	1.94
1984	Simeoni (FRG)	2.07
1988	Kosadinova (BUL)	2.01

BRONZE

1928	Wiley (USA)	1.56
1932	Dawes (CAN)	1.60
1936	Kaun (GER)	1.60
1948	Ostermeyer (FRA)	1.61

1952	Chudina (URS)	1.63
1956	- -	
1960	- -	
1964	Chenchik (URS)	1.78
1968	Kozir (URS)	1.80
1972	Gusenbauer (AUT)	1.88
1976	Blagoyeva (BUL)	1.91
1980	Kirst (GDR)	1.94
1984	Huntely (USA)	2.00
1988	Bykova(URS)	1.99

Shot Put

GOLD

1948	Micheline Ostermeyer (FRA)	13.75m
1952	Galina Zybina (URS)	15.28m
1956	Tamara Tyshkevich (URS)	16.59m
1960	Tamara Press (URS)	17.32m
1964	Tamara Press (URS)	18.14m
1968	Margitta Gummel (GDR)	19.61m
1972	Nadyezda Chizhova (URS)	21.03m
1976	Ivanka Khristova (BUL)	21.16m
1980	Ilona Slupianek(GDR)	22.41m
1984	Claudia Losch (FRG)	22.48m
1988	Lisovskaya (URS)	22.24m

SILVER

1948	Piccinini (ITA)	13.09
1952	Werner (GER)	14.57
1956	Zibina (URS)	16.53
1960	Luttge (GDR)	16.61
1964	Garisch (GDR)	17.61
1968	Lange (GDR)	18.78
1972	Gummel (GDR)	20.22
1976	Chizhova (URS)	20.96
1980	Krachevskaya (URS)	21.42
1984	Loghin (ROM)	20.47
1988	Neimke (GDR)	21.07

BRONZE

1948	Schafer (AUT)	13.08
1952	Tochonova (URS)	14.50
1956	Werner (GER)	15.61
1960	Brown (USA)	16.42
1964	Zibina (URS)	17.45
1968	Chizhova (URS)	18.19
1972	Khristova (BUL)	19.35
1976	Fibingerova (TCH)	20.67
1980	Pufe (GDR)	21.20
1984	Martin (AUS)	19.19
1988	Meisu (PRC)	21.06

Discus

GOLD

1928	Helena Konopacka (POL)	39.62m
1932	Lillian Copeland (USA)	40.58m
1936	Gisela Mauermayer (GER)	47.63m
1948	Micheline Ostermeyer (FRA)	41.92m
1952	Nina Romashkova (URS)	51.42m
1956	Olga Fikotova (TCH)	53.69m
1960	Nina Ponomaryeva (URS)	55.10m
1964	Tamara Press (URS)	57.27m
1968	Lia Manoliu (ROM)	58.28m
1972	Faina Melnik (URS)	66.62m
1976	Evelin Schlaak(GDR)	69.00m
1980	Evelin Jahl (GDR)	69.96m
1984	Ria Stalman (HOL)	65.36m
1988	Hellman (GDR)	72.30m

SILVER

1928	Copeland (USA)	37.08
1932	Osborn (USA)	40.12
1936	Wajsòwna (POL)	46.22
1948	Gentile (ITA)	41.17
1952	Bagryantseva (URS)	47.08
1956	Beglvakova (URS)	52.54

1960	T. Press (URS)	52.59
1964	Lotz (GDR)	57.21
1968	Westermann (FRG)	57.76
1972	Menis (ROM)	65.06
1976	Vergova (BUL)	67.30
1980	Vergova-Perkova (BUL)	67.90
1984	Deniz (USA)	64.86
1988	Gansky (GDR)	71.88

BRONZE

1928	Svedberg (SWE)	35.92
1932	Wajsowna (POL)	38.74
1936	Mollenhauer (GER)	39.80
1948	Mezeas (FRA)	40.47
1952	Dumbadze (URS)	46.29
1956	Romashkova (URS)	52.02
1960	Manoliu (ROM)	52.36
1964	Manoliu (ROM)	56.87
1968	Kleiber (HUN)	54.90
1972	Stoeva (BUL)	64.34
1976	Hinzmann GDR)	66.84
1980	Lyesovaya (URS)	67.40
1984	Craciunescu (ROM)	63.64
1988	Kristova (BUL)	69.74

Javelin

GOLD

1932	Mildred Didrikson (USA)	43.68m
1936	Tilly Fleischer (GER)	45.18m
1948	Herma Bauma (AUT)	45.57m
1952	Dana Zatopkova (TCH)	50.47m
1956	Ines Jaunzeme (URS)	53.86m
1960	Elvira Ozolina (URS)	55.98m
1964	Mihaela Penes (ROM)	60.64m
1968	Angela Nemeth (HUN)	60.36m
1972	Ruth Fuchs (GDR)	63.88m
1976	Ruth Fuchs (GDR)	65.94m

1980	Maria Colon (CUB)	68.40m
1984	Tessa Sanderson(UK)	69.56m
1988	Felke (GDR)	74.68m

SILVER

1932	Braumuller (GER)	43.49
1936	Kruger (GER)	43.29
1948	Parviainen (FIN)	43.79
1952	Chudina (URS)	50.01
1956	Ahrens (CHI	50.38
1960	Zatopkova (TCH)	53.78
1964	Rudas (HUN)	58.27
1968	Penes (ROM)	59.92
1972	Todten (GDR)	62.54
1976	M. Becker (FRG)	64.70
1980	Gunba (URS)	67.76
1984	Lillak (FIN)	69.00
1988	Whitbread (UK)	70.32

BRONZE

1932	Fleischer (GER)	43.00
1936	Kwasniewska (POL)	41.80
1948	Carlstedt (DEN)	42.08
1952	Gorchakova (URS)	49.76
1956	Konyayeva (URS)	50.28
1960	Kalediene (URS)	53.45
1964	Gorchaova (URS)	57.06
1968	Janko (AUT)	58.04
1972	Schmidt USA)	59.94
1976	Schmidt (USA)	63.96
1980	Hommola (GDR)	66.56
1984	Whitbread (UK)	67.14
1988	Koch (GDR)	67.30

Pentathlon

GOLD

1964	Irina Press (URS)	5246pts.

1968	Ingrid Becker (FRG)	5098pts.
1972	Mary Peters (UK)	4801pts
1976	Siegrun Siegl (GDR)	4745pts
1980	Nadyezda Tkachenko (URS)	5083pts
	Heptathlon (Replaced Pentathlon in 1984)	
1984	Glynis Nunn (Aus)	6390pts.
1988	Joyner (USA)	7291

SILVER

1964	Rand (UK)	5035
1968	Prokop (AUT)	4966
1972	Rosendahl (FRG)	4791
1976	Laser (GDR)	4745
1980	Rukavishnikova (URS)	4937
1984	Joyner (USA)	6385
1988	John (GDR)	6897

BRONZE

1964	Bistrova (URS)	4956
1968	Toth (HUN)	4959
1972	Pollak (GDR)	4768
1976	Pollak (GDR)	4740
1980	Kuragina (URS)	4875
1984	Everts (FRG)	6363
1988	Behmer (GDR)	6858

Track and Field Medals (including Tug-of-war)

	Men(Gold)	Women(Gold)
United States	235	26
Soviet Union	29	25
Great Britain (U.K.)	42	4
Germany (FRG)	11	12
Finland	46	-
Sweden	19	-
GDR	11	21

Australia	6	10
France	7	3
Canada	9	2
Italy	12	3
Poland	9	6
Hungary	6	3
Greece	3	-
Romania	-	8
Czechoslovakia	5	3
Jamaica	4	-
New Zealand	7	1
Kenya	6	-
South Africa	4	1
The Netherlands	-	5
Japan	4	-
Norway	3	-
Cuba	2	1
Belgium	2	-
Ethiopia	5	-
Bulgaria	-	1
Brazil	3	-
Ireland	4	-
Mexico	3	-
Argentina	2	-
Austria	-	1
Trinidad	1	-
Tunisia	1	-
Denmark	1	-
Portugal	1	-
Morocco	1	1
Luxemburg	1	-
Uganda	1	-

ON THE BLOCKS
Sprinters use starting blocks that are fixed to the track. They provide a firm base for the foot to push against at the start of the race. Blocks can be

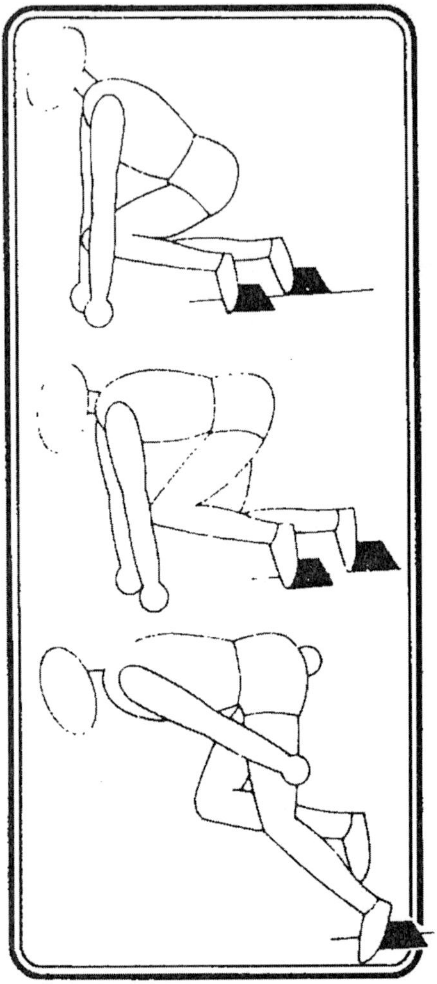

connected to a device that detects any false start - when an athlete's foot leaves the blocks before the gun goes off.

ONE THOUSAND FIVE HUNDRED METRES

The four lap race over 1 mile or 1500 metres is for many people their favourite athletics event.It is long enough for strategies to develop and short enough to sustain the maintenance of interest. Its practitioners must balance speed and endurance with keen sense of harnessing their abilities to particular races and tactics appropriate to them.The popularity of the event has been reflected by the intensity of competition over the years. There is such a wealth of talent at the top that even such outstanding athletes as Steve Cram and Seb Coe have Said Aouita, Steve Scott, Sydney Maree, Jose Luis Gonzales, Jose Abascal and others in keen contention for major honours.

1500m (WORLD RECORDS)

TIME	COMPETITOR	VENUE	DATE
3.55.8	Abel Kiwiat (USA)	Cambridge,Mass	8-6-12
3.54.7	John Zander(SWE)	Stockholm	5-8-17
3.52.6	Paavo Nurmi(Fin)	Helsinki	19-6-24
3.51.0	Orro Peltzer (GER)	Berlin	11-9-26
3:49.2	Jules Ladoumegue(FRA)	Paris	5-10-30
3:49.2	Luigi Beccali(ITA)	Turin	9-9-33
3:49.0	Luigi Beccali(ITA)	Milan	17-9-33
3:48.8	Bill Bonthron(USA)	Milwaukee	30-6-34
3:47.8	Jack Lovelock(NZL)	Berlin	10-8-41
3:47.6	Gunder Haegg (SWE)	Stockholm	10-8-41
3:45.8	Gunder Haegg(SWE)	Stockholm	17-7-42
3:45.0	Arne Andersson(SWE)	Gottenburg	17-8-43
3:43.0	Gunder Haegg (SWE)	Gottenburg	7-7-44
3:43.0	Lennart Strand (SWE)	Malmo	15-7-47
3:43.0	Werner Lueg (GER)	Berlin	29-6-52
3:42.8	Wes Santee (USA)	Compton	4-6-54
3:41.8	John Landy (AUS)	Turku	21-6-54
3:40.8	Sandor Iharos (Hun)	Helsinki	28-7-55
3:40.8	LasloTabori (HUN)	Oslo	6-9-55
3:40.8	Gunnar Nielsen (DEN)	Oslo	6-9-55
3:40.6	Istvan Rozsavolgyi(HUN)	Tata	3-8-56

3:40.2	Olavi Salsola (FIN)	Turku	11-7-57
3:38.I	Stanislav Jungwirth(TCH)	Stara Boleslaw	12-7-57
3:36.0	Herb Elliott (AUS)	Gothenburg	28-8-58
3:35.6	Herb Elliott (AUS)	Rome	6-9-60
3:33.1	Jim Ryun(USA)	Los Angeles	8-7-67
3:32.2	Filbert Bayi (TAN)	Christchurch	2-2-74
3:32.I	Sebastian Coe(GBR)	Zurich	15-8-79
3:32.I	Steve Ovett (GBR)	Oslo	I5-7-80
3:31.6	Steve Ovett(GBR)	Koblenz	27-8-80
3:31.24	Sydney Maree(USA)	Cologne	28-2-83
3:30.77	Steve Ovett (GBR)	Rieti	4-9-83
3:29.67	Steve Cram (GBR)	Nice	16-7-85
3:29.46	Said Aouita (MOR)	Oslo	23-8-85

OPITZ, MARTINA

East Germany (born 12th Dec.,1960) - A sociology student who improved nearly 6m. in 1983. She should dominate the event for years to come. In discus she earned a gold in 1983 World Championships. In the same year she won another gold in European Cup.

ORGANIZATIONS

The Sports Council and AAA in Great Britain are the sources of lists of clubs,sports centres, fitness-testing centres and injury clinics, and an enquiring letter along with a S.A.E.to both these organizations will provide invaluable information.

The Sports Council - 16, Upper Woburn Place, London WC 1 H 0QP
Amateur Athletic Association - Francis House, Francis Street, London SW 1 P 1DL.

Other running organisations include:
Scottish AAA - 16 Royal Crescent, Glasgow, G3 7SL.
Welsh AAA - 54 Charles Street, Cardiff.
Northern Ireland AAA - 20 Karnan Park, Portadown, Country Armagh.
Women's AAA - Francis House, Francis Street, London SW 1P 1DL
Road Runners Club - 10 Honeywood Road, Colchester, Essex.
Fell Runners Association - 165 Penistyone Road, Kirkburton, Huddersfield.

British Orienteering Federation National Office - 41 Dale Road, Matlock, Derbyshire, DE4 3LT.

American Organisations:

New York Road Runners Club- P.O. Box 881, FDR Station, New York 10150.

The Boston Athletic Association - 180 Beacon Street, Boston, Mass 01867.

ORTHOTICS

Where foot or leg imbalance occurs or there are other joint problems, it is now possible to construct custom-made shoe inserts, which are built up in specific areas, in order to correct imbalances during the running action. Many athletes have found that orthotics have cured long-standing injury problems.

OTKALENKO, N.

U.S.S.R. (born 23rd May, 1928)-In 1951 she won the Soviet 800 m. title in a record time of 2 min. 12.0 sec. In 1954 she again won the European Championship. Her final season of major competition was 1961 when she clocked a respectable 2 min. 08.6 sec.

OTTEY, MERLENE

Jamaica (born 10th May,1969) - One of the most accomplished of Commonwealth born female sprinters ever, she entered real world class in 1980, placing third in that year's Olympic 200 metres final in 22.20 before going on to capture the 1982 Commonwealth 200 metres title and a silver in the 100m. Her finest performance to date came when placing second in the 200 metres at the inaugural World Championships in which she also gained 4x100 metres relay bronze medal.

OTTLEY, DAVE

U.K. (born 5th Aug., 1955) - He broke the UK javelin record in 1980 throwing 85.52 m. His major championship results since 1977 have on the whole, been disappointing but he did well to place 4th in his event at both the 1979 and 1983 European Cup finals.

OVETT, STEVE

U.K. (born 9th Oct.,1955) - Fourth place in the 1500m final at the 1983 World Championships brought an end to his reign as the world's leading mile/ 1500m competitor. In 1980 Olympics bronze and gold in 1981 World Cup for 1500m were just the tips of his achievements. His reputation as one of the world's greatest tactical middle distance runners was well and truly shattered three years later in the inaugural World Championships when he allowed himself to become hopelessly boxed in at the bell and could not claw his way back to Steve Cram, Steve Scott and Said Aouita on the last lap. His latest triumph came at Reiti in Italy in Sept.,1983 when he gained world record 1500m from Sydney Maree with a time of 3 min. 30.78sec. Now established as a television star.

OWENS, J.C.

U.S.A. (born 12th Sep.,1913) - He was the supreme physical genius of his age is less an opinion than a statement of fact. His sparkling career culminated in his quadruple success at the 1936 Olympics. In 1936 Olympics he won gold medals in the 100 m.,200m. long jump and 4 x 100 m. relay. In the Berlin Olympics he pulled a magnificent leap of 25 ft. 9 (1/4)in. His best mark in long jump was 26 ft. 8 (1/2)in. He began his career at an early age with some of his school figures still the envy of modern day athletes, including a 7.61 metres long jump. After his success in Berlin, Owens turned professional and in 1948 he was still long jumping at around 7.90 metres. In 1955, at the age of 41, he ran the 100 metres in 9.8 sec. It was a tribute that both Harrison Dillard and later Carl Lewis based their early training on him.

OXYGEN DEBT

The amount of oxygen that an athlete must absorb via respiration, following all out effort, to replenish that utilized by the muscles during the effort.

P

PACEMAKER
A runner who leads the rest of the field during a middle or long distance race.

PADDOCK, C.W.
U.S.A. (1900- 1943) - In 1920 Olympics, he won gold medal in 100m. and silver medal in 200 m. In 1924 Olympics he won a silver medal in 200 m. During 1921 and 1924 he equalled the 100 yd. record of 96 sec. five times. In 1926, he broke the record at 95 sec. . The record he made in 110 yds. in 10.2 sec. remained unbeaten for 29 years.

PAMICH, A.
Italy (born 3rd Oct, 1933) - He has been the walker of the highest class. He made world tracking records at 30km. (4 hr. 4min 56.8 sec.) and 50 Km. (4 hr. 14min. 02.4 sec.). He was 7th in 1954 European, 4th in 1956 Olympics, 2nd in 1958 European, 3rd in 1960 Olympics 1st in 1962 European Championships, 1st in 1964 Olympics and 1st in 1966 European Championships. He won three gold medals, a silver and a bronze.

PAN-AMERICAN GAMES
The Pan-American Games were instituted in 1951, the first being held in Buenos Aires. Subsequent venues have been Mexico City 1955, Chicago 1959, Sao Paulo 1963, Winnipeg 1967, Cali (Colombia) 1971, Mexico City 1975, San Juan 1979, Caracas 1983 and Indianapolis 1987.

PARSONS, GEOFF
U.K. (born 14th Aug.,1964) - The tallest ever UK international, he achieved

the unique feat, in 1983, of setting a UK senior record when winning an English Schools title.

PEACOCK, TYKE

U.S.A. (born 24th Feb.,1961) - Peacock ranked number one in the World in 1981 World Cup in high jump. He also captured silver in World Championships 1983.

PEDERSEN, T.O.

Norway (born 9th Feb., 1943) - In 1960 Olympics, he was the youngest at 17 to reach a final in javelin throwing. In 1964, he broke the world record with 285 ft. 10in. Later the same year he broke his own record with 300 ft. 11 in.

PENES, M.

Romania (born 22nd July,1947) - In 1964 Olympics in Tokyo, she was the champion in javelin throwing 198ft. 7 (1/2)in. She was the youngest athletic champion of all time - only 17 years and 2 months old. In 1966 European Championships she finished second.

PENNEL, J.T.

U.S.A. (born 25th July, 1940) - In 1963, he established seven world records in pole vault highest being 17 ft. 1/4 in. He established another record in 1966 at 17 ft. 6 (1/4)in.

PENTATHLON

It is a five event test of all-round ability. In the men's event are included long jump, javelin, 200m.,discus and 1,500 m. All these are performed in that order in one day. The women's event consists of 80 m. hurdles, shot and high jump on the first day and long jump and 200 m. on the second. The game was included in the Olympics in 1964. The game is generally played in U.S.A., U.S.S.R. and West Germany.

World record holder at ten-yearly intervals

1935 Gisela Mauermayer (GFR)
1945 Gisela Mauermayer (GFR)
1955 Aleksandra Chudina (USSR)
1965 Irina Press (USSR)
1975 Burglinde Pollak (GDR)
1985 Sabine Paetz (GDR)

PERMIT MEETINGS

International invitation athletics meetings for which an official permit has been granted by the world athletics governing body, the IAAF. Considered of greater international significance than other invitation meetings, these permit meetings are more closely controlled and directly sanctioned by the IAAF.

PERSONAL BEST

An individual athlete's best performance in a particular athletics event throughout his/her athletics career.

PETER, JORG

East Germany (born 23rd Oct.,1955) - Has won four of his 13 marathons during 1980-8, including at Kosice 1987. Third at Tokyo 1988 in national record.

PETERS, J.H.

U.K. (born 24th Oct., 1918) - In 1946 marathon he won the AAA 6 mi. In 1947 he won the 10 mi. title. In 1948, his timing was 30 min. 07.0 sec. for 6 mi. and came ninth in the Olympic 10,000m. In 1951, he ran from Windsor to Chiswick in the British record time of 2 h. 29m. 24 sec. In 1952, he created his first world record of 2 hr. 20 m. 42.2 sec. Again he created world record and his timing was 2 hr. 17 min. 39.4 sec. for 10 miles.

PETERS, MARY

Ireland (born 6th July, 1939) - After 17 years in the Pentathlon Mary received her just reward when she beat Heidi Rosendahl by 10 points to win the 1972 Olympics title with a new world record. Northern Ireland's finest athlete, her first Commonwealth Games medal was a silver in the shot in 1966 and in 1970 she was a double gold medallist in the shot and pentathlon. She retained the pentathlon title at 1974 Commonwealth Games. A superb ambassador for the sports.

PHOTO FINISH

The finish of a track race for which a photograph is required to determine the final placings where several competitors have crossed the finish line almost simultaneously, making it impossible to judge the finish accurately with the naked eye alone.

PIRIE, D.A.G.

U.K. (born 10th Feb., 1931) - In 1951, he won his first AAA 6mi. title in the English record time of 29 min. 32.0 sec. In 1952, he broke more national records. In 1953, he captured three English cross-country titles. In 1956, he created a record in 5000 m. with a time of 13 min. 36.8 sec. The remarkable achievement he tied the 3000m. world record of 7 min. 55.6 sec. and won over 1500 m. in 3 min. 43.7 sec. against Klaus Richtzenhain, the German who was destined to win the Olympic silver medal later in the year.

PLANT

The action of inserting the far end of the vaulting pole into the vaulting box beneath the uprights, immediately before the pole vaulter takes off at the end of his run-up.

POLE VAULT

Pole vault is an excellent field event enjoyed equally by the competitors as well as the spectators. The event involves speed of a sprinter and agility

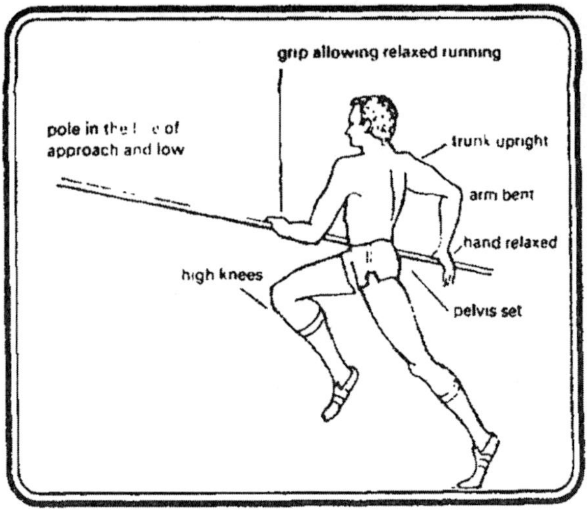

and strength of a gymnast. It *is essential that* a vaulter has exceptional neuro-muscular coordination together with leg speed and arm and shoulder strength. It is observed that tall men with long arms make good vaulters.

Generally poles are made of steel, aluminium or bamboo. A beginner may start practice with any one of these. However, a vaulter has to be very careful in the selection of the pole for competition. He must aim to the use of fibre-glass pole after he has attained a good experience and developed sufficient coordination.

Specifications for Pole Vault

(a) Landing Area	Length: 5 metres Width: 5 metres
(b) Distance between Uprights	Minimum 3.66 metres Maximum 4.32 metres
(c) Length of Cross Bar	Minimum 3.86 metres Maximum 4.52 metres
(d) Weight of Cross Bar	Maximum 2.26 Kilogrammes
(e) Support for Cross Bar extension	75 millimetres
(f) Planting box	Length: 1 metre

Width at Front end: 600 millimetres
Thickness Metal Sheet: 2.5 millimetres.

Length of the sheet from the front of the box towards stop board : 800 millimetres.

Rules of Pole Vault

1. Any competitor may have the uprights moved in either direction, but they must not be moved more than 2feet from the prolongation of the inside edge of the top of the stop board.
2. The judges should make a remeasurement to ensure that there is no variation in height.
3. The take off for the pole shall be from a wooden or metal box as per the specifications given earlier. The front edge of the box must be in level with the run up and finally fixed to the ground.
4. The pole may be of any material and any length or diameter, but the basic surface of the metal must be smooth.
5. An athlete fails in the competition if:
   - (a) in the course of a vault he dislodges the bar so that it falls from the pegs.
   - (b) Without first having cleared the bar, he touches any part of his body,or the pole, or the ground beyond the vertical plane of the upper part of the stop board.
   - (c) he makes three runs without completing the vault.
   - (d) he leaves the ground to make a vault and fails to clear the bar.
   - (e) he clears the bar himself but lets the pole go off and allows it pass under.
   - (f) While he is making the vault or after leaving the ground places his lower hand above the upper one or moves the upper hand higher up on the pole.

World record at ten-yearly intervals

1905	3.74m	Fernand Gonder (Fra)
1915	4.02m	Marcus Wright (U.S.A.)
1925	4.25m	Charles Hoff (Nor)
1935	4.39m	Keith Brown (U.S.A.)
1945	4.77m	Cornelius Warmerdam (U.S.A.)
1955	4.77m	Cornelius Warmerdam (U.S.A.)

1965	5.28m	Fred Hanson (U.S.A.)
1975	5.65m	Dave Roberts (U.S.A.)
1985	6.00m	Sergey Bubka (U.S.S.R.)

POLLOCK, J.F.

Australia (born 25th June,1940)- In 1962, she ran 440 yd. in 54.2 sec. She won a bronze medal at the Tokyo Olympics. In 1965, she set a world record of 52.4 sec. for 440 yd. In 1966 she won the Commonwealth title.

POLYTECHNIC MARATHON

Polytechnic marathon held annually in Windsor, was first held in 1909. The West London Club Polytechnic Harriers duly arranged the first such event on 8 May, 1909. They had already organized one of the pre-Olympic trial races as well as the actual 1908 Olympic marathon from Windsor in the White City Stadium. In succeeding years the Polytechnic became one of the world's most prestigious marathons. Until 1932 it was held between Windsor and Samford Bridge. From 1938 until 1972,perhaps its most illustrious era, it was held on a course between Windsor and the Polytechnic Stadium at Chiswick. In 1975, for lack of support, the race was not held at all, but was revived in 1976 following new sponsorship from Goldenlay Eggs. In 1978, women competed for the first time.

PONOMARYEVA, N.

U.S.S.R. (born 27th April, 1929) - She was one of the most distinguished discus thrower. In 1952 Olympics she won the gold, in 1956 the bronze and in 1960 again a gold . She was a world record holder. In 1954, she was European Champion.

POTGIETER, G.C.

South Africa (born 16th April , 1937) - In 1956, he beat the world record for 440 yd. hurdle with 50.7 sec. In 1958, he created a new world record with 49.7 sec. in winning at the Commonwealth Games. In 1960, he set a fresh record of 49.3 sec. In 1966, he won the South African decathlon title with 6,534 points.

PRAVEEN KUMAR

India (born 6th Sep., 1948) - He was born in village Sarhali near Amritsar in Punjab and received his education in the border town graduating from Khalsa College. He was attracted to sport at the age of 14 and with his lanky six feet two frame was an instant favourite and winner.

Praveen who threw the discus to a golden distance in the 1966 and 1970 Asian Games in Bangkok.

PRELIMINARY HEATS

In handicap sprint races run in lanes, with more than one round of preliminary heats, the winners only of the first round shall be entitled to take further part in the competition. Not more than 6 competitors shall take part in the final heat.

PRESS, I.

U.S.S.R. (born 10th March, 1939) - In 1959 she set the pentathlon, world record at 4,880 points. In 1960 Olympics she won the 80 m. hurdles with a world record of 10.3 sec. In 1964 Olympics she won the pentathlon with a world record of 5,246 points.

PRESS, T.

U.S.S.R. (born 10th May, 1937) - In European Competitions , she won gold medal in discus and bronze medal in shot in 1958, gold medal in shot and silver medal in discus in 1960 and gold medals both in discus and shot in 1964. In 1965 she made world records both in shot 61 ft. o in and discus.195 ft. 10 (1/2)in.

PROGRAMME

A draw shall be made to decide the order in which competitors shall take their trials and this order should be printed on the programme. The judges shall have the power to alter this order.

Q

QUALIFYING STANDARDS

For all major international track and field celebrations, athletes wishing to compete are expected to achieve certain qualifying standards in their chosen events within a specified period prior to the competition, before they can be considered to represent their national teams.

QUARRIE, DON

Jamaica (born 25th. Feb.,1951) - He took both sprints in 1970 and 1974 Commonwealth Games. He was selected as a 17 year old for the Mexico Olympics but was injured in training in Mexico City. He had to miss out on the 1983 World Championships when he collided with an official while warming up for his semi-final.

QUARTERING WIND

The wind direction most helpful to the discus thrower, i.e. blowing towards the front of the throwing circle from an angle, rather than head-on.

QUICK MARCH

Walkers differ from runners in that they must have at least a part of one foot in contact with the ground at all times. Walking races are usually over longer distances than running races.

QUINTON, C.L.

U.K. (born 11th July, 1936) - In 1958 she won silver medal in hurdles in the Commonwealth Games and relay in the European Championships. Again in 1960 Olympics she won silver medal in hurdles.

QUOW, ELLIOT

U.S.A. (born 3rd March, 1962) - He was the American champion over 200m., and won silver in 1983 World Championships.

R

RADFORD, P.F.

U.K. (born 20th Sep., 1939) - He won a gold medal in relay and got fourth position in 100 yd. at the Commonwealth Games and 3rd in the European 100 m. in 1958. He improved his 100 yd. time to 9.4 sec. in 1959 and repeated that in 1960. He created a world record in 220 yd. in 20.5 sec. In 1960 Olympics he helped the British relay team to win a bronze medal. In indoor 50 m. he was equal to the world's best 5.5 sec.

RAND, M.D.

U.K. (born 10th Feb., 1940) - In 1957 she set her first national record in the pentathlon (4,046pts.). In 1958 Commonwealth Games she won a silver medal in long jump and remained fourth in hurdles in 1960 Olympics. In 1962 she earned a bronze medal in the European long jump, and shared the world relay record in 1963.

REITZ, COLIN

U.K. (born 5th April,1960) - He got one of Helsinki's luckiest medals, one which had him launching the last 30m to the line. He won bronze in 3000 steeplechase of 1983 World Championships and again silver in European Cup.

RELAY RACING

Relay racing is a team event; the dictionary definition being a race between teams, the members of which are replaced at fixed points. In other words, each member of the team runs only a part of the total distance, and then hands on to the next runner, and so on until all the members of the team have run.

In athletics, there are two main types of relay race, the shuttle relay, in which the runners race up and down a straight course, and the normal type of relay which takes place round the oval running track.

The normal distance of each 'leg' on a 400 m. track is 100 m but younger athletes, under thirteen years of age, are advised not to run relay distances of more than 50-80 m.

The first runner of each team carries a baton which is handed on to the next runner. This baton can be a small smooth stick or a piece of stiff cardboard tubing. In adult competition there are definite rules about its size and weight, but in the early stages these are not so important.

Whilst the speed with which each athlete runs is very important even more vital is the skill with which he hands over the baton to the next runner. For if it is dropped and has to be picked up, or if the outgoing athlete does not get away quickly enough, valuable time is wasted, and more often than not the race is lost.

An added difficulty in the baton change over is that the rules state

that the change must take place within a distance of 20m. This is known as the change over zone.As the incoming runner nears the change over zone, the outgoing runner starts to move forward,so that as little time is wasted as possible. At this point several things are of vital importance:

1. He must judge the moment of starting to move, so that the change over actually takes place near the far end of the zone.
2. He must not move too soon so that the incoming runner cannot reach him to hand over the baton within the zone, and thus force him either to stop or even go back to get the baton.
3. His hand must be in the best possible position to receive the baton without any fear of its being dropped.

In sprint relay races the technique of baton change is known as non-visual or unseen, which means that the outgoing runner does not look at either the incoming athlete or the baton, when the change is being made, for if this is done, valuable fractions of a second would be lost.

Having received the baton the second runner sprints away with it held in the correct position for it to be put into the waiting left hand of the third runner. This involves alternate changing from left to right at the last. When a team wants to pass from left to right at each take over, the outgoing runner must change the baton from his receiving hand to his left as soon as he is given it.

Relay Records

4 x 100m relay (Men)			
World record	37.83	USA on	11th Aug., 1984
European record	38.02	SU on	6th Sep., 1987
Commonwealth record	38.39	Jam on	19th Oct., 1968
African record	38.73	Nig on	13th Sep., 1979
Olympic record	37.83	USA on	11th Aug., 1984
Asian record	39.05	Chn on	5th Sep., 1987

4 x 400m relay (Men)			
World record	2:56.16	USA on	20th Oct., 1968
European record	2:58.86	UK on	6th Sep., 1987
African record	2:59.32	Nig on	11th Aug., 1984

Asian record	3:02.33	Jap on	5th Oct., 1986
Olympic record	2:56.16	USA on	20th Oct., 1968

4 x 100m relay (Women)

World record	41.37	GDR on	6th Oct., 1985
Commonwealth record	42.43	UK on	1st Aug., 1980
African record	43.44	Nig on	9th Aug., 1987
Asian record	44.61	Chn on	25th Nov., 1987
Olympic record	41.60	GDR on	1st Aug., 1980
European rëcord	41.37	GDR on	6th Oct., 1985

4 x 400m relay (Women)

World record	3:15.92	GDR on	3rd Jan., 1984
Commonwealth record	3:21.21	Can on	11th Aug., 1984
African record	3:27.08	Nig on	12th Aug., 1987
Asian record	3:31.55	Ind on	5th Sep., 1987
Olympic record	3:18.29	USA on	11th Aug., 1984

RESISTANCE TRAINING

Hill running, in which the gradient of the slope makes the body work harder, is the simplest form of resistance. A potential problem of sandhill running is Achilles tendon strain, which can occur if too much sandhill running is done in too short a time. In general, it is probably best used by runners who have regular access to the sand. Other forms of resistance training include barefoot running in the sea upto calf level,and running in heavy army boots, although the value achieved through their additional weight is perhaps undermined by the often cumbersome running action which has to be adopted. Harness training is favoured by some sprinters, in which they attempt to sprint while restrained by a harness around their waist held by a colleague who endeavours to hold them back, while walking or running behind.There is no limit to the different and ingenious methods devised by runners and coaches over the years to add value to the training sessions by making them harder. The reasoning behind resistance training could in some ways perhaps be aligned to that of the man who kept hitting his head against a wall because it will be so nice when he stops.

REST

One of the most frequently overlooked components of a successful training programme is the value of rest. During training, muscle tissues are damaged, chemical waste accumulates, glycogen in the muscles is depleted.

For the body to restore itself to a condition ready for another dose of hard training, some easing down between the longest and most draining sessions is needed. A complete rest day each week has a lot to commend it, mentally as well as physically. Some runners can cope with everyday training. Ironically, runners at all levels often produce their fine performances after they have been prevented from training for some time by injury or illness. Method to increase relaxation and promote recovery could include taking a sauna, a massage, or listening to music in the dark.

RHEIM, HEINZ KARL

West Germany (born 31st March,1951) - Rheim a lover of classical music, is rated as the best hammer thrower never to win an Olympic medal. He won bronze at European Championships 1978. In European Cup he won gold in 1975,1977 and 1979.

RICHARDS, R.E

U.S.A. (born 20th Feb.,1926) - In both 1952 and 1956 Olympics he was Olympic champion in pole vaulting. In 1951 and 1955 he was Pan-American champion. Between 1948 and 1957, he was American champion indoors and outdoors. He was three times American champion in decathlon.

RITCHIE, MEG

U.K. (born 6th July,1952) - The first British woman's discus thrower of real world class, she set a Commonwealth discus record of 67.48 m in 1981. She won her first major title in 1982 at the Commonwealth Games with a throw of 62.98 m, her longest in major competition. She also set women's shot record in 1983.

ROAD RUNNING SHOES

Road runners' feet undergo an enormous amount of stress during each race, so their shoes must give support and be very comfortable.

ROBINSON, JAMES

U.S.A. (born 27th Aug.,1954) - One of the most durable 800m. runners. He won silver in the World Cup during 1979 and 1981. He was still good enough at almost 29 to take fifth place in Helsinki.

ROELANTS, G.

Belgium (born 5th Feb.,1937) - He came fourth in 1960 steeplechase. In 1962 he won European title. He scored another great victory at the 1964 Olympics. He was world record holder for the 3000m steeplechase. In 1966 he slashed over a minute off the Australian's figures for 20,000m and carried on to add over a quarter of a mile to his one hour record. He is also holder of the European 10,000m record.

RONO, HENRY

Kenya (born 12th Feb.,1952) - Rono's small collection of gold medals does not do justice to his enormous talent. In 1978 he won two Commonwealth golds, two African Games golds and created four world records.

RONO, KIP

Kenya (born 4th Jan.,1958) - The little front running Kenyan is always game to inject an exciting surge of pace, but he has yet to develop the necessary sprint finish that wins the major Games titles. He won gold in 1979 World Cup and bronze in 1978 Commonwealth Games.

ROSE, NICK

U.K. (born 30th Dec.,1951) - An outstanding track and cross-country runner with a 1977 European Cup final 5000 metres win and a third place in the 1980 World Cross-Country Championships. In 1979 he clocked 46 min.37sec. for 10 miles. His 10 km time of 27.43 in a New York road race in 1981 was thought to be a world best, but the course was later found to be short.

ROUND

All athletics field event competitions comprise several rounds. In the horizontal jumps and throws a round consists of a series of jumps or throws, one for each and every competitor contesting the event, regardless of whether the attempt is valid or not.

ROWE, A.

U.K. (born 17th Aug.,1936) - In shot putting in 1956 he attained 51ft. 7in and 55ft. 7in (British record). He triumphed at both the Commonwealth Games and European Championships in 1958 and 1959. He carried the European record out to 61ft.0in. In 1961, he raised the European and British records to 64ft.2in.

R.R.C.

The Road Runners Club, a national body, was founded following the inaugural London to Brighton road race, held in August 1951.During the fifties and sixties, road running was still considered to be a minority part of the athletics spectrum, but the RRC was vigorous then in campaigning for greater recognition and better organization. In recent years,the enormous boom in road running activities led to the formation. The RRC concentrates more on the serious side of distance running than the fun run.

RUDOLPH, W.G.

U.S.A. (born 23rd June,1940) - At the Melbourne Olympics, she won a bronze medal as a member of the United States sprint relay team. She developed into the finest female runner. In 1960 Olympics at Melbourne she won three gold medals. She was world record holder for 200m (22.9sec). She won both individual sprint with some three yards to spare her time for the 100m being a phenomenal 11.0sec.

RULES OF TRACK EVENTS

1. Athletes should wear clean clothes, not subject to any objection.
2. An athlete can participate in a game bare-footed or with footwear on one foot or both. The footwear should be such as does not give them additional help for play.
3 A competitor who obstructs the play of others or retards their progress may be disqualified.
4 Each athlete shall bear marks distinctly on his chest and back. He will not be able to run without number.
5. In lanes races, a competitor shall confine himself to his lane from the beginning to the end of a play.
6. An athlete knowingly, running out of his lane may be disqualified. If in the opinion of the referee he has not done it knowingly, the referee may or may not disqualify him.
7. A player leaving his track of his own will not be allowed to continue his race
8. A judge can order an athlete to take part in a different way if track and field events start simultaneously.
9. A point shall be scored against an athlete who makes an unnecessary delay in field events and he shall not be permitted to participate in trial. If he persists in it, he shall not be permitted to participate in one more trial, but his first performance shall be reckoned. Normally two minutes are given for field events and three minutes for pole vault.
10. Use of intoxicants and such other drugs is forbidden for an athlete. He cannot even keep them with him during the event. The competitor keeping such drugs is liable to be disqualified.
11. In 800 metres race,the starter shall say in his own language "On your marks''....."set'' and when all athletes are ready ,pistol shot shall be fired and the athletes start the race. For races above 800m only these words shall be said, "On your marks'', and when the players get ready, the pistol shot shall be fired.
12. A competitor shall not touch the floor in front of him or start line with his hands or feet when he is in a position 'On his marks'.
13. If an athlete crosses the start line before the pistol shot, his start shall be a foul. He shall be given a warning for it. If he persists in it he shall be disqualified in Pentathlon and

Decathlon.

14. The position of the competitors is decided on the finish line first with toes is considered to have reached across first.
15. A competitor in hurdle race shall be disqualified if
    (i) he obstructs other players by extending his hand and feet.
    (ii) he covers the hurdle of others lane
    (iii) in the opinion of a referee he fells the hurdle knowingly.
16. A competitor shall not be disqualified due to some reason other than the above mentioned rules.

RUNNER'S KNEE

Runner's or jumper's knee is a catch all name for an irritating injury that can be tendinitis, tenosynovitis or torn cartilage. Depending on the extent of the condition, many trainers have found that you can still practice and compete with runner's or jumper's knee so long as you warm it up with heat before practice and treat it with ice after practice. It also helps if you take a slow,long warmup and jog before competition.

RUNNING CLUBS

For serious runners and for aspiring athletes, there are literally hundreds of clubs throughout the country. The Amateur Athletics Association has a list of all of them. A letter to your regional A.A.A. office, enclosing a stamped addressed envelope,should get you the information you want.

RUNNING IN COMPANY

'Boring' is one of the biggest criticisms levelled against running particularly training runs as many sedentary sceptics wonder just how the runner occupies his/her mind while doing those long, lonely stretches along the road. It is a fair comment, as not everyone is able to keep the brain ticking over as the miles are ticked off, and many find the mental demands greater than the physical ones. For such people it is a tremendous help to train with others and simply talk those miles away. Go to a club where there are runners or joggers of a similar standard to yourself and latch on to them. If you find this company helps, then join the club and make these social runs the cornerstone of your training. Not only can it relieve the monotony, it may actually improve your running by dragging you along to distances you might not be able to cope with on your own.

RYUN, J.R.

U.S.A. (29th Apr., 1947) - He captured the world record of 1 min 44.9sec. for 880yd. and a share in the American 2mi. record of 8min. 25.2sec. as well as being the second fastest 1500m performer (3min. 36.1sec.) of all time. He has already levelled 1 mile time twelve times- his latest 3mi.51.3sec. in 1966.

S

SALAZAR, ALBERTO

U.S.A. (born 7th August,1958) - In 1981, he ran the Big Apple race again and this time did a world's best. Salazar was lucky to be running at all. For in the Falmouth seven mile road race in 1978 he collapsed and was given the last rites. Fortunately, he recovered.

SALMON, GRAHAM

U.K. (born 5th Sep.,1952) - Graham holds the British Blind record for high jump and 100 metres, European and World Blind records for 400 metres and has broken the World Blind 400 metres record 5 times. Before taking up running in 1977, Graham tried cross-country skiing and represented Great Britain in the 1976 Disabled Winter Olympics.

SAMOLENKO, TATYANA

U.S.S.R. (born 12th Aug.,1961) - The European silver medal was her only loss at 1500m in 1986. Added three gold medals and a silver at World Championships in 1987. Fast finisher, who also stepped down in distance to win European Cup 800m.

SAMUELSON, JOAN

U.S.A. (born 16th May, 1957) - Has won eight of her thirteen marathons, climaxed by her sensational Olympic victory, made possible by winning the US Trials race just 17 days after undergoing arthroscopic surgery on her right knee. Won 1985 Chicago marathon.

SANDERSON, TESSA

Jamaica (born 14th March,1956) - She earned a silver in javelin 1978 European Championships. Won a gold in Commonwealth Games and silver in European Cup 1981.

SANEYEV, VIKTOR

U.S.S.R. (born 3rd Oct.,1945) - Russian triple jumper Saneyev was a supreme competitor, winning three Olympic golds and narrowly failing to equal Center's unique fourtimer at Moscow in 1980 when at 34 he was beaten by fellow countryman Jaak Uudmae. His first success, in 1968, came in that memorable competition in which the world record was surpassed five times, twice by Saneyev himself, who went on to notch his third world record with 17.44 metres in 1972.

SARUL, EDWARD

Poland (born 16th Nov.,1958) - One of the biggest shock,when Sarul won the gold in the shot at 1983 World Championships. His best of 20.64m did not even put him in the all time 50 tops. Yet he beat all the big names and showed his victory was no fluke by winning the European Cup final in 1983 with a gold.

SCARTEZZINI, MARIANO

Italy (born 7th Nov.,1954) - His best time of 8·12.5 would have got him a silver in Moscow, but he did it a month later,not having competed in the Moscow Olympics. He won gold in 1979 and 1981 European Cup steeplechase.

SCHMIDT, J.

Poland (born 28th Mar.,1935) -As a jumper he won European Championship in 1958 and 1962 and gold medals in 1960 and 1964 Olympics. In 1960, achieved world record of 55ft.10(1/2)in.

SCHILDAUER, WARNER

East Germany (born 5th June,1959) - He won silver in 10,000m and 5000m during World Championships 1983. Again he repeated the same in European Championships. He also won gold in 1981 World Cup in 10,000m.

SCHMID, HARALD

West Germany (born 29th Sept.,1957) - He won 1983 World Championships in 400m hurdles with a silver. He again captured gold in European Championships 1978,1982. In European Cup of 1979 1981 and 1983 he won gold in 400m hurdles.

SCHUL,R.K.

U.S.A. (born 28th Sept.,1937) - He achieved world record of 8min 26.4sec for 2mi. and won gold medal in 5000m in 1964 Olympics.

SCORING TABLE

Official tables used to ascribe points values to specific performances in the track and field events which go to make up the multi events.

SCOTT, STEVE

U.S.A. (born 5th May,1956) - Scott has been the U.S. 1500 metres champion every year since 1977, except in 1981 when he was beaten. Californian was always second best. Even when he set his best time for a mile in 1982, he won silver in 1500m. World Championships of 1983.

SCRATCH LINE

The white line drawn across the width of the track, or across each individual lane, immediately behind which the athlete takes up his starting position to begin a race. In the field events the foul line at the end of the javelin runway is also referred to as a scratch line.

SCUTT, MICHELLE

U.K. (born 17th June,1960) - Good enough to reach the 400 metres semi-finals and share in the British quartet's third place in the 4x400 metres relay final at the 1980 Olympic Games, she had an even better year in 1982. That year she set a Commonwealth and UK 400 metres record of 50.63 and went on to take the 400 metres silver medal at the Commonwealth Games at Brisbane.

SECTOR

The designated area of the stadium infield within which implements used in the throwing events must land.

SEDYKH, YURIY

U.S.S.R. (born 11th July,1955) - Unquestionably the greatest hammer thrower and competitor of modern times, Sedykh has mastered the art of throwing for the major occasion. Gold in Olympic Games 1976,1980, silver in World Championships 1983, gold in European Championships 1978,1982, another gold in World Cup 1981, and still another gold in European Cup 1981. He is the technical innovator in his event,but may be past his best now.

SEKO, TOSHI

Japan (born 15th July,1956) - The fastest Japanese marathoner of all time when he recorded 2hr 8:38 to win the 1982 Tokyo Marathon. He confirmed his world class in 1984 by finishing Ist in the Fukuoka marathon in 2hr 08:52.

SHAHANGA, GIDAMIS

Tanzania (born 4th Sept.,1957) - Shahanga's victory in the Edmonton Commonwealth Games was achieved, according to him, when he was only 17. In Brisbane after his 10,000 metres victory he was still insisting he was 21 and stating that contrary to common belief his Christian name is spelt Gidamis not Gidimas.

SHARP, CAMERON

U.K. (born 3rd June,1958) - Emerging from Alan Wells' shadow in 1982 Sharp was selected for the European Championships and against all odds took the 200 metres silver medal, clocking 20.47 behind the winner. At the Commonwealth Games later in the year he won three bronze medals, in the individual 100 and 200 metres and the 4x100 metres relay, in which he had also picked up bronze.

SHCHELKANOVA, T.

U.S.S.R. (born 18th April,1937) - In 1961, she broke the world record in shot put at 21ft.3in improving it further every year until 1964 when she reached 21ft. 11(3/4)in. In 1965, she became the second woman to surpass 22ft. and in 1966 she covered 22ft.10in.

SHORTS

Shorts can be a very neglected item as there is a feeling that anything will do. It most certainly won't when running long distances, and although the most glaring example has been highlighted (Bermuda Shorts), even some football and beach shorts can shape as well as restrict your stride. Freedom shorts are best, but don't always rely on the built-in briefs and make sure they are not too tight at the waist. You will need at least two pairs.

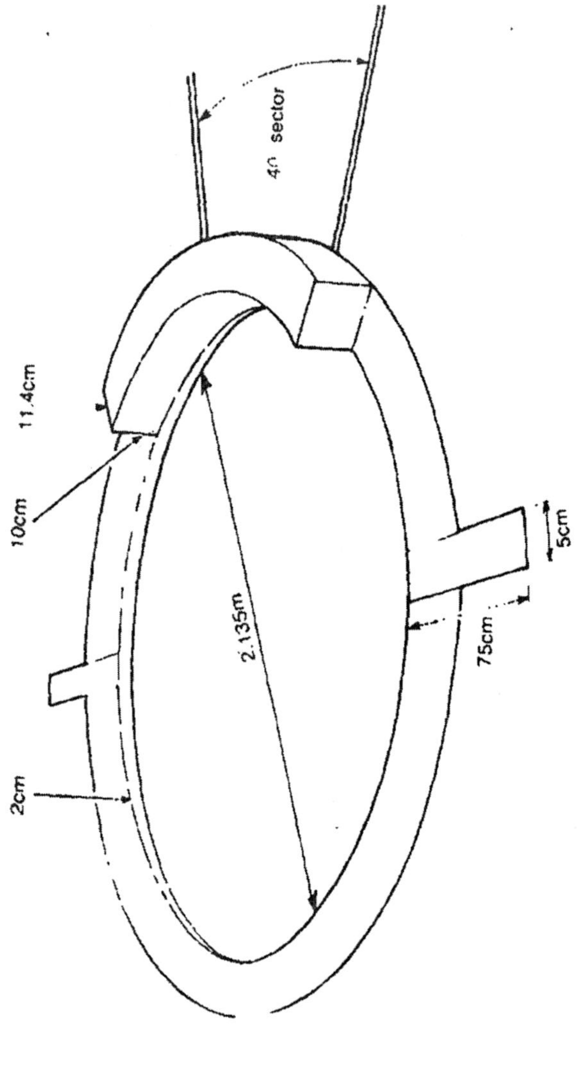

The shot put circle

Shot-Put
9.5-11 cm
wome-
11-13 cm
men
2
3
4
5
6
7

SHOT PUT

The shot is a heavy, cannonball-like ball. It is held in one hand against the side of the chin and propelled by pushing it away from the body - actually throwing it is against the rules. As for all throwing events, different weights are used for men and women and for different age groups.

Rules of the putting the shot

1. In making his puts the competitor may rest his feet against but not on top of the stop board.
2. The shot shall be put from the shoulder with one hand only.
3. At the time the competitor takes his stance in the ring, the shot shall not be dropped below this position during the act of putting. The shot must not be brought behind the line of the shoulders.
4. For a valid put the shot must fall so that the point from which measurement is to be made is within the inner edges of lines marking a sector of about 65 degree set out on the ground so that the radii lines touch, with their edges, the extremities of the stop board and cross at the centre of the circle.
5. Immediately after each put the measurements should be made.

World record at ten-yearly intervals (Women)

1925	10.68m	Violette Morris (Fra)
1935	14.38m	Gisela Mauermayer (Ger)
1945	14.89m	Tatyana Sevryukova (USSR)
1955	16.67m	Galina Zybina (USSR)
1965	18.59m	Tamara Press (USSR)
1975	21.60m	Marianne Adam (GDR)
1985	22.53m	Natalya Lisovskaya (USSR)

SHRUBB, A.

U.K. (1897-1964) - He has been one of the most outstanding runners. His eminence can be judged considering the number of records he made and the period for which these remained unbeaten. He held nearly every British record from 1(1/2)miles to one hour, many of them surviving for over 30 years and the last for 49 years. He held world record of 10mi in

50min.40.6sec for 24 years, 9 mi. in 9min 09.6sec for 22 years, 3 mile in 14min. 17.2sec for 18 years, 11mi, 1,137yd. hour run for 9 years,6mi in 29min 59.4 sec. and 10,000m. in 31min 02.4sec. for7 years.

SIDE STITCHES
Side stitches, which can occur during a run, are severe pains below the rib cage in the abdominal area and you feel as if a knife were sticking into your body. They occur when the diaphragm is deprived of oxygen. They will disappear if you slow your pace and use more stomach muscles to inhale and exhale more deeply. You can also squeeze your side as you run, which may relieve the pain.

SIMEONI, SARA
Italy (born 11th April,1953) - Tall, graceful Simeoni earned gold in 1980 Olympics high jump event. She also earned gold in 1978 European Championships and silver in 1979 European Cup.

SIMPSON, A.
U.K. (born 22nd May, 1940) - He has been Britain's faster mile and most prolific sub-four minute performer. He was the holder of world indoors 5000m best. He was fourth in the 1964 Olympics 1500m and 2nd in the 1966 Commonwealth Games mile.

SINKIM, DAN
North Korea (born 3rd July,1938) - She established herself as the fastest female quarter miler. In 1959, she established a world record of 2min.04.3sec. for 800m. and in 1961 reduced it to 2min 01.2sec. In 1964, she completed 800m. in 1min.58.0sec and 400m. in 51.2sec.

SKOGLUND, LOUISE ANN
Sweden (born 28th Jun.,1962) - Has met peak form at the European Championships. She won in 1982 with a Swedish record which she

improved in 1986 when she was fourth. Missed 1987 season after operation on injury.

SLANEY, RICHARD

U.K. (born 16th May,1956) - The top UK discus thrower in 1982 and 1983, by exceeding UK record by 32 cm, but the performance was never ratified as a new national mark. He narrowly failed to win his first major championship medal at the 1982 Commonwealth Games by throwing just 20cm short of the bronze medal winning mark.

SLUPIANEK, BRIESENICK LLONA

East Germany (born 24th Sept.,1956) - Her hand injury undoubtedly cost her the first World Championship gold, but whenever she competes she seems to upset some people.She was suspended, and then reinstated, after being found guilty of taking anabolic steroids. This blots her record as the finest shot putter of modern times.She earned gold in shot of 1980 Olympic Games.

SLY, WENDY

U.K. (born 5th Nov.,1959) - Is primarily responsible for ending the recent decline in British women's middle distance standards. She first approached real world class in 1982, taking second place in the Commonwealth Games women's 3000 metres and setting a Commonwealth record of 8:46.01 for that distance. Her big break-through came at the inaugural World Championships where she was placed fifth at both 3000 and 12500 metres, clocking a superb 8:37.06 at 1500 m.

SMITH, CALVIN

U.S.A. (born 8th January,1961) - He is the fastest man of all time. He won gold and silver in 200 and 100m sprints of 1983 World Championships. There was little in his career to suggest that the quietly spoken boy from the deep south would become one of the all time greats.

SMITH, JOYCE

U.K. (born 26th Oct.,1937) - An international track athlete since 1956, with a 1974 European Championships 3000 metres bronze medal to her credit, she finally turned to the marathon in 1979. She set six British women's Marathon bests in all, her finest performances coming in the 1981 and 1982 London marathons, in the first of which she achieved her first sub 2(1/2) hours clocking (2:29:57)(1982).

SMITH, T.C.

U.S.A. (born 12th Jan.,1944) - He was a furlong-cum-quarter mile runner of high order. In 1966, he set four world records - 200m. and 220yd straight and turn.

SMOKING

Undoubtedly long term health risks are related to smoking, cigarettes have short term negative effects on an exercise like running, which is so dependent on the efficiency of the lungs and oxygen utilization. Carbon monoxide gas, reduces the oxygen carrying power of the haemoglobin in the blood by 10-15 per cent, limiting in turn the body's ability to function at its peak ability. At best, smoking is a dangerous handicap.

SNELL, P.G.

New Zealand (born 17th Dec.,1938) - He won the titles in the 1960 Olympics 800m, 1962 Commonwealth 880 yds and mile and 1964 Olympics 800m and 1500m. In 1962, he established mile world record of 3min. 54.5sec. and also established world record at 800m (1min. 44.3sec) and 880yd.(1min. 45.1sec)

SOCKS

The function of socks is fivefold: (1) they provide a desirable aesthetic appearance, (2) they fill up the spaces between the foot and the shoe, holding the foot firmly and protecting the skin from pressure points of the shoe that may lead to blisters, (3) they are claimed in some cases to provide extra cushioning, (4) they provide warmth to the foot,the ankle and the Achilles tendon and (5) they plug the gap between the ankle and the inside of the shoe, keeping out uncomfortable mud when running over wet fields or trails.

SOLEBERG TRINE

Norway (born 18th April,1966) - She was the top goal scorer in Norwegian second division handball in 1984, and but for her interest in the javelin would have been a candidate for the national team.

SPLITS

Times recorded at intermediate points during a race of 400 metres or longer to give an indication of whether the overall pace is fast or slow.

STAGGERED START

Start of a race run in lanes in which the competitors in the outer lanes start from scratch lines several metres ahead of those in the lanes inside them, to counteract the extra distance involved in running wide round a bend.

STAMINA

Sprinters need stamina to keep them going once they have reached their maximum speed. Distance runners need stamina to keep running lap after lap. Building up stamina is a matter of conditioning your legs and your breathing. This means running regularly and gradually building up your training programme. It is possible to run too much in training or do things that may do more harm than good. Anyone who thinks seriously of taking up running as a sport should seek the advice of a coach.There are certainly several theories. Finding the method that suits you best might involve much trial and error. But you have to have confidence in your training programme.

START TO FINISH

Races are started by firing a starting pistol. In top class meetings, this triggers a highly accurate electronic timing device; ordinary stopwatches are used in lower levels of competition. The athlete is judged to have finished the race when his torso crosses the line (not his arms, legs, head or neck).

STEEPLECHASE

The standard distances are:-

Adults - 3000 metres, 28 hurdles and 7 water jumps

Senior Boys - 2000 metres, 17 hurdles and 4 water jumps

Inter.Boys - 1000 metres, 8 hurdles and 2 water jumps

The 3000 metre steeplechase, an event for men only, is a branch of middle distance running. This game also demands the ability to cross the hurdle, overcome 28 hurdle jumps, and even water jumps are usually included in the race. The exact distance of each lap is not specified in the rules since the water jump position depends on whether it is inside or

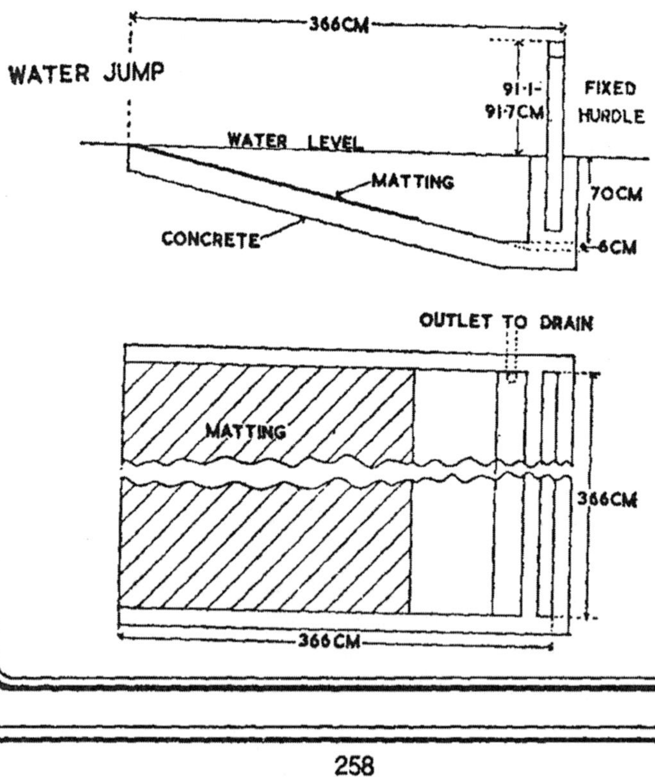
WATER JUMP
366CM
91·1-
91·7CM
FIXED
HURDLE
WATER LEVEL
MATTING
70CM
CONCRETE
6CM
OUTLET TO DRAIN
MATTING
366CM
366CM

outside the normal track, but there is a run-in distance from the start to the beginning of the first lap, then several laps, each including four hurdle jumps and one water jump. With its heavy wooden hurdles that do not tip over when struck by the athlete as do those used in the other athletic hurdle races, the steeplechase is a race for the few determined. Steeplechaser needs to be a very fit and able hurdler with a good tactical brain to keep out of trouble in a crowded field of jostling runners. Each hurdle is 0.914 metres high and 3.96 metres wide and competitors must pass over each one without trailing their legs to the sides. The water pitch is 3.66 metres in length and width. The bottom is 0.7 metres in front of the hurdle and slopes up to ground level at the end. Competitors must go over or through the water.

World record at ten-yearly intervals

1945	8:59.6	Erik Elmsater	Swe
1955	8:40.3	Jerzy Chromik	Pol
1965	8:26.4	Gaston Roelants	Bel
1975	8:09.7	Anders Garderud	Swe
1985	8:05.4	Henry Rono	Ken

STEPHENS, H.H.

U.S.A. (born 3rd Feb., 1918) - She won nearly 100 races. In 1935, she set world records of 10.8sec for 100 yd. and 11.6sec.(twice) for 100yd. In 1936 Olympics she won gold medals in the 100m in 11.5 sec. and the 4x100m relay.

STONES, DWIGHT

U.S.A. (born 6th Dec.,1953) - Stones returned to the amateur ranks after a period as a professional, but although he regained his place in the United States team he found Europe's young lions too hard to beat. Won bronze in 1976 Olympics in high jump. Captured silver in 1977 World Cup.

STOPBOARD

A curved piece of wood 10cm (4 in) thick affixed to the front of the shot put circle. When throwing, the shot putter braces his foot against the stopboard to avoid falling forwards out of the circle.

STRAIGHT

Long, straight section of the standard track adjoining the bends. The straight situated nearest the main stand is termed the homestraight and the other, the backstraight.

STRESS FRACTURES

Also called fatigue fractures or march fractures, stress fractures are small but painful cracks in a bone structure due to strain, jolting, or pounding. They usually occur in the ball or heel of the foot and disappear after two or three weeks of rest. If you must run with a stress fracture, do so in moderation under a doctor's supervision and only on soft surfaces.

STRIDE PATTERN

The calculated number of strides that a hurdler must take between the obstacles to arrive at the correct take off point, and on the correct take off leg, at each obstacle.

STRONG, SHIRLEY

U.K. (born 18th Nov.,1958) - Most talented British female sprint hurdler for many years, she finally broke into real world class in 1983. Three times she broke the UK 100 metres hurdles record. Her earlier career highlights include a second and first in the Commonwealth Games 100 metres hurdles finals .

STUDS

Most commonly required by orienteers and fell runners but sometimes used in cross-country. They usually have deep, well spaced studs to give maximum grip in muddy or loose terrain, especially when running downhill. Some companies attempt to provide a waterproof upper and, by and large, the shoes are heavy for competition purposes. The market awaits a really excellent racing stud.

SUPINATION

This involves movement at the front of the foot, from the inside to the outside, and excessive motion is over-supination, though this is nowhere near as common as over-pronation.

SYNTHETIC TRACK

A general term used to describe all types of artificial surface tracks.

SZEWINSKA, IRENA

Poland (born 24th May, 1946) - She enjoyed the title of European queen of athletics for many years.Beginning as an 18 year old at the Tokyo Olympics she won the silver medal for the long jump gained another in the 200 metres in a European record time and then helped Poland win the 4x400 metres in a world record. She set world records for both sprints in 1965 and then won the 200 metres and the long jump at the European Championships a year later, as well as helping Poland win the sprint relay.

In 1968, in Mexico, she won the Olympics 200 metres gold with a world record of 22.58 sec and also picked up a bronze in the 100 metres. More bronze medals followed in the European Games and the Olympics of 1972 before she started serious 400 metres running in 1973, setting world record leading up to the breaking of the 50 sec barrier.

She emphasised her tremendous ability by winning the 400 metres in the 1976 Montreal Olympics in a world record 49.28sec. She even competed in the Moscow Olympics her fifth but at 34 her career came to an end with a leg injury and she was eliminated in the semi-final stage.

T

T.A.C.

The Athletics Congress (USA)

TAKEOVER ZONES

Zones marked in each lane of a standard 400 metres track within which relay baton changeovers must be executed.

TAPE

Band or cord stretched across the track or race finish, at about waist height above the finish line, to help the competitors judge the exact finishing point of the race.

TAYLOR, ANGELLA

Canada (born 28th Sept., 1958) - One of the new breed of Canadian runners from the West Indies. Canada is benefiting from the Carribean, just like Britain.

TEAM EVENT

This realy is the only athletics event in which teams compete directly against each other. A baton is passed between four team members, who each run either 100m or 400m.

TEN THOUSAND METRES

No other area of athletics, save perhaps the 1500 m and mile, has been so graced with celebrated, evocative names as the long distance event of

5,000m and 10,000m. The sympatico between long distance runner and trackside viewer is an intangible the sprinter could never hope to capture. To watch someone like Zatopek, shoulders rolling in apparent agòny, mouth creased in torment, repeatedly circling in front of you, forges a lifelong affiliation.

Ten thousand metres world record at ten yearly intervals

1905	31:02.4	Alfred Shrubb (UK) Glasgow	5 Nov, 1904
1915	30:58.8	Jean Bouin (Fra)Colombes,Paris	16 Nov, 1911
1925	30:06.I	Paavo Nurmi(Fin)Kuipio	31 Aug, 1924
1935	30:06.1	Paavo Nurmi as above	
1945	29:35.4	Viljo Heino (Fin)Helsinki	25 Aug, 1944
1955	28:54.2	Emil Zatopek (Cs)Brussels	1 Jun, 1954
1965	27.39.4	Ron Clarke (Aus) Oslo	14 Jul, 1965
1975	27:30.80	David Bedford (UK) London	13 Jul, 1973
1985	27:13.81	Fernando Mamede (Por)Stockholm	2 Jul, 1984

THERMAL WEAR

The use of thermal wear in running has been turned inside out. The garments which are being marketed, that is T-shirts, long sleeve shirts and leg tights, can be worn under garments, but most commonly they are used by runners as protection for exposed limbs in extremely cold weather, and the tights are worn under shorts, and long sleeve shirts under competition singlets.

The materials most commonly encountered are polypropylene, polyester, or a blend of polyester and Viloft.

THE FINISH

The finish should be a line drawn across the track at right angles to the inner edge.

THE RACE

Any competitor wilfully jostling or running across another so as to impede his progress shall forfeit his right to be in the competition.

THE SPRINTS

Whether it be in the 100 metres, where power and short-term energy are all-important, or the 400 metres, where sustained energy is needed to avoid the burn-out over the final 200 metres, the technique in sprints is very much in the hands of the coaches.

These races are timed accurately up to one hundredth of a second *by electronic timing device. The athlete is expected to have an explosive* start, great acceleration from start up to around 30m (pick-up stage), a sustained speed for the middle portion, and then a slight deceleration for the remainder of the race. The athlete has to strive for maximum stride length and leg speed. The start is the main deciding factor of the sprint. Two styles of starts are the crouch start and the standing start. Depending on one's experience, one can develop any type of start.

At the start, the feet of the athlete must be in contact with the ground, fingers behind the start line. When all athletes are steady on the start mark, the starter gives the command 'set' and 1.5 to 3.0 sec after that he fires the gun. The first step should be accompanied by powerful drive from the lead legs with vigorous arm actions. If any athlete has two false starts, he is

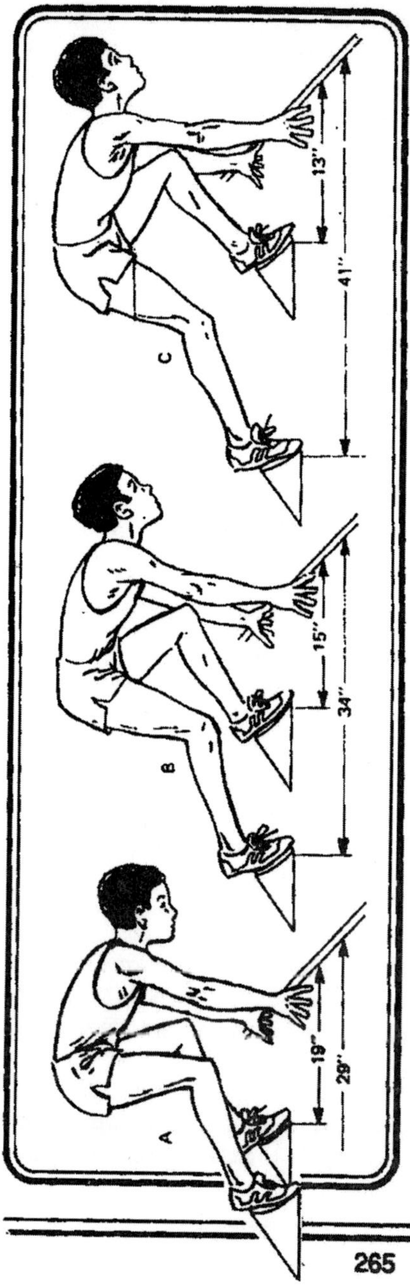

disqualified. The official finish is the finishing line, where photo-finish cameras determine first, second and third positions. The athlete should continue the sprint in full speed even at the finish line drawn across the track at right angles to the inner edge and a tape is held right above this line. The competitors have to break the tape by torso. The competitors try to do so by inclining their body forward.

The lists of the world record holders and Olympic medallists at the sprints are dominated by athletes from U.S.A.

100 Metres World record at ten-yearly intervals-

Year	Sec.	Name	Country
1905	10.8	Luther Cary	USA
1915	10.5	Richard Rau	Ger
1925	10.2	Charles Paddock	USA
1935	10.2	Charles Paddock	USA
1945	10.2	Jesse Owens	USA
1955	10.1	Lloyd La Beach	Pan
1965	10.0	Armin Hary	GFR
1975	9.8	Steve Williams	USA
1985	9.93	Calvin Smith	USA

The 200 metres race is run on a curve in lanes with a staggered start, with the blocks set on the outside of the bend. The runner has thus to run the bend with just the right body angle to maintain speed.

200 metres race as consisting of four important phases:

(i) The start and the straight line acceleration to the point where this straight line forms a tangent to the inside of his lane and is very similar to the 100 metres start.

(ii) The run for the 200 metres runner presents technical difficulties, since he must continue accelerating and hope to reach to top speed while running part of a circle. In order to run in a circle close to the inside line of his lane he must lean into the centre to maintain balance. The right leg has to swing across the body to hold it into the curve in the left leg support phase. An unbalanced runner or one who tends to carry weight on the right leg will have trouble running a bend well. Runners with strong lateral movements, such as the short stocky 'power' type runners, will find this style as not effective in the 200 metres bend since the feet need to drive under the body in the line of movement. The smooth flowing stylists are often the 200 metre specialists. On the bend, then, the outside leg and arm must work hard to maintain the lean-in. There is some coasting period in this part of the 200 metres, and stamina is needed to ensure that the athlete comes out of the bend with top sprinting speed.

(iii) Coming out of the turn into the straight requires a change of posture again, so that a central balance is achieved. This is a crucial stage of the race because the style of running has to change. The turn requires a fast cadence, but as the athlete enters the straight the emphasis is on a stronger leg action.

(iv) The straight part of the 200 draws on the mental and endurance reserves of the runner, for he must maintain his form and try to lose as little speed as possible as he nears the finish. The danger is in 'tying up' with tense muscles as fatigue sets in.

The 200 metres runner, like the 100 metres athlete, must train for greater speed through high-quality sprinting, paying special attention to particular points of technique during repetition runs. In addition he must train at high speed bend running, and he must work for stamina with full and over distance repetitions.

200 Metres World record for 220y (Straight Track) at ten yearly intervals

1905	21.2	Bernie Wefers (USA)
1915	20.8	Albert Robinson (USA)
1925	20.8	Charles Paddock (USA)
1935	20.3	Jesse Owens (USA)
1945	20.3	Jesse Owens (USA)
1955	20.2	Mel Patton (USA)
1965	20.0	Dave Sime (USA)
	20.0	Frank Budd (USA)
1975	19.5	Tommie Smith (USA)

World Record for 200m around a turn at ten yearly intervals

1905	21.4	(for 220y)James Maybury(USA)
1915	21.2	(for220y) William Applegarth(UK)
1925	21.2	(for 220y)H.T.Evans(USA)
	21.2	Charles Paddock(USA)
1935	20.6	(for 220y) James Carlton(Aus)
1945	20.6	James Carlton (Aus)
1955	20.6	(for 220y) Andy Stanfield (USA)
	20.81	Andy Stanfield (USA)
1965	20.2	(for 220 y) HenryCarr (USA)

1975	19.83	Tommie Smith (USA)
1985	19.72	Pietro Mennea (Ita)

400 Metres: This is a sprint for the well-trained athlete. The distribution of energy has to be carefully controlled because very few can maintain an all-out sprint over the entire distance. It is very important for the 400 metre runner to judge pace and to be able to assess his own ability in relation to the competitors. An evenly paced race will be more economical and effective; for example, it is better to run each 200 metres in 25 seconds and 27 seconds than in 23 seconds and 30 seconds. It is the total time that counts, and even if that last example ended with 29 seconds, the rapidly slowing athlete would act as incentive for other competitors to chase and overtake him. The first 200 metres is generally run faster than the second because of the fatigue in the second, but an even faster time will not necessarily cancel out the slower time recorded in the second half. A common pattern is to try for a good start and first bent, a comfortable fast stride down the back straight, and a big effort on the last bend while trying to maintain relaxation and speed to the finish. The good 400 metre runner often has a buoyant, (relaxed style with a long stride, keeping mainly on the ball of the foot).

400 Metres world record at ten-yearly intervals

Women

1925	60.8	Eileen Edwards	(UK)
1935	56.8	Nellie Halstead	(UK)
1945	56.8	Nellie Halstead	(UK)
1955	53.9	Maria Itkina	(USSR)
1965	51.2	Shin Keum Dan	(NKo)
1975	49.9	Irena Szewinska	(Pol)
1985	47.6	Marita Koch	(GDR)

THOMAS, SHIRLEY

U.K. (born 15th June,1963) - A bright sprint prospect for the future, she took the 100 metres silver medal at the 1981 European Junior Championships, clocking 11.43, and added European and World Championship sprint relay silver medals to her collection in 1982 and 1983, respectively. She also showed promise in reaching the World Championships individual 100 metres semi-finals in the later year.

THOMPSON, D.J.

U.K. (born 20th Jan.,1933) - In 1955, he won the race from London to Brighton (25 mi) for the first of eight successive years. He also established his first natural 50,000m title. On the track he set UK records at 20min. 30mi. In 1960 Olympics in Rome he won the 50,000m road walk in record time of 4hr.25min. 30sec.

THORPE, J.H.

U.S.A. (1888 - 1953) - He won two gold medals in pentathlon and decathlon at the Olympics but was stripped off them because of his having turned professional. But there is no doubt that he was the outstanding athlete of his times.

After his imposed professionalism, Thorpe went on to play not only baseball but football also and he received the consolation of being voted the greatest footballer in America.

THREE THOUSAND METRES

Who can halt the Soviet bloc? Romania's Maricica Puica claimed the Olympic 3,000m title, profiting perhaps from Decker's controversial exit. But Puica is now into her mid thirties. With Decker dedicating 1986 to motherhood, the expectations fall on the slender shoulders of Zola Budd, innocent party in Decker's Olympic debacle, and rapidly maturing into a distance runner of the highest possible class.

3000 m (Women) WORLD RECORD

Time	Competitor	Date	Venue
8:53.0	Lyudmilla Bragina (URS)	12.8.72	Moscow
8:52.8	Lyudmilla Bragina (URS)	6.7.74	Durham
8:26.78	Syvetiana Ulmasova (URS)	25.7.82	Kiev
8:22.62	Tatyana Kazankina (URS)	26.8.84	Leningrad

TIMEKEEPING

The IAAF lays down that there should be three official timekeepers and one or two alternate timekeepers for every event. Where two of the official watches agree, that time is the official time. If all three watches disagree, the middle time becomes the official time. The time is taken from the flash of the starting pistol to the moment at which any part of the athlete's torso (which includes the neck) reaches the edge of the finish line which is nearer to the start. Times are recorded to one-tenth of a second in races up to and including the mile to one-fifth of a second in longer events.

TOOMEY, W.

U.S.A. (10th Jan.,1939) - In 1959, he won his first AAA 3mi. title and set his first British record in 1960. In 1901, he set a European 3 mi. record of 13min. 12.0sec. In 1962, he made mile in four minutes, made U.K. 2mi. record and won European 5000m. championship. In 1966, he set a European 6mi. record.

TRACK EVENTS

Races of up to one lap in length are run in eight "lanes". Because the distance around the outside of the track is greater than the inside, the athletes start in a staggered line, so that each one runs an equal distance

TRACK SHOES

Athletes who race on the track use tight-fitting, lightweight shoes with spiked soles. The spikes provide the best grip on the track and allow sprinters to reach speeds of up to 40 km /h (25mph).

TRAINING BOTTOMS

These garments have filled a gap in the market which appeared when tracksuits with tapered legs virtually disappeared. Even if these types of suit were still easily accessible, separate training bottoms would be just as necessary as with these suits, the bottoms always wear out first.

Training bottoms are available in different fabrics but probably the best and certainly the best known are "Tracksters"(TM), made from light-weight stretch nylon, which keeps the legs warm, yet offer little resistance or restriction when running. Being 100% nylon, they are easily washed and dried. Matching Trackster tops are also made which, together with the bottoms, give an excellent lightweight training suit.

TRIAL EVENTS

Specially staged track and field events, the results of which assist athletics team selectors to determine the best of the athletes available to represent teams competing usually in major competitions.

TRAINING SCHEDULES

100 and 200 metres (Boys and Girls)

Monday	Easy fartlek running, hill springing, steep hills or step running, 15 to 30 minutes.
Tuesday	High knee-lift exercises, long striding exercises, running-tall exercises, relaxed striding, 4 x 200 metres.
Wednesday	Repeat Monday's session.
Thursday	Repeat Tuesday's session.
Friday	Leg speed, 4-6 x 100 metres.
Saturday	2-3 x 400 metres at 3/4 effort.
Sunday	Easy fartlek running, 15 to 30 minutes.

100 and 200 metres (Adults)

Monday	Easy fartlek running, hill springing, steep hills or step running, 1/2 hour.
Tuesday	High knee-lift exercises, long striding exercises, running-tall exercises, relaxed striding, 4 x 300 metres.
Wednesday	Repeat Monday's session.
Thursday	Repeat Tuesday's session.
Friday	Leg speed, 10 x 120 metres.
Saturday	3 x 800 metres at 3/4 effort.
Sunday	Easy fartlek running, 1 hour.

400 metres (Boys and Girls)

Monday	Long aerobic running, 1/2 to 3/4 hour.
Tuesday	Long aerobic running, 3/4 to 1 hour.
Wednesday	Easy fartlek running, 1/2 to 3/4 hour.

Thursday	Repeat Tuesday's session.
Friday	Relaxed striding, 6 x 200 metres.
Saturday	Long aerobic running, 3/4 to 1(1/4) hours.
Sunday	Easy fartlek running, 1/2 to 1 hour.

400 metres (Adults)

Monday	Long aerobic running, 1/2 hour.
Tuesday	Long aerobic running, 1 hour.
Wednesday	Easy fartlek running, 3/4 to 1 hour.
Thursday	Repeat Tuesday's session.
Friday	Relaxed striding, 6 x 200 metres.
Saturday	Long aerobic running, 1 to 1(1/2) hours.
Sunday	Repeat Wednesday's session.

800 and 1,500 metres (Boys and Girls)

Monday	Easy fartlek running, 1/2 to 3/4 hour.
Tuesday	Long aerobic running, 1 to 1(1/4) hours.
Wednesday	Time trials, 3,000 metres.
Thursday	Repeat Tuesday's session.
Friday	Easy fartlek running, 1/2 hour.
Saturday	Time trials, 5,000 metres.
Sunday	Long aerobic running, 1 to 1(1/2) hours.

800 and 1,500 metres (Men)

Monday	Easy fartlek running, 1 hour.
Tuesday	Long aerobic running, 1(1/2) hours.
Wednesday	Time trials, 5,000 metres.
Thursday	Repeat Tuesday's session.
Friday	Easy fartlek running, 3/4 hour; and hills
Saturday	Time trials, 10,000 metres.
Sunday	Aerobic running, 1(1/2) hours or more.

800 and 1500 metres (Women)

Monday	Easy fartlek running, 3/4 to 1 hour.
Tuesday	Long aerobic running, 1 to 1(1/2) hours.
Wednesday	Time trials, 3,000 metres.
Thursday	Repeat Tuesday's session

Friday	Easy fartlek running, 3/4 hour.
Saturday	Time trials, 5,000 metres.
Sunday	Long aerobic running, 1(1/2) hours or more.

3,000 metres (Boys)

Monday	Long aerobic running, 1 hour.
Tuesday	Long aerobic running, 1 to 1(1/2) hours.
Wednesday	Time trials, 5,000 metres.
Thursday	Repeat Tuesday's session.
Friday	Easy fartlek running, 1/2 to 3/4 hour.
Saturday	Time trials, 10,000 metres.
Sunday	Long aerobic running, 1(1/4) to 1(1/2) hours.

3,000 metres (Women)

Monday	Easy fartlek running, 3/4 to 1 hour.
Tuesday	Long aerobic running, 1 to 1(1/2) hours.
Wednesday	Time trials, 5,000 metres.
Thursday	Repeat Tuesday's session.
Friday	Easy fartlek running, 3/4 hour.
Saturday	Time trials, 10,000 metres.
Sunday	Long aerobic running, 1(1/2) hours or more.

5,000 and 10,000 metres (Boys and Girls)

Monday	Easy fartlek running, 3/4 to 1 hour.
Tuesday	Long aerobic running, 1 to 1(1/2) hours.
Wednesday	Time trials, 5,000 metres.
Thursday	Repeat Tuesday's session.
Friday	Repeat Monday's session.
Saturday	Time trials, 10,000 metres.
Sunday	Long aerobic running, 1(1/2) hours or more.

5,000 and 10,000 metres (Adults)

Monday	Easy fartlek running, 1 hour.
Tuesday	Long aerobic running, 1(1/2) hours.
Wednesday	Time trials, 10,000 metres.
Thursday	Repeat Tuesday's session.
Friday	Repeat Monday's session.

Saturday	Repeat Wednesday's session.
Sunday	Long aerobic running, 2 hours or more.

3,000metresSteeplechase (Men)

Monday	Easy fartlek running, 1 hour.
Tuesday	Long aerobic running, 1(1/2) hours.
Wednesday	Time trials, 5,000 metres.
Thursday	Repeat Tuesday's session.
Friday	Easy fartlek running, 3/4 hours (hills).
Saturday	Time trials, 10,000 metres.
Sunday	Long aerobic running, 1(1/2) hours or more.

Marathon (Beginners)

Monday	Long aerobic running, 1/2 to 3/4 hour.
Tuesday	Long aerobic running, 1 hour.
Wednesday	Repeat Monday's session.
Thursday	Repeat Tuesday's session.
Friday	Repeat Monday's session.
Saturday	Long aerobic running, 1 to 2 hours.
Sunday	Long aerobic running, 3/4 to 1 hour.

Experienced Runners

Monday	Long aerobic running, 1 hour.
Tuesday	Long aerobic running, 1(1/2) hours.
Wednesday	Easy fartlek running, 1 hour, on hills.
Thursday	Repeat Tuesday's session.
Friday	Jogging, 1 hour.
Saturday	Long aerobic running, 2 hours or more.
Sunday	Repeat Tuesday's session.

TRIPLE JUMP

In addition to the training done as a sprinter the triple jumper must devote much of his training time to ploymetrics - the explosive type, eccentric muscle contraction work of depth jumping. A few examples of this training method are:

1. Jumping from the top of a box (typically 1 metre high), on to one leg, followed by a hop, step and jump.

Hop
Step
Jump

2. Jumping from the top of a box of the floor, immediately rebounding from one or both feet to another box, to the floor, to a box etc.
3. Hopping, or double foot bounding, over low hurdles placed about 2 metres apart.
4. Vertical jumps in rapid sequence while holding dumb bells.

This type of training ensures that the muscles concerned are attempting to contract while they are being stretched by the much larger force of the landing. The tensions in the muscles and tendons are very much greater in this so-called eccentric contraction than in normal concentric contraction at the appropriate joints. In addition the movement is of an intense, short-duration in which the muscles are called upon to exert a very large force in a short time, which is exactly what is required of them in the triple jump take-off.

In triple jump the hop is made first so that the competitor lands first upon the same foot as that from which he has taken off. In the step he lands on the other foot, from which subsequently the jump is performed.

The rules allow an unlimited length of runway (minimum 40 metres), and, in addition to the rules defining failures which include those for the long jump, they also specify that : If a competitor while jumping touches the ground with the 'sleeping' leg it shall be considered a failure''. Simple sounding rules, but then simple rules quite often define highly technical events - as is the case with the triple jump. Because the objective is to triple jump as far as possible, one may think that an enormous hop is the best way to start the movement of the take-off board. However, even the strongest triple jumpers have to keep this phase under control if the rest is not to suffer.

World record at ten-yearly intervals

1915	15.52m	Daniel Ahearne (USA)
1925	15.52m	Daniel Ahearne (USA)
1935	15.78m	Jack Metcalfe (Aus)
1945	16.00m	Naoto Tajima (Jap)
1955	16.56m	Adhemar Ferreira (Bra)
1965	17.03m	Jozef Schmidt (Pol)
1975	17.89m	Joao Carlos de Oliveira (Bra)
1985	17.97m	Willie Banks (USA)

T-SHIRT

For less serious runners, these are all-the-year-round racing wear and usually carry some kind of slogan, advertising or proof of having been somewhat exotic! Fine. For the serious runner, they are a useful garment for training in both cool or cold weather; in cool weather, as a garment under something else, such as a tracksuit or foul weather suit.

TUG-OF-WAR

This sport was part of the athletics programme 1900-1920. Three men won a record two golds and one silver from 1908 to 1920. John Shepherd, Frederick Humphreys and Edwin Mills, all from Great Britain.

Gold	
1900	Sweden/Denmark
1904	USA
1906	Germany
1908	Great Britain
1912	Sweden
1920	Great Britain

TYLER, D.J.B.

U.K. (born 14th Mar.,1920) - In 1936 and 1948 Olympics she cleared the height of the winner but in accordance with the rules then in force, she was declared second in both. She won the Commonwealth titles both in 1938 and 1950. In 1939 she set a world record of 5ft.5(1/2)in. She was second in both the 1950 European and 1954 Commonwealth Games competitions. In 1952 and 1956 Olympics she was 7th and 12th respectively.

TYPES OF TRACK

Older tracks are made from grass or cinders but modern tracks are made from synthetic rubber and polyurethane materials, and are used for training and racing in all weathers.

TYPING UP

A condition sometimes experienced by runners during the later stages of the longer sprint events, where lactic acid builds up in the leg muscles to such an extent that their function becomes temporarily impaired causing the athlete to slow dramatically towards the finish of the race.

TYSON, CAROL

U.K. (born 15th Dec.,1957) - One of the more recent pioneers of women's race walking, she set world marks on the track at 3 km and 5 km in 1979 whilst only 21. In addition to several WAAA titles at 5 and 10 km she also holds the unofficial UK record for the mile walk, which she set during a 3 km race back in 1977 when still only 19.

TYUS, W.

U.S.A. (born 29th Aug.,1945) - In 1964, she got the first position in the 70yds (7.5sec). In the Olympics at Tokyo she won the gold medal to equal world record in 100m in 11.2sec. She also equalled the world record in both 110yd (10.3sec) and 100m (11.1 sec) in the following season.

U

ULMASOVA, SVETLANA

U.S.S.R. (born 4th Feb.,1953) - The world's leading women's 3000 metres runner for several years,she finally broke the 6 year old world record in 1982 recording 8:26.78. In addition to a World Cup 3000 metres win in 1979, she became the first woman to retain a European Championships 3000 metres title with her second win in Athens in 1982. She finished fourth in 1983 World Championships.

UNOFFICIAL OLYMPICS

An unofficial Olympic celebration was staged in Athens in 1906. For the record, the winners were as follows:

100m	A Hahn (USA)	11.2 sec.
400m	P.H.Pilgrim (USA)	53.2 sec.
800m	P.H.Pilgrim (USA)	2 min. 11.2 sec.
1500m	J.D.Lightbody (USA)	4 min. 12.0 sec.
Marathon	W.J.Sherring (Canada)	2 hr. 51 min. 23.6sec.
110mh	R.G. Leavitt (USA)	16.2 sec.
high jump	C.Leahy (Ireland)	5ft. 9 in.
pole vault	F. Gonder(France)	11 ft. 6 in.
long jump	M.Prinstein (USA)	23 ft. 7(1/2)in.
triple jump	P.J.O'Connor (Ireland)	46ft. 2 in.
shot	M.J.Sheridan (USA)	40 ft. 5 in.
discus	M.J.Sheridan (USA)	136ft. 1/4in.
javelin	E. Lemming (Sweden)	175 ft. 6 in.

USHA, P.T.

India (born 20th May,1964) - Her phenomenal starting from birth and childhood in a remote, miniscule village in Kerala, she has been blazing the trail of Indian athletic scene ever since she was 13 years of age by breaking one record after another. Her spirited performance at the 1984 Los Angeles Olympics, where she narrowly lost a medal by one-hundredth of a second. Her subsequent feast of 6 medals at Jakarta and 5 medals at Seoul 1986 Asian Games have won her much acclaim.

V

VAINIO, MARTTI

Finland (born 30th Dec.,1950) - He burst into the limelight in 1978 at the European Championships, when his long prancing style took him to the 10,000 metres title. Vainio made a supreme effort in the 500 metres, throwing himself over the line for a medal.

VALENT, GEJZA

Czechoslovakia (born 3rd Oct.,1953) - Leapt into world class in the 1980s after a decade of little progress. His father,Gejza, had a personal best discus mark of 53.84m in 1956, which ranked him 16th in the world.

VAN DIJCK, WILLIAM

Belgium (born 24th Jan.,1961) - Won the 1986 Grand Prix at 3000m steeplechase, with a series of fine wins, although he disappointed with fifth place at Stuttgart.

VEROULI, ANNA

U.K. (born 13th Nov.,1956) - Verouli sent the Athens crowd into ecstasy when she won the European Championships 1982 javelin gold. In World Championships 1983 she earned bronze.

VETERAN

Athlete still competing at the age of 40 or over in the case of a male or 35 and over in the case of a female.

VIGNERON,THIERRY

France (born 9th March,1960) - The first man to pole vault 19 feet, he is a prolific record breaker in this event yet has continually failed to perform well under major competition pressure. In 1979, he set a world junior pole vault record which still stood at the end of 1983, in 1980 he twice vaulted a world record 5.75 m but placed only 7th at the Olympics. In 1983, he placed only 8th at the World Championships and then set another record of 5.83 m.

VILLETON, JOCELYNE

France (born 17th Sept.,1954) - Has surprised with high placings in both European and World Championships. Ran short course 2:28:02, and third New York in 1987.

VIREN, LASSE

Finland (born 22nd July, 1949) - Viren became the hero of Finland when he followed in the traditions of Finnish greats by completing the double of 5,000 and 10,000 metres gold medals at the Munich Olympics, the latter at which he set a world record of 27min 38.4sec, despite falling during the race. Four years later, despite looking an also-ran in the in between years, he went to Montreal and retained both his titles and then ran into 5th place in the marathon only 24 hours after winning the 5,000m. gold.

After another four years of mediocre performances dotted by injuries and illness, Viren attempted to do the impossible at Moscow and when he took the lead in the 10,000 metres with 1200 metres to go, he appeared to have achieved it, only to be beaten on the final lap and eventually finished in fifth place.

His first notice on the athletic scene had been posted when he set a world two mile record shortly before Munich and then added a 5,000 metres best later that year.

His only other medal of note, however, came in the 1974 European Championships when he gained the bronze in the 5,000 metres.

VOLKOV, KONSTANTIN

U.S.S.R. (born 28th Feb.,1960) - The world's leading vaulter of 1981, he placed first in the World Students Games, European Cup and World Cup competitions and achieved a vault of 5.84 m at an unofficial meeting to exceed the then world record by 3 cm. His finest performances include silver medal winning vaults at both the 1980 Olympic Games and 1983 World Championships and he has remained a tremendously consistent vaulter over several seasons in one of athletics' most difficult events.

VOSS, TORSTEN

East Germany (born 24th March,1963) - Added 121 points to his personal best to win the 1987 world title, when he set no individual event personal bests, but performed consistently close to them.

W

W.A.A.A.

Women's Amateur Athletic Association.

WAFFLE SOLED SHOES

The waffle soled running shoe, with its dozens of small rubber studs, owes its name to its inventor,Bill Bowerman, the distinguished University of Oregon track. coach from 1948 to1973. He is closely involved in the foundation of the Nike Company in the USA in 1972.

WAITZ, GRETA

Norway (born 1st Oct.,1953) - Mrs. Waitz is the greatest woman long distance runner of all time. When she won the World Championships marathon in Helsinki in 1983, there was never a more popular and fitting winner. Slimily built and blond, she first came to the forefront in 1974 by winning the bronze medal at 1500 metres at the European Championships, as Greta Andersen. It was 12 months later that she decided to increase her distance and shattered the world 3,000 m record with 8min 46.6sec and then lowered it by almost a second in 1976, the year of the Olympics.

With a longer distance than 1500m. for women still a way off, Mrs. Waitz failed to make the final- and lost her world record shortly. In 1978, she moved into marathon running. In New York she lowered the existing world record by over two minutes with a time of 2hr.32min 30sec. She has dominated cross-country at which she has won five out of the six world titles- and in 1979 set world record for the 10,000m., the 10 miles and again the marathon in New York. In 1980, she set a new world record for the 15 km, the 10,000m., the indoors 3,000m. and astonishingly, the marathon record in New York for the third successive time.

WAKIIHURI, DOUGLAS

Kenya (born 26th Sept.,1963) - Went to Japan in 1983 to train under the late Kiyoshi. Made his marathon debut in 1986, and then to win the world title in 2:11:48.

WALASIEWICZ, S.

Poland (born 11th April,1911) - In 1932 and 1936 Olympics in 100m she won gold and silver medals respectively. In 1938, in European Championships 100m and 200m she won the titles and in the long jump silver medals. In the 1930 Women's World Games she was first in 60m. and second both in 100m and 200m walking.

WALKER, JOHN

New Zealand (born 12th Jan.,1952) - The first man ever to duck under 3:50 for a mile, Walker suffered a serious Achilles tendon injury in the late 1970. Walker's greatest achievement was winning the 1976 Olympics 1500 metres title in Montreal but it was as a world record breaker that he achieved his fame, especially on the European circuit. In 1974, Walker first came to notice in a race that he lost. The occasion was the 1974 Commonwealth Games in Christchurch when Filbert Bayi smashed the 1500 metres world record of Jim Ryun, a time that Walker also got inside in second place, a defeat he made up for in Helsinki later in the year. He came to Europe a year later and was the first man in racing history to break 3 min 50 sec for the mile, he ran 3 min 49.4sec. He broke the 2,000m. world record of Michel Jazy shortly before the 1976 Olympics with 4 min 51.4 sec, a time that stands today, despite the attempts of Wessinghage, Coe and Ovett. A great competitor, Walker not often outspoken, upset officialdom in 1983 by warning them of the increasing dangers of drugs that he claimed were in widespread use at the World Championships at Helsinki in 1500 metres. He won gold in 1500m Olympic Games 1976.He also won silver in 1981 World Cup.

WALKING

Walking may appear to be the natural link between ordinary walking and running, and in some respects this is true - with increase in speed, the force-time decreases. However, the horizontal forces at right-angles to the direction of movement do not reveal this tidy progression, because although ordinary walking and running produce only small wasted forces in this direction, race walking shows much the largest peaks which represent a significant energy.

A study of the body movements involved in these activities pinpoints the cause. In normal walking and running the knee of the supporting leg is bent as it passes through the vertical position but in race walking the knee of this leg is straight in the vertical position. This means that the rest of the body must make compensatory movements to maintain the path of the centre of mass on an efficient line.

50 Km Walk (Road) Men

World record	3:38:17	Ronald Weigel (GDR) in	1986
Commonwealth record	3:46:34	Willi Sawall (Aus) in	1980
Asian record	3:52:51	Li Baojin (Chn) in	1987
African record	4:14:30	Eddie Michaels (RSA) in	1967
European record	3:38:17	Ronald Weigel (GDR) in	1986
Olympic record	3:47:26	Raul Gonzalez (Mex) in	1984

50Km Walk (Track) Men

World record	3:41:38.4	Raul Gonzalez (Mex) in	1979
European record	3:46:11.0	Mykola Udovenko (SU) in	1980
Commonwealth record	4:05:47.3	Chris Maddocks (UK) in	1984
Asian record	4:20:45.0	Kazuo Shirai (Jap) in	1980
African record	4:21:44.5	Abdelwahab Ferguene (Alg) in	1984

5000m Walk (Track) Women

World record	21:16.0	Kerry Saxby in	1987
Asian record	21.20.2	Yan Hong (Chn) in	1987
European record	21:30.92	Oksana Shcastnaya (SU) in	1987

Commonwealth record	21:16.0	Kerry Saxby in	1987
African record	24:51.7	Sabeha Mansouri (Alg) in	1987

10,000m Walk (Track) Women

World record	43.52.1	Chen Yaoling (Chn) in	1987
Asian record	43.52.1	Chen Yaoling (Chn) in	1987
European record	44:32.50	Yelena Kuznetsova (SU) in	1986
Commonwealth record	45:08.13	Kerry Saxby (Aus) in	1986
African record	54:18.6	Sabeha Mansouri (Alg) in	1987

10km Walk (Road) Women

World record	42:52	Kerry Saxby (Aus) in	1987
Commonwealth record	42:52	Kerry Saxby (Aus) in	1987
European record	43:22	Olga Krishtop (SU) in	1987
Asian record	43:45	Jin Bingjie (Chn) in	1987
African record	61:09	Amani Mohamed Ali (Egy) in	1987

WARMERDAM, C.A.

U.S.A. (born 22nd June,1915) - In 1940, he created a world record with his fifteen foot pole vault. He improved upon his world record by 15ft.7 (1/2) in outdoors in 1942 and 15ft. 8in indoors in 1943. He leapt 15ft. or over on 43 occasions. That no other athlete could manage to scale 15ft. till 1951, speaks of his supremacy in the game.

WARMING UP, WARMING DOWN

Pre-and post-competition exercises, the former preparing muscles for strenuous competitive activity and the latter helping to prevent muscles stiffening up after such activity.

WATER STATIONS AND REFRESHMENTS

Refreshment stations should be located at intervals of 3km/2 miles or less and near the start and finish. Refreshments, which may be either provided by the organizers or by the athlete himself, shall be available at the stations nominated by the competitor.

The organizers shall provide, midway between two refreshment stations points where water only will be supplied. In warm weather, additional water stations may be provided,equipped with hoses and showers.

WATSON, LESLIE

U.K. (born 4th Feb.,1948) - A prolific marathon and ultra distance runner, she competed in as many as 20 marathons during 1981, in which year she also set a world best mark of 6h. 02 min. 37 sec. for 50 miles on the road. Smashed the 50 mile track world record with 6h. 20 min. 42 sec.

WEATHER SUITS

Weather suits of great variety are in the market and, certainly for winter wear, they are being worn more and more instead of tracksuits. They vary considerably in their performance, from those that keep out the elements completely. There is also a considerable variation in price.

The ones that keep out the wind only are obviously not going to offer a great deal of protection from rain, and this has to be remembered when making a purchase. Rainsuits themselves vary a lot in performance. Some lightly coated or proofed nylon suits will keep the wearer dry for a short period of time in rain, but eventually water will soak through. Heavily proofed fabrics will keep water out, but also keep water, i.e. perspiration, in. But this is usually all right because at least you will be warm and wet inside, with the cold rain on the outside. You have to rely on layers of clothing inside these rainsuits to soak up perspiration. Other fabrics are in the market which claim to breathe, that is,they have a layer of material in the construction which contains microscopic holes. These holes are too small to allow liquid water to penetrate, but large enough to allow molecules of water vapour to pass through.

There are other in-between suits made from proofed polyester/ cotton/nylon blend fabrics, with a mesh lining to the body which breathe, and which have enjoyed considerable success. When looking at the price of weather suits, the more that goes into it, or the better the performance, the more you have to pay. The very best suits are quite expensive.

WEBER, HARTMUT

West Germany (born 17th Oct.,1960) -The bespectacled Weber, champion in Athens in 1982 could well turn to the 400m hurdles in the future. In European Cup 1981 he won a gold, and repeated again in European Championships 1982.

WEIGEL, RONALD

East Germany (born 8th Aug.,1950) - A relatively undistinguished career, since his second place in the 1977 European Junior Championships 10km and a world best indoors 20 km in 1980, was dramatically transformed at the 1983 World Championships when he achieved a decisive victory in the 50km event.

WEIR, ROBERT

U.K. (born 4th Jan.,1961) - He achieved his first major success at the 1982 Commonwealth Games, taking the gold medal with a new UK hammer record of 75.08 m. He is also a top international class discus thrower and placed a very respectable fifth in that event at the European Cup finals of 1981 and 1983.

WELLS, ALLAN

Scotland (born 3rd May,1952) - In 1978, Allan Wells was on his way to becoming one of the world's leading sprinters, taking gold and silver in the Edmonton Commonwealth Games.He won gold in 100m sprints of Commonwealth Games and yet another gold in 200m sprints. In World Cup 1981 he won gold and silver in 100m and 200m sprints. It was thought that the IAAF ruling that all sprinters must use blocks, which Wells had scorned, would affect him, but he adapted magnificently to achieve success in Moscow where the absence of the US team took some glory off his achievement. He won the Commonwealth Games 100m again in 1982, but then had to settle for a dead heat in the 200 metres with Mike McFarlane.

WESSIG, GERD

East Germany (born 16th July,1959) - The only high point of his remarkable career came in Moscow with a gold in Olympic Games 1980.He managed more than 8000 in the 10 discipline event last year but did not jump in any of the international meetings.

WESSINGHAGE, TOMAS

West Germany (born 22nd Feb.,1952) - He won gold in 5000m of European Championships and bronze in 1974. Again in 1975 he won yet another gold in 1500m.

WHITBREAD, FATIMA

U.K. (born 3 March, 1961) - World silver javelin medallist in 1983. Fatima is unequalled in British throwing history. In 1979, she became the only British woman ever to win the Junior European title and her World silver in 1983 was the first major throwing medal for Britain in 59 years.

WHITFIELD, M.G

U.S.A. (born 11th Oct.,1924) In both 1948 and 1952 Olympics 800m he won gold medals, both the times taking 1min. 49.2sec. In 1948 Olympics he also got another gold in 4x400m relay. In 1952, in addition to gold he won silver medal in relay. In 1948 Olympics he got a bronze medal in 400m.

WHITLOCK, H.H

U.K. (born 16th Dec.,1903) - In 1931, he was second in the RWA 50,000m. championship. In 1933, he won his first title. In 1936, he won the Olympic race and in 1938 he won the European title. He won the RWA championship in 1936 in his fastest time for 50km. in 4hr.30min. 38sec.

WILEY, CLIFF

U.S.A. (born 21 May, 1955) - He claimed the American title, winning against the Soviets and also triumphed at the World University Games. He won gold in 400m. World Cup 1981.

WINCH, MIKE

U.K. (born 20th July,1948) - Ranked second only to shot put record holder Geoff Capes among British throwers during his career, he has thrown further than any other Briton barring Capes having reached his best ever distance of 20.43 m. His outstanding international achievements include silver medal winning efforts at both the 1974 and 1982 Commonwealth Games.

WIND READING

Wind velocity measurement that has a bearing on performances in the sprints and horizontal jumps, especially where records are concerned.

WIND UP

A phase of the hammer thrower's technique in which the athlete rotates in the throwing circle, swinging the hammer around in a wide arc at an ever increasing speed.

WOCKEL, BARBEL

East Germany (born 21st March,1955) - Although not the fastest female over 200 metres she has certainly been the most competitive, winning every major 200 metres title that she has contested, including both the 1976 and 1980 Olympic titles, the 1982 European title and the European Junior title in 1973. She was placed second in the 1982 European Championships 100 metres.

WOMEN'S AMATEUR ATHLETIC ASSOCIATION

The WAAA, which was founded in 1922, is the governing body for women's athletics in England and Wales. The Association promotes annual Championships, which like those of the AAA are unofficial British Championships.

WOODERSON, S.C.

U.K. (born 30th Aug.,1914) - In 1937, he made a world record of 4min.06.4sec.for mile. In 1938, he made world record of 1min. 48.4sec. for

800m and 1min. 49.2sec. for 880yd.in the European Championships. In European Championships in 1946 he won the 5000m in 14min. 08.6sec.

WOODRUFF, J.Y.

U.S.A. (born 5th July,1915) - In 1936 Olympics won a gold medal in 800m. clocked in 50.3sec. He won another gold in reducing the time to 1min. 47.7sec in 1940.

WORLD ATHLETE OF THE YEAR

The American magazine *Track and Field News*, one of the most authoritative publications on athletics, annually selects, by a poll of international experts, its world athlete of the year. Male athlete of the year has been selected sice 1959 and woman athlete since 1976. For the years 1967 to 1975 the woman athlete of the year was similarly selected by *Women's Track and Field World.*

WORLD CHAMPIONSHIPS

From parochial British origins, the Wold Cross -Country Championships have developed into the main athletics event of the winter. The first international was staged between the four home countries in 1903 and the competition was dominated by England until it came under the jurisdiction of the IAAF in 1973, when it was renamed the IAAF World Cross-Country Championships. Since then, only one British runner Ian Stewart, of Scotland has won the men's individual title.

WORLD CUP

The IAAF's inaugural World cup competition, held in Dusseldorf in 1977, was a resounding success both as a major world athletics event and as a source of finance for the federation to divert towards the development of athletics in the Third World. The format of the world's strongest individual nations competing against continental teams proved immensely popular with the world's leading athletes battling not only for their own honour, but for the pride of their nation or continent. Although the second World Cup in Montreal in 1979 was much less spectacular, the 1981 event in Rome was another great success. The competition was temporarily suspended in 1983 because of the IAAF's decision to hold it once every four years instead of bi-annually in order to fit their World Championships into the athletics diary.

BEST WORLD CUP PERFORMANCES

Men	Min:sec		
100m	10.00	Ben Johnson (Can)	1985
200m	20.17	Clancy Edwards (USA)	1977
400m	44.47	Mike Franks (USA)	1985
800m	1:44.04	Alberto Juantorena (Cub)	1977
1500m	3:34.45	Steve Ovett (UK)	1977
5000m	13:13.82	Miruts Yifter (Eth)	1977
10000m	27:38.43	Werner Schildhauer (GDR)	1981
3000m steeple	8:19.89	Boguslaw Marminski (Pol)	1981
110mh	13.32	Greg Foster (USA)	1981
400mh	47.31	Edwin Moses (USA)	1981
4x100mr	38.03	USA	1977
4x400mr	2:59.12	USA	1981
	metres		
High jump	2.31	Petrik Sjoberg (Swe)	1985
Pole vault	5.85	Sergey Bubka(USSR)	1985
Long jump	8.52	Larry Myricks (USA)	1979
Triple jump	17.58	Willie Banks (USA)	1985
Shot put	22.00	Ulf Timmermann(GDR)	1985
Discus	69.08	Gennadiy Kolnootchenko (USSR)	1985
Hammer	82.12	Juri Tamm (USSR)	1985
Javelin	96.96	Uwe Hohn (GDR)	1985

Women	Min.sec.		
100m	11.02	Evelyn Ashford (USA)	1981
200m	21.83	Evelyn Ashford (USA)	1979
400m	47.60	Marita Koch (GDR)	1985
800m	1:57.48	Lyudmila Veselkova(USSR)	1981
1500m	4:03.33	Tamaa Sorokina (USSR)	1981

3000m	8:36.32	Svyetlana Ulmasova (USSR)	1979
10000m	32:07.50	Aurora Cunha (Por)	1985
100mh	12.67	Grazyna Rabsztyn (Pol)	1979
400mn	54.45	Sabine Busch (GDR)	1985
4x100mr	41.37	GDR	1985
4x400mr	3:19.50	GDR	1985
	metres		
High jump	2.00	Stefka Kostadinova (Bul)	1985
Long Jump	7.27	Heike Drechsler (GDR)	1985
Shot put	20.98	Ilona Slupianek (GDR)	1979
Discus	69.78	Martina Opitz (GDR)	1985
Javelin	70.08	Antoaneta Todorova (Bul)	1981

WORLD STUDENTS GAMES

The Universiade or World Students Games organized by the Federation Internatonale du Sport Universitaire is well established as one of the world's most important meetings.

Championship best performances

Men	**Hr.min.sec**		
100m	10.07	Lee McRace (USA)	1987
	9.97	Andres Simon(Cub)(heat)	1985
200m	19.72	Pietro Mennea (Ita)	1979
400m	44.98	Harald Shmid (GFR)	1979
800m	1:43.44	Alberto Juantorena(Cub)	1977
1500m	3:38.43	Said Aouita (Mor)	1981
5000m	13:41.25	Mikhail Zhelobovskiy(USSR)	1973
10000m	28.48.90	Dane Korica (Yug)	1973
Marathon	2:17.10	Osvaldo Faustini (Ita)	1983
3000m. Steeple	8:21.26	John Gregorek (USA)	1981
110mh	13.21	Alejandro Casanas (Cub)	1977
400mh	48.44	Harry Schulting (Hol)	1979
4x100mr	3:00.98	Italy	1979
4x400mr	1:24.03	Guillaume Le Blanc(Can)	1983

	metres		
High jump	2.41	James Lott (USA)	1987
Pole vault	5.75	Konstantin Volkov (USSR)	1981
	5.75	Rodion Gataullin (USSR)	1985
Long jump	8.21	Yussuf Alli (Nig)	1983
	8.23	Laszlo Szalma (Hun)	1981
Triple jump	17.86	Charlie Simpkins (USA)	1985
Shot put	21.13	Remigius Machura (Cs)	1985
	20.85	Alessandro Andrei (Ita)	1985
Discus	69.46	Luis Delis (Cub)	1983
Hammer	77.74	Klaus Ploghaus (GFR)	1981
Javelin	89.52	Dainis Kula (USSR)	1981
Decathlon	8194 pts	Josef Zeilbauer (Aut)	1979

Women	Min:sec		
100m	11.00	Marlies Gohr (GDR)	1979
200m	21.91	Marita Koch (GDR)	1979
400m	50.35	Maria Pinigina (USSR)	1979
800m	1:57.81	Doina Melinte (Rom)	1981
1500m	4:05.35	Gabriella Dorio (Ita)	1981
3000m	8:53.78	Breda Pergar (Yug)	1981
10000m	32:58.45	Marina Rodchenkova (USSR)	1985
100mh	12.62	Lucyna Langer (Pol)	1979
400mh	54.97	Yekaterina Fesenko(USSR)	1983
4x100mr	42.82	USA	1983
4x400mr	3:24.97	USSR	1983
5km walk	22:21.10	A. Grigoryeva (USSR)	1985

	metres		
High jump	2.01	Silvia Costa (Cub)	1985
Long Jump	7.04	Irina Valyukevich(USSR)	1985
	7.06w	Anisoara Cusmir (Rom)	1983
Shot	20.82	Nadyezhda Chizhoiva(USR)	1973
Discus	67.48	Florenta Craciunescu(Rom)	1981
Javelin	71.82	Ivonne Leal (Cub)	1985
Heptathlon	6616.pts	Malgorzata Nowak (Pol)	1985

WSZOLA, JACEK

Poland (born 30th Dec.,1956) - When he was only seventeen he was fifth in the Rome European Championships. Two years later and still a teenager, he shocked Dwight Stones and won the Olympic title in High Jump in 1976 and silver in 1980. In 1979 World Cup he won silver and bronze in 1977.The Poles had a contract with Adidas that Wszola would wear Tiger shoes and he refused to change them. So he was pulled out.

WULBECK, WILLI

West Germany (born 18th Dec.,1954) - Wulbeck has been a leading world performer since before the Montreal Olympics, when he finished fourth behind Alberto Juantorena. He won gold in 800m. of 1983 World Championships; and repeated the same feat in European Cup.

Y

YARDS, MILES AND METRES

Some race distances are measured in yards and miles. Here is a list to show roughly what these measurements mean:

100 yards	91 metres
120 yards	110 metres
220 yards	201 metres
1/2 mile	805 metres
1 mile	1610 metres
3 miles	4830 metres
6 miles	9660 metres
10 miles	16100 metres

YIFTER, MIRUTS

Ethiopia (born 15th May,1944) - He won gold in 5000m of Olympic Games 1980 and bronze in 10,000m. In World Cup 1979 he won another gold in 5000m. His Olympic record is 13:21.00 in 5000m of 1980 Olympics.